The Collection Program in Schools

**Recent Titles in
Library and Information Science Text Series**

The Collection Program in Schools

Concepts, Practices, and Information Sources

Fourth Edition

KAY BISHOP

Library and Information Science Text Series

LIBRARIES
U N L I M I T E D
A Member of the Greenwood Publishing Group
Westport, Connecticut • London

Library of Congress Cataloging-in-Publication Data

Bishop, Kay, 1942-
The collection program in schools : concepts, practices, and information sources. –
4th ed. / Kay Bishop.
    p. cm. – (Library and information science text series)
    Rev. ed. of: The collection program in schools / Phyllis J. Van Orden and Kay
Bishop ; with the assistance of Patricia Pawelak-Kort. 3rd. ed. 2001
    Includes bibliographical references and index.
    ISBN–13: 978–1–59158–583–1 (alk. paper) – 978–1–59158–360–8 (pbk.:
alk. paper)
    1. School libraries–Collection development–United States. 2. Instructional
materials centers–Collection development–United States. I. Van Orden, Phyllis.
Collection program in schools. II. Title.
   Z675.S3V334 2007
   025.2′1878–dc22   2007009005

British Library Cataloguing in Publication Data is available.

Library of Congress Catalog Card Number: 2007009005
ISBN-13: 978–1–59158–583–1
        978–1–59158–360–8 (pbk.)

First published in 2007

Libraries Unlimited, 88 Post Road West, Westport, CT 06881
A Member of the Greenwood Publishing Group, Inc.
www.lu.com

Printed in the United States of America

The paper used in this book complies with the
Permanent Paper Standard issued by the National
Information Standards Organization (Z39.48–1984).

10 9 8 7 6 5 4 3

Contents

Illustrations

Figures

Tables

Author's Comments

This book is dedicated to the many school library media students that I have helped educate in the past several years in New York, Florida, Kentucky, and Mississippi. I hope all of you are out there in schools making a difference in the lives of students and positively affecting their learning. It has been my pleasure to be a part of your education.

I would like to thank the following persons for their assistance in the preparation of the manuscript of this book: Sue Janczak, my wonderful program assistant at the University of Buffalo (UB), who provided both content and editorial suggestions; David Mead, who drew the computer graphics used in the book; Donna Taylor, a UB graduate student who spent many hours updating and adding to the Appendix; and UB research graduate assistants Ryan Philips and Angela Rhodes, who located article titles for possible use in the "Additional Readings" at the end of several chapters.

Introduction

Collection development can be an exciting challenge that demands special knowledge, skills, and a positive attitude. Although the general principles and techniques of collection development are applicable to most library settings, the unique characteristics of each media program generate new and changing demands that require flexibility and creativity. To help media specialists face these challenges, this text

- describes the environment in which the collection exists;
- presents principles, techniques, and common practices of collection development and management;
- raises issues that affect all collections, but that must be resolved in accordance with the goals and needs of a particular collection;
- suggests approaches to handling collection management situations and demands; and
- identifies helpful resources, including suggested readings, Web sites, selection aides, and documents.

This introductory text provides an overview of the processes and procedures associated with developing, maintaining, and evaluating a collection at the building level. The book reflects the opinion that the collection is a key element of the media program, providing the means for meeting the information and instructional needs of the school population. To serve these needs, media specialists must consider the collection as a physical entity, composed not only of its internal resources, but also of the informational and instructional materials available through the community, resource-sharing plans, and telecommunications.

An underlying assumption is that collection development activities interact in a cyclical pattern. Policies and procedures for each of the activities are discussed in detail. Additional important topics and policy statements, such as students' rights, intellectual freedom, copyright and fair use guidelines, and acceptable use of Internet materials are addressed.

Chapter 1 focuses on definitions and characteristics of the collection, while Chapter 2 provides a brief overview of collection development activities. Chapters 3–12 discuss specific collection development activities in more detail, focusing on policies and procedures that need to be addressed for each activity. Chapter 13 deals with issues and ethics related to the development and management of school media center collections. The impact of the curriculum on the collection is discussed in Chapter 14. Chapter 15 looks at how the collection can meet the needs of special groups of students, such as ESL students, gay and lesbian students, reluctant readers, minorities, and students with physical disabilities. Fiscal issues that relate to the collection, such as licensing, raising funds, and writing grants, are discussed in Chapter 16. Information related to creating, moving, and closing collections is included in Chapter 17.

The Appendix is an annotated bibliography of resources that can be used for the various collection development activities. If resources are mentioned in the text of chapters, they have been included in the Appendix, with complete ordering information. Items listed in the "Additional Readings" at the end of each chapter are usually not included in the Appendix so readers should also refer to the listings in "Additional Readings" to obtain other valuable information on the topics covered in the chapters.

New and Updated Features

Chapters were rearranged in this edition of the book to present a logical sequence of topics for those students who are writing policy and procedure manuals as course assignments. Suggested readings and Web sites at the end of chapters have been updated. Other new topics added to the text include the following:

- Licensing online resources, such as subscription databases
- Creating a collection development policy that meets curriculum standards
- Addressing special programs and educational trends that affect school library collections
- Circulating and promoting the collection
- Using online selection and evaluation tools
- Providing remote access to school library collections
- Addressing the needs of additional special groups of students

The Appendix, "Resources," has also been expanded and updated.

1

The Collection

What is a media center collection? Before the 1990s, it would have been fairly easy to answer this question—a collection describes the resources (mainly print, but perhaps also some audiovisual items) that are housed in a single room of a school. *Tangibility* (the physical presence of an item) and media center *ownership* were two basic concepts of a traditional school media center collection.

Today, however, it is much more difficult to define a school library media center collection. Does it include the online databases to which a media center subscribes? Are Web sites that a library media specialist "marks" or "collects" for student use considered to be in the media center's collection? If a media specialist provides links to virtual libraries, are the items in the virtual library part of the media center collection? If a media specialist can access titles on a union catalog and get them for students through interlibrary loan, are they considered part of the media center collection? And if a student can access thousands and possibly millions of Web sites while seated at a computer in a media center, are all those sites included in a media center collection? Few would argue that with advances in information technology the concept of the media center collection has changed significantly and expanded its scope. The collection undoubtedly goes beyond the walls of a single room in a school.

For the purposes of this book, a media center collection is defined as a group of information sources (print, nonprint, and electronic) selected and managed by the media specialist for a defined user community (students, faculty, and sometimes parents in a school). This definition excludes the thousands of Web sites accessed by students while sitting at media center computers, but it does include online databases to which a media center subscribes, Web sites selected and managed by a media specialist, materials in virtual libraries that can be accessed by the media specialist, and items provided in a union catalog through interlibrary loan. If you ascribe to this definition, which includes viewing media specialists as both collection developers and managers, the concept of collection development policies becomes all-important since one needs guidelines to develop and manage a collection. Writing and implementing development policies and procedures for media centers is a major portion of this book. The chapters of this book provide tools to write and implement an effective collection development policy for a specific school media center.

Physical Entity and Accessibility

The collection housed in the school library media center is a physical entity composed of individual items that collectively create a whole. In collection development and management the value of a single item must be viewed in relation to other items in the collection. When deciding whether to add or withdraw a specific item to one's immediate physical collection, the following questions should be considered:

- Is the same information already in the collection, but in a different format?
- Will an alternative format make the information accessible to more people?
- Is the same or a similar item quickly accessible through a resource sharing network or the Internet?
- Does this item uniquely fill a particular need?

Questions like these help identify the relationship of one item to another in the collection.

With access to information through resource sharing and electronic means, media centers are moving away from a philosophy of ownership to one of accessibility. The immediate physical collection provides only a starting point for students as they begin to search for information. Through online catalogs students can learn about information resources in other schools, public libraries, community college libraries, or other sites. The collection as a physical entity provides an initial point for coordinated collection development practices and resource sharing with other media centers, libraries, and institutions.

Although answers to students' questions were traditionally found in the collection housed in the school media center, the answers today may or may not be found within the materials on the shelves of the media center. The collection goes beyond the walls of the immediate media center that is connected electronically to a far-reaching world of sources and information.

Two types of barriers can limit access to information: physical barriers and a lack of policies and practices that demonstrate a commitment to intellectual freedom. Examples of potential physical barriers are height of shelving, width of aisles, and lack of necessary equipment for using materials. A small child or short person may not be able to reach an item on a shelf. A person in a wheelchair or on crutches may not be able to move freely and make needed turns between the shelving. A partially sighted person may not be able to view a document without being able to enlarge the image.

A principle for information access and delivery is that "the library media program is founded on a commitment to the right of intellectual freedom" (American Association of School Librarians & Association for Educational Communications and Technology, 1998, p. 91). This commitment is not new; it is part of the profession's history. The position is equally significant today as we help students become critical thinkers and competent problem solvers who can contribute in a democracy.

The Media Center Program and the Collection

In the 1998 guidelines for school library media programs, *Information Power: Building Partnerships for Learning*, the learner is the main focus. The focus of today's media center programs is to provide authentic learning activities that help students achieve information literacy. A creative, energetic media program incorporates the nine information literacy standards for student learning described in *Information Power: Building Partnerships for Learning* (American Association of School Librarians & Association for Educational Communications and Technology, 1998).

The media center collection plays an important role in ensuring that the media program is integrated with the overall school program and that it provides access to information within and outside the school. To meet the school's media needs effectively, the media program should

- be a vital part of the total school program;
- respond to the curricular needs and interests of teachers, administrators, and other staff members;
- consider the multicultural diversity of the student population, the developmental levels and learning styles of students, and the needs of students with disabilities;
- provide guidance in the use of and access to a full range of resources— print, nonprint, and electronic;
- cooperate with other institutions to provide the widest possible access to information, which may involve interlibrary loan, coordinated collection development, and other forms of resource sharing;
- exemplify the total media concept, providing access to materials in a variety of formats, appropriate equipment, trained personnel, and resources housed inside and outside the media center; and
- be managed by a staff that adequately plans and carries out the selection, maintenance, and evaluation of resources.

The media specialist is the person responsible for ensuring that these conditions exist and these functions take place.

The responsible media specialist supports the philosophy, goals, and objectives of the school in which the media program functions. This person collaborates with teachers and administrators in the planning process to ensure that the media program is an integral part of the school program, manages the media program's operations, selects materials and other resources (including electronic formats), and instructs students and teachers. The media specialist who understands the value of the media program acts as its chief advocate by (a) offering informational, instructional, consultative, and production services; (b) evaluating the services and collection; and (c) promoting the media program through public-relations activities.

All members of the school faculty share responsibility for the media program. A media specialist cannot run an effective, integrated program alone. The leadership and human-relations skills of the media specialist are called upon to involve others in the program. It is necessary for the media specialist to collaborate with teachers in curricular planning, and, in turn, teachers should collaborate with the media specialist in planning and evaluating the media program.

A media specialist may find it difficult to involve administrators, teachers, and students in planning, implementing, and evaluating the media program. However, collection-related activities (using print, nonprint, and electronic resources) provide a range of opportunities for involvement. The media specialist can increase participation in collection development by

- identifying the characteristics of the media center users and the demands of the curriculum;

- taking steps to involve administrators, teachers, and students in the development of media center policies;

- inviting others to participate in the selection of materials and online resources for the collection;

- facilitating interagency borrowing and lending of materials; and

- involving teachers, students, and administrators in the evaluation of the materials and policies.

The media specialist makes many decisions about the collection: what to add, what to access through resource sharing, and what to remove. While others can help with these decisions, it is the media specialist who must develop an overview of the total program, take responsibility for the decisions, and manage a responsive collection while involving others in the planning and evaluation process.

Roles of the Media Specialist and the Collection

Information Power: Building Partnerships for Learning (American Association of School Librarians & Association for Educational Communications and Technology, 1998) identifies the following key roles of the media specialist as they relate to the total learning program: teacher, instructional partner, information specialist, and program administrator. Three basic ideas or strategies—collaboration, leadership, and the use of technology—are identified as the unifying themes for guiding the effective media specialist.

The collection can be viewed as one element in the school's media program. From this perspective, the collection is a tool that supports the roles and activities of the media specialist. The media specialist's roles can be characterized as direct or indirect. The roles operate in a cyclical pattern as shown in Figure 1.1. The direct roles involve interaction with patrons. These *direct* roles include professional services as teacher, instructional partner, and information specialist for students, teachers, staff, parents, and community members. The role of helping students evaluate the information they find is increasingly important as students face the multiple and varied information sources available through the Internet. The media specialist's *indirect* roles provide the means for carrying out the direct roles. In these roles the media specialist serves as program administrator, including developer and evaluator of the collection. The direct and indirect roles are interdependent. Acting as a teacher, an instructional partner, and an information specialist, the media specialist gains knowledge that is then used in making decisions about the collection.

Figure 1.1. Roles of the media specialist

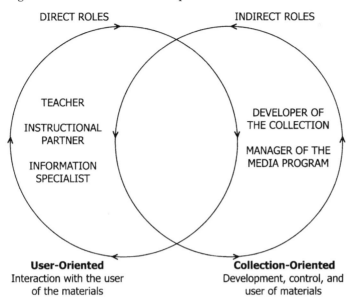

As teachers, media specialists help students develop skills in accessing, evaluating, and using information from multiple sources. They work with classroom teachers and administrators to help them develop skills in information literacy, including the uses of information technology.

As instructional partners, media specialists join teachers in linking student information needs, curriculum content, learning outcomes, and a wide range of information resources. Media specialists work with individual teachers to design and assess student learning tasks and to integrate these with the information and communication skills required in subject matter standards.

As information specialists, media specialists acquire and evaluate information resources, while working collaboratively with teachers, administrators, and students to make them aware of information issues. Media specialists demonstrate a mastery of sophisticated electronic resources and maintain a focus on the quality and ethical uses of information resources.

As program administrators, media specialists are responsible for the management of staff, budgets, equipment, facilities, and evaluation of the program and collection. They must interpret and communicate all these tasks to school personnel and the public. In carrying out these responsibilities, media specialists work to ensure that programs meet goals directly related to the collection. These include (a) providing intellectual access to information and (b) providing physical access to information by selecting and organizing the local collection and by acquiring information and materials from outside sources.

In any particular setting, the collection must support the media specialist's roles as teacher, instructional partner, information specialist, and advocate for the effective use of information and information technology.

Relationships that Influence the Collection

District Level

Many building-level media programs (those designed to meet the needs of a single school) are units of a school district media program. The district's goals and objectives apply to the building-level media program, and the district-level media program personnel and resources provide a wide range of services to the building-level program. The district may provide centralized purchasing and processing of materials. The online catalog or union catalog may include bibliographic and location information about items owned by the district and housed in the media centers throughout the system.

Collections housed in the district media center often include items that supplement materials owned by individual schools. District collections may contain materials that are expensive or heavily used at limited intervals, museum items with curricular value, and backup equipment. They also may include video or DVD libraries, professional collections, and materials examination collections. District-level collections are available to all school personnel within the district. Some districts also provide the transportation of items in their collections to individual schools.

Regional Level

The media program and the media specialist have formal and informal relationships with groups and agencies within the county and regions of the state. County-level and regional-level professional associations provide programs and contacts useful to the media specialist. Some states, such as New York, have several separate BOCES (Boards of Cooperative Education Services), which provide shared educational programs and services to school districts. School library systems function within a BOCES, providing access to information and library resources and conducting professional development activities.

State Level

In the United States, education is the responsibility of each state. Each has its own philosophy, goals, and objectives for its educational programs. These responsibilities are assigned to the state education agency. The agency staff may serve as consultants and information disseminators, and their products and services may include printed publications, sponsorship of list-servs or other electronic services, statewide online catalogs for the holdings of all the schools in the state, and the maintenance of materials examination centers. For media specialists working without the benefit of a district-level media program, the state media consultant is a key contact. In addition to consultants, state educational agencies may offer recommendations and standards for the media program and collection, as well as other useful guidelines for media specialists.

Other state agencies are information resources. They provide information about all aspects of the state, sponsor Web sites, or offer lists of resources available from the state.

National Level

The school and the media program are elements within the education and information systems of our society. Society's concerns can influence the school media program. A few examples illustrate this relationship. Society's concerns about people with physical disabilities have spawned several pieces of federal legislation that affect media programs and collections. In 1990 the Americans with Disabilities Act (ADA) mandated that public services and facilities be accessible to people with disabilities. The media specialist should assess whether the media center fulfills this mandate.

Other pieces of legislation that directly affect the operation of a media center are the Copyright Act of 1976, the Digital Millennium Copyright Act passed by the U.S. Congress in 1998, and the Teach Act passed in 2002. Designed to balance the interests of authors and artists with the user's ability to access information, these laws guide media specialists in carrying out their responsibilities.

The U.S. Congress also passes legislation that affects K-12 education and consequently impacts media center programs and collections. The *No Child Left Behind* (NCLB) legislation signed by President George W. Bush in 2002 focuses on accountability for schools, including a high-stakes testing program for students in K-12 schools. This legislation has strongly impacted curriculum and instruction in schools in the United States. Some grant programs are part of the *No Child Left Behind Legislation. NCLB* programs that especially affect school media centers include *Improving Literacy through School Libraries*, *Early Reading First Initiative*, and *Reading First Title I*, which provides financial aid to schools with high percentages of children living in poverty, has also added library materials to some schools. Although federally funded, most of these programs administer the programs through state or local agencies (U.S. Department of Education, n.d.).

The Libraries and Services Technology Act (LSTA) was signed into law by the U.S. Congress in 1996. Originally known as the *Library Services Act* (LSA), the program has been in existence in various forms since 1956. Funds are available to school library media centers, public libraries, academic libraries, qualified private/research libraries, special libraries, library consortia, and libraries in correctional institutions to improve patron services. *LSTA* emphasizes improving library services to the underserved, especially to children living in poverty (New Hampshire State Library, n.d.). The Institute of Museum and Library Services (IMLS) administers *LSTA*.

Some national professional associations provide guidance and information to school media specialists. Two professional associations directly involved with media programs are the American Association of School Librarians (AASL), a division of the American Library Association, and the Association for Educational Communications and Technology (AECT). The joint efforts of these two associations led to the publication of *Information Power: Guidelines for School Libraries* (1988) and *Information Power: Building Partnerships for Learning* (1998).

Global Level

With the increasing availability of Internet, the opportunity to tap into resources on a global basis is growing. Teachers and students can "surf" the Internet for sites throughout the world. LM_NET, a listserv (discussion group), is dedicated to school library media specialists worldwide and to people involved with the school library media field. School media specialists can join this listserv and discuss various topics that focus on topics of interest to the school library media community (LM_NET, 2004).

The International Association of School Librarianship (IASL) shares information about school library programs and materials for children and youth throughout the international community. Their Web site includes information and documents that are helpful to school library media specialists (International Association of School Librarianship, 2005).

Conclusions

The concept of the school library media center collection has changed in recent years. Today's collection includes not only the items that are owned by the media center and are physically present on the shelves, but it also includes materials that are electronically accessible through resource sharing, as well as Internet items that are selected by the media specialist. By being actively involved as a teacher, instructional partner, information specialist, and program administrator, the media specialist can align the media program and collection with the needs of its users and with the school program.

References

American Association of School Librarians & Association for Educational Communications and Technology. (1988). *Information power: Guidelines for school library media programs*. Chicago: American Library Association.

American Association of School Librarians & Association for Educational Communications and Technology. (1998). *Information power: Building partnerships for learning*. Chicago: American Library Association.

International Association of School Librarianship. (2005). *School libraries online*. Retrieved December 12, 2006, from http://www.iasl-slo.org

LM_NET. (2004). Retrieved December 12, 2006, from http://www.eduref.org/lm_net

New Hampshire State Library. (n.d.). *What is LSTA?* Retrieved December 12, 2006, from http://www.state.nh.us/nhsl/grants2000whatis.html

U.S. Department of Education. (n.d.). *No child left behind*. Retrieved December 12, 2006, from http://www.ed.gov/nclb/landing.jhtml?src=pb

2

Collection Development

Although pre-service media specialists may think collection development involves only selecting the items that become part of a media center collection, it is, in fact, much more complex. Collection development is comprised of numerous activities that are dependent upon one another. The following are collection activities that are necessary to maintain and develop an effective media center collection:

- Becoming knowledgeable about an existing collection.
- Becoming familiar with the school and community.
- Assessing the needs of the school's curriculum and other programs.
- Assessing the specific needs of the users.
- Establishing collection development policies and procedures.
- Identifying criteria for selection of materials.
- Planning for and implementing the selection process.
- Acquiring and processing materials.
- Participating in resource sharing.
- Maintaining and preserving the collection.
- Providing physical and intellectual access to materials.
- Evaluating the collection.

This chapter provides a general overall explanation of these activities. Many of these activities will be addressed in more depth in subsequent chapters.

Learning about the Existing Collection

If a collection is to serve as a communication and information base, the media specialist must know both the users' needs and the collection's available resources. Browsing is an easy way to learn about a collection. Walk through a collection and note whether you recognize titles and equipment. Ask yourself the following types of questions:

- Are you familiar with all the formats you find?
- Are signs clear and accurate?
- Are materials housed in unusual areas?
- Will students overlook any materials?
- Does the online catalog help students locate items?
- Are encyclopedias available in print, on CD-ROM, or online?
- How do users access electronically delivered information?
- Is the collection accessible only in the media center or can students and teachers access it from classrooms or from home?

While browsing, try out the online public access catalog (OPAC) and make notes about materials that are new to you. Create a list of areas that need signs to make materials easier to find. Note whether equipment is housed in an area convenient to the materials that require it. Look to see if there is a ready-reference area and note whether these materials are duplicated in the circulating collection.

Remember that some collections extend to materials housed outside the media center but that are still on the school campus. Professional journals or other materials may be located in the teachers' lounge or department offices. Check other resources in the school. Do the guidance offices collect vocational materials or materials about colleges? Are there other departmental collections? Does the online catalog indicate the storage locations throughout the school?

As you gather these first impressions, check the media center's procedure manual for explanations of unusual situations. For example, ten copies of one book title may seem unusual, but perhaps the books are used in classrooms that conduct literature-based reading programs.

Although these procedures will help you gain information about the collection, it is important to remember that it is impossible to become totally familiar with a collection in your first semester or even your first year as a media specialist. However, as you participate in the day-to-day operations of the media center (circulating materials, shelving books, etc.) and become involved with teachers and students, you will gain valuable knowledge about the collection.

Knowing the Community

A basic consideration of all collection development activities is the interaction of the media program with the school, other educational or informational institutions and agencies, and the external environment. The community (its geographical, political, economic, cultural, and social characteristics) influences the collection. Changes in a school's mission or goals, in access to other collections, or in citizens' attitudes about education influence decisions about the collection.

Today, the global community is a key resource. Students have computers in their homes and access to them at school and in their public libraries. Teachers electronically communicate with colleagues around the world. Telefacsimile (fax) machines and Internet access can speed the delivery of an article for a student's report. All these factors affect a media center's collection development activities. See Chapter 3, "Community Analysis and Needs Assessment," for more discussion of community analysis.

Assessing Needs

To ensure that the collection fulfills the informational and instructional needs of its users, the media specialist must identify those needs. Whom does the collection serve? What are the users' informational needs? What are the subjects taught in the school? What are the teachers' instructional needs? Are there groups of students with special needs?

You can begin to find the answers to these questions by accessing the school's Web site for pertinent information, examining curriculum guides, asking the administrative staff for student demographic statistics, and attending departmental meetings. Analyzing media center reports, such as circulation statistics or interlibrary loan requests, will also help provide information about the needs of the users. Conducting a survey of the students and teachers to determine how a collection can assist in meeting specific needs is also a valuable means of assessing user needs.

More information on assessing needs is included in Chapter 3, "Community Analysis and Needs Assessment."

Describing the Program

Students and teachers need to know when they will be able to physically access the materials in the collection. Clearly post the media center's hours of operation for your users. Also, let users know how the media center is scheduled. Do you have flexible scheduling, fixed scheduling, or a mixture of flexible and fixed scheduling?

You should also note whether there are special reading programs that the collection supports, such as Battle of the Books, Scholastic's *Reading Counts*, or Renaissance Learning's *Accelerated Reader*. You can answer numerous other program questions in a policy and procedures manual:

- Does the media center sponsor special programs, such as author visits or National Library Week?
- Do media center personnel conduct book fairs?
- Are there orientations for students and new faculty members?
- Are there opportunities for students to serve as volunteers or aides?
- How does the media center assist with student or faculty research?
- Are copy and printing services available?
- Are there provisions or materials for students with special needs?
- Do media center personnel conduct professional development workshops for teachers?
- How are the media center programs and services evaluated?

All of these areas of the program may not relate directly to the collection (although many do), but it is important to have this type of information included in a media center manual or in a publication that is available to students and teachers. Chapter 4, "The Media Center Program," includes more information about areas of the media program that impact the collection.

Selecting Materials

Selection policies articulate the media program's commitment to the right of intellectual freedom, and they reflect professional ethics, rights of users, and concern for intellectual property. These policies are carried out using specific selection procedures.

Criteria, or the standards used to evaluate items, are a major component of selecting materials. One must establish criteria for assessing each item and its relationship to the collection as a whole. Generally criteria used to evaluate materials include literary quality, currency, accuracy of information, appeal and value to students, application within the curriculum, quality of presentation, and format. You will also need to establish selection criteria and policies relating to specific formats, including electronic formats that are accessed online through the Internet.

Selection is the process of deciding whether an item will be a valuable addition to the collection. During this process, keep the set criteria in mind and make decisions within established policies. Personal examination and favorable reviews can provide the basis for selection decisions. Sources that provide reviews include selection tools and reviewing journals. Some of the most useful selection tools for school media specialists are listed and described in the Appendix, "Resources."

If you have the opportunity to accept gift materials to add to the media center collection, utilize the same criteria for accepting donated materials that you use for purchasing collection items.

Some materials that you select, such as videocassettes and CD-ROMS, require equipment. Therefore it is necessary for you to also establish criteria and procedures for the purchase of equipment. Many school districts provide guidelines for such purchases.

Established criteria, policies, and procedures are not the only factors that can influence a media specialist's choices. It is possible that one's values, interests, and even prejudices may influence selection decisions. To make sound decisions, you should set aside personal biases and make objective choices. Soliciting and gathering input from teachers, administrators, and students can also assist in the selection process.

The selection of materials is a major portion of collection development and includes establishing criteria for selection of many types of formats. Thus, three chapters of this book (Chapters 6, 7, and 8) address this topic.

Acquiring and Processing Materials

After selecting materials and equipment to add to the collection, you must then make decisions relating to the process of acquiring and processing these items. In schools where clerical assistance is available in a school media center, an aide or clerk can be very helpful in these activities. Frequently a school bookkeeper or financial officer is also involved in the acquisitions process.

For items such as books or magazines you may want to acquire your materials through a jobber. A *jobber* is a company that handles titles from several publishers. There are many advantages of using jobbers, including savings of money and time spent by media center personnel. You may also decide to order some items directly from publishers or local bookstores. Some audiovisual vendors handle and distribute materials from several companies. For some selections, such as reference databases, you may need to make decisions about whether to purchase the item in a CD-ROM format or online. Purchases that involve online access are generally more complex than acquiring a physical item and often involve licensing issues.

Many items can be purchased already processed, including catalog records, spine labels, and perhaps barcodes, security strips, plastic book jackets, and school media center stamp identification. Purchasing "shelf-ready" items (those that are processed by the jobber or publisher) can save you and your staff an enormous amount of time. The cost is very affordable and varies due to the extent to which the items are processed. If you choose to do some of the processing on your own, you will need some written procedures for this activity.

More detailed discussions of acquisition and processing activities can be found in Chapter 9, "Acquisitions and Processing."

Resource Sharing

Participation in resource sharing will influence your selection and acquisition decisions. Networks involving more than one library provide access to information materials and services housed outside the school's facility. A school that participates in a cooperative network has access to a plethora of resources and services; however, participation carries with it certain responsibilities and perhaps financial obligations. Some networks offer cooperative purchasing programs, cataloging and processing, computerized databases, delivery systems, production services, examination centers, serials cooperatives, and other forms of resource sharing. Generally there are policies and procedures that are written cooperatively by representatives from the libraries involved in this type of resource sharing. These should be included in your policies and procedures manual. You can also participate in informal resource sharing, such as inquiring by phone or e-mail as to the availability of a particular item in another school in your district or perhaps faxing a journal article from one media center to another or hand delivering an item that is needed in a nearby school.

Fitting resource sharing into a continuum of collection development activities is somewhat difficult since resource sharing can impact multiple collection development activities, including selection, acquisitions, and circulation. More information relating to resource sharing can be found in Chapter 9, "Acquisitions and Processing," and in Chapter 16, "Fiscal Issues Relating to the Collection."

Maintaining and Preserving Materials

Collection maintenance is an important and often neglected function of collection development. The media specialist must make decisions about removing (de-selecting or weeding), mending, rebinding, and replacing materials. Equipment must also be kept in working condition.

You can do many things to help preserve and maintain your collection and equipment. These include teaching students the proper handling of materials, providing copy machine access, utilizing a security system, and maintaining appropriate temperature and humidity in the media center, to name just a few. Conducting systematic inventories of materials also helps maintain a usable collection. It is important to establish policies and procedures for these maintenance and preservation activities. Chapter 10, "Maintenance and Preservation," provides additional information about how to effectively maintain a collection.

Accessing and Circulating Materials

While some librarians may not consider accessing and circulating materials as collection development activities, they are the reasons that the other activities take place. The ultimate purpose of collection development is to make materials accessible to users. As mentioned in Chapter 1, media specialists need to provide physical and intellectual access to materials. Physical access includes having times (during school, before school, after school) when students and teachers are able to use the collection.

You will also need to develop circulation policies and procedures to provide some guidelines for the use of the collection. Some questions to consider are:

- Which types of formats circulate and to whom?

- For how long can students check out materials?

- Is there a limit on the number of items that can be checked out?

- Does the limit on items vary depending on a student's grade level?

- How do the check-out policies differ for teachers?

- Are fines charged for overdue items?

- Do students need to pay for materials that are damaged during the time the materials are checked out?

Students and teachers also need electronic access to materials. It is the media specialist's responsibility to provide and manage this access. This may involve working closely with the person responsible for setting up the school's network and with the school's technology committee. It is also important that acceptable use policies be written for the use of electronic materials. If there is not such a policy in place, then you should take the initiative to develop a policy. Teachers and administrators should be involved in developing an acceptable use policy since it is a policy that needs to be adopted and utilized throughout the school.

Your policy and procedures manual should contain a statement endorsing intellectual freedom. Some official documents, such as the *Library Bill of Rights* written and amended by the American Library Association Council, are valuable additions to your manual, either in the text of the manual itself or in an appendix. Such documents will be beneficial if you receive complaints about materials in your collection and you need to defend intellectual freedom. Your manual should also include a list of very specific procedures to follow if an item is formally challenged. This list should be a part of your policy and procedures manual before a challenge occurs.

Copyright issues also affect access. Your manual should include a statement noting that media center personnel uphold the U.S. copyright laws and fair use guidelines. In most schools the media specialist is responsible for enforcing those laws and guidelines within the media center and is responsible for providing information to the faculty and students regarding copyright. This does not mean that media specialists should serve as "copyright cops" outside the media center (a responsibility of school administrators); however, the media center manual should include how copyright information is provided to users. It is helpful to have a list of some of the guidelines that affect teachers and students.

In some instances intellectual freedom and copyright issues are addressed in the selection portion of a policy and procedures manual. It does not matter whether you have a separate section relating to access and circulation to address these issues or whether you place them in the selection portion of your manual, but it is essential that they be included.

Circulation of materials is covered in more detail in Chapter 11, "Circulation and Promotion of the Collection," while intellectual freedom and copyright issues are discussed in Chapter 13, "Ethical Issues and the Collection."

Evaluating the Collection

Gathering information on how students and teachers utilize the materials will assist you in evaluating the collection. Some evaluation techniques that involve users include examining circulation statistics, determining the in-house use of materials, and conducting surveys. Collection-centered techniques, such as directly examining the collection and comparing the materials to lists or bibliographies, can also be used to evaluate a collection. Your manual should include a plan for systematically evaluating the collection, including who conducts the evaluation, what types of measures are used, and how often the collection is evaluated. More information related to how to carry out an evaluation of a collection is found in Chapter 12, "Evaluation of the Collection."

Interaction of Collection Development Activities

One can view collection development activities as a continuum in which one activity leads to and influences the others (see Figure 2.1). Activities are not isolated; rather, their interactions are cyclical. Thus a change in one activity affects others. For instance, if there is a change in the curriculum (part of the community analysis) and several science courses are added, this will affect selection. You should establish policies that provide guidance, but you also need to keep in mind that policies may need to be altered to meet changes. With the rapid developments in technology, media specialists can expect to add new formats to the collection; selection criteria for these formats will then need to be incorporated into the policy.

Other Factors that Affect Collection Development

The media specialist is responsible for developing and implementing collection development activities. However, the media specialist cannot control all the factors that influence collection development activities. The

Figure 2.1. Interaction of collection development activities

media center program must operate within policies that the local board of education adopts and must also meet the goals of the district and the school. The "attendance districts" established by the school board may change yearly and impact the composition of the student body or potential users of the collection. State or federal legislation may dictate requirements about the student population, the curriculum, and other school programs. Shifts in the student population will impose new demands on the collection that collection development activities must accommodate. The constantly changing availability of electronic access creates continual shifts in the equipment needed and requires the media specialist to seek updating skills.

District Media Program

A building-level media program that is part of a district media program offers many advantages to the entry-level media specialist. The system's media program coordinator or director is someone you can turn to for guidance. The district-level guidelines for media programs and the selection policy that the governing body adopts also aid the media specialist. District-level media programs offer many services to help establish and maintain the collection program. For example, there may be opportunities to examine new materials or view exhibits and demonstrations at district-level media program meetings.

Regional centers also provide personnel and services, including consultants or technicians, cooperative collections, examination centers, staff development workshops, and clearinghouses for information about new technology. Providing distance-learning opportunities is another way these centers can extend the resources of the building media center.

Although district and regional programs offer many benefits, they may also impose constraints on the school media program. An approved buying list generated by a district-wide committee may limit the equipment that a media specialist can purchase or the media specialist may be allowed to order from only specific jobbers. If you encounter these situations, you should ask district-level personnel if there are procedures for ordering other items. In some districts, you must also order titles at specified times.

Financial Support and Control

The school's and district's funding policies, including policies regulating use of outside funding sources, impose constraints on collection development. Accrediting agencies may also make budget demands. Media specialists operate within the limits set by budget allocations. In addition to the size of the budget, the accounting system can affect collection activities. For example, funds designated for computer software cannot be used for books. Collection development is more successful when budgeting allows program objectives and needs to determine priorities.

The school board's or the administrator's position on the use of outside funding also affects the collection. Some school districts opt not to use outside funds; others encourage media specialists to seek grants or endowments. Such grants or endowments may specify materials to be purchased or may limit the type of use or user for whom materials may be purchased. For example, some funding may be used only for materials for student use.

At some point in your career as a media specialist, a school official may inform you that you must spend a large sum of money earmarked for materials for special uses within seven to ten days. This situation does not encourage thoughtful planning or selection, but it sometimes occurs with outside funding opportunities. Try to be knowledgeable regarding what materials can be funded by outside sources and be aware when the funding will occur. A file of materials that you are currently considering for purchase is essential in these situations.

School Facilities

Limitations of the physical plant or the physical facilities of the media center can affect the collection. For instance, the lack of an adequate number of safe electrical outlets limits the use of some media. Media center usage by after-school programs or programs for preschoolers may influence collection development activities. Many formats in the collection (such as picture books, large study prints, art prints, and maps) require specialized storage units. As media centers change from predominately print collections to ones with electronic collections, less shelving space is needed, but more computer workstations are required. These are all examples of ways that the school or media center facilities can affect collection development. In some instances, such as a lack of an adequate number of electrical outlets, you may need to advocate for additional wiring to be put into the media center or you may need to find funding to provide the additional computer workstations that are required for electronic resources.

Conclusions

Collection development is comprised of many activities that interact with one another. Changes in one activity often affect other collection development activities. Policies and procedures should be written to address each of the activities, but media specialists should be prepared to make alterations in order to meet changing needs. Other factors, such as district-wide policies and services, financial support, and school facilities can also impact collection development.

Additional Readings

Hughes-Hassell, S., & Mancall, J. C. (2005). *Collection management for youth: Responding to the needs of learners.* Chicago, IL: American Library Association.

Kachel, D. E. (1997). *Collection assessment and management for school libraries: Preparing for cooperative collection development.* Westport, CT: Greenwood Press.

Lukenbill, W. B. (2002). *Collection development for a new century in the school library media center.* Westport, CT: Libraries Unlimited.

McGregor, J., Dillon, K., & Henri, J. (2003). *Collection management for school libraries.* Blue Ridge Summit, PA: Scarecrow Press.

Shankles, R. (2002). Not limited by space any more. *Arkansas Libraries, 59*(6), 16–17.

Helpful Web Sites

Graf, N. (2006). *Collection development in the information age.* Retrieved July 14, 2006, from http://www.sagebrushcorp.com/support/collectiondev.cfm

Resources for school librarians. (n.d.). *Collection development.* Retrieved March 11, 2006, from http://www.sldirectory.com/libsf/resf/coldev2.html

3

Community Analysis and Needs Assessment

Effective collection development must be based on reliable knowledge about the collection's users (in the case of a school media center—the students, teachers, administrators, and perhaps parents being served). The gathering of information about a population that a library serves is generally called *community analysis*. The demographics that should be collected about users of a school media center include (1) community information and (2) school information.

Learning about the Community

If the students in your school live in a large city, you should include in your community analysis information about the city itself (for instance, the location of the city and its population), but additional demographics should relate to primarily the neighborhood area in which most of the students live. For smaller towns, where neighborhoods may not be especially unique, the data for the entire town may be reported.

How do you learn about the community? Some good sources of information are the school district, the local chamber of commerce, the news media, government agencies, service and civic clubs, government census data, and the public library. These sources can provide maps, surveys, brochures, community profiles, lists of local activities, and projections for future population shifts. They can also lead you to other information sources, such as planning commissions or historical societies. Almost all communities have official Web sites that can provide some of the information you will need to collect, and many of the groups and institutions often have their own Web sites. If the public library has recently surveyed the community's information needs, their findings can be helpful. United States census data, which are available online (http://www.census.gov/), provide much information for a community analysis.

The following information is helpful to include in a community analysis:

- Geographic setting
- Topographic features (near mountains, oceans, etc.)

- Population
- Age distribution of the population
- Ethnic and racial groups
- Educational levels of the population
- Economic levels of the population
- Employment opportunities
- Businesses
- Political activities
- Modes of transportation
- Educational institutions
- Availability of libraries and museums
- Information agencies (newspapers, radio stations, TV stations)
- Technological resources (availability of Internet via cable TV, fiber-optic cable to the home, high-tech industries, etc.)
- Recreational facilities
- Religious institutions
- Housing
- Governmental units
- Medical care facilities and organizations

In addition to the topics listed above, a community analysis might also include information that is unique to the community, such as historical development, cultural data, or future trends and plans.

How does this profile help the media specialist with collection development and programming? The demographics can provide useful guidance. Census data about racial, ethnic, and language backgrounds indicate some types of materials the collection needs. Ethnic organizations, such as a Hispanic council, might be willing to help meet the needs of young Hispanic students. In communities with large populations of refugees and immigrants, you will also need materials that help students and teachers understand the new members of their community.

Stability of the population also affects the collection. A community without an influx of young families may face a decline in student population, leading to closing or consolidating schools. If you are in a school with low-income workforces, there is likely to be a certain amount of transience. Children of inner-city factory workers or migrant farm workers may spend only a few weeks in your school. A migrant family's need to move may happen suddenly. When working with children from such families, you may need to emphasize materials in less permanent formats. In these situations, it may be better to select less costly paperback books and not fret about the loss of materials.

The location of the community, its climate, and its recreational patterns also make demands on the collection. Schools in areas where skiing, snow-mobiling, or water sports are regular activities need appropriate materials in the media center collection.

Many communities support recreational and educational programs. Young people may regularly participate in functions at museums, zoological gardens, art institutes, and concert halls. These interests result in demands on the collection. For instance, if a community has a planetarium that is open to students, the collection will need stronger astronomy resources than one in a community without such a facility. Active Scout or 4-H programs may also indicate a need for specialized materials in the collection.

A community of young families may be more likely to support educational programs than a community of fixed-income people. The educational level of the population may be another clue to the willingness of citizens to financially support schools. Active participants in community groups might be more receptive to the importance of a media program. Remember that neighborhoods in large school districts differ drastically. You may find pockets of support, or opposition, in various neighborhoods.

Learning about the School

Your community analysis should also include a detailed description of the school itself. It is extremely important to have knowledge about the students, teachers, and administrators who utilize the media center. The best sources for such information include the school Web site, the guidance office, and the school secretary or administrative assistant. Some states also maintain Web sites on individual schools. These Web sites can provide you with information such as student enrollment, the number of students on free or reduced lunches, and student test scores. The following is information to be included in a school analysis:

- Enrollment
- Grade levels
- Ethnic make-up of the student body
- Number of students whose second language is English
- Socioeconomic status of the students
- Number of students on free or reduced lunches
- Drop-out rate
- Number of students enrolled in advanced courses
- Percentage of students going to college
- Special education population
- Standardized test scores
- Courses or units of study emphasized in the curriculum
- Extracurricular activities available
- Number of faculty members
- Background of faculty members (Do the teachers live in local neighborhoods? Do they have advanced degrees? Do they come from diverse backgrounds?)

Other types of information, such as the number of high school students who have jobs or the number of transient students in a school, can also influence collection development. The purpose of a school has implications for the collection. If you are a media specialist in a magnet school, such as a performing arts or technical school, or in a parochial school where specific religious beliefs are taught, certain titles may need to be included in the collection (or perhaps excluded).

In what other ways can the information you gather in a school analysis impact the collection? Schools with a high percentage of students in advanced placement classes will have demands different from those schools where students are entering the military or job force, rather than going on to higher education. Students taking courses through Advanced Placement or International Baccalaureate programs are likely to need materials available through interlibrary loan or on the Internet. On the other hand, students who attend vocational programs for a part of the school day will need specialized materials, such as car repair or hair fashions, that support their vocational curriculum. If an elementary school has many students whose first language is not English, you will want to include many bilingual materials in the collection.

As a media specialist, you also should assess the needs of the teachers in your school. A good, useful professional library will be greatly appreciated by the faculty, as will instruction in accessing online materials for their courses. It could be beneficial to determine whether there are teachers in the school who are working on advanced degrees. They may need your assistance in locating print or online materials to help them complete requirements for the courses in which they are enrolled.

Other Libraries

Some of your most valuable allies may be the public library's children and young adult specialists. If you are a new media specialist, investigate the following: What services do libraries and other information agencies offer to students? Is there a branch library near your school, or do students use a bookmobile? Do students have access to the Internet at the public library? Can they access the public library's online catalog from their home or from the school? Do school and public libraries offer cooperative programs or services? Can you borrow public library materials for classroom use? Has the school established a procedure for alerting the public library of forthcoming assignments? Do the two libraries participate in resource sharing plans? Have the libraries jointly applied for grant funds?

Visit local community college, college, and university libraries. Their collections probably include reference materials, bibliographies, and selection tools too expensive for the school's collection. If special libraries (industry, hospital, government, etc.) in the community are open to student use, their resources can be of particular interest to high school students completing research papers or science projects.

Assessing User Needs

While completing a community and school analysis can provide valuable information for collection development, other means of assessing student and faculty needs should also be utilized. Conducting separate surveys for students and teachers can be helpful. These surveys should include questions relating to the needs of the users and to the collection. The questions on the student survey should be written so students can clearly understand them. The wording of questions will vary greatly, depending on grade levels included in a school. Sample survey questions for classroom teachers might include:

- What units of study are you planning for this school year?
- Does the media center currently have adequate materials to support your curriculum?
- Do students in your courses need materials from the media center to complete assignments?
- Will you be bringing students to the media center for research?
- How can I help your students with their research?
- What areas of professional development are of particular interest to you?
- Are you currently working on an advanced degree? If so, in what area of study?

A few sample questions for students include:

- Is English your first language? If not, what other languages do you speak or read?
- What are your favorite leisure activities?
- What are your reading interests?
- Do you have any hobbies?
- Do you participate in extracurricular activities? If so, what are some of those activities?
- Do you check out materials from the public library?
- Are there materials needed for reports that you have not been able to find in the media center collection? If so, name some of them.

The data from such surveys should be analyzed and presented in a report that includes some graphic representations, so the survey results can easily be understood, not only by a media specialist, but by other interested parties as well. Include in your report recommendations based on the survey results. Perhaps you will need to add materials in particular areas of the collection. For instance, if the survey indicated a large percentage of students whose first language is Spanish, you might consider applying for a grant to add bilingual materials to your collection. If you find the eighth grade science teachers are beginning a new unit of study on oceanography, you will want to include in your budget funds to help strengthen that area of the collection.

In addition to conducting formal surveys that can impact collection development, you should also use informal means to assess user needs. One informal way to gather this information is to attend grade level or department meetings to learn about what types of projects, assignments, or units of study are being planned by classroom teachers. In the media center, at lunch in the cafeteria, or at faculty meetings you can informally chat with teachers about what types of materials and services they would like to see available in the media center. Providing a suggestion box on the media center circulation desk makes it possible for students or teachers to comment on materials they were not able to locate in the collection or to suggest titles of special interest to them.

Conclusions

In order to determine the needs of the users of a media center, a media specialist should conduct a community analysis, including demographics relating to both the community and the school itself. Carefully designed and administered surveys can also provide accurate and reliable data about user needs. Media specialists can assess the needs of students and teachers through informal means, such as attending department or grade level meetings. Information gathered in a community analysis and through needs assessments should be major influences for collection development and the school media center program.

Helpful Web Sites

Brooker, R. (n.d.) *ALA community scan*. Retrieved November 15, 2006, from http://www.ibrc.Indiana.edu/presentations/community_scan.html

Curry, A. (n.d.). *LIBR 520: Collection management*. Retrieved November 15, 2006, from http://www.slais.ubc.ca/courses/libr520/02-03-wt1/1520-Community.htm

Greer, R. C., & Hale, M. L. (2003). *The community analysis process*. Retrieved November 15, 2006, from http://skyways.lib.ks.us/pathway/article.html

Lamb, A., & Johnson, L. (2004). *Community analysis*. Retrieved November 15, 2005, from http://eduscapes.com/sms/community.html

South Carolina State Library. (2004). *Community analysis resources on the WWW*. Retrieved November 19, 2006, from www.state.sc.us/scsl/lib/commscan.html

Upper Hudson Library System. (n.d.). *Community analysis and community survey form*. Retrieved November 15, 2006, from http://www.uhls.org/uhls/communityanalysis/

4

The Media Center Program

Recent research has proven that school media centers play critical roles in improving academic achievement (Baumbach, 2002; Burgin & Bracy, 2003; Todd, Kuhlthau, & OELMA, 2004; Loertscher & Todd, 2003). Research studies clearly indicate that in order to succeed, students need strong media center programs (Lance, Rodney, & Hamilton-Pennell, 2001; Rodney, Lance, & Hamilton-Pennell, 2002; Todd, Kuhlthau, & OELMA, 2004). As part of those programs, all students need access to current, quality, high-interest, and extensive collections (American Association of School Librarians, 1999). The media center program provides a setting where students can develop the information skills that they will need as adults—being able to locate, evaluate, organize, use, and create information.

Scheduling of the Media Center

Patrons need to be informed of the operating hours of the media center, including the times they can check out materials or use the media center computers. These hours are generally affected by the media specialist's employment contract, the number of professional media specialists in a school, and the presence of clerical or paraprofessional assistants. Having more media center personnel usually makes it possible to have expanded hours of access for patrons. For instance, in a high school setting where at least two professional media specialists are on staff, it may be possible to stagger work hours so the media center can be open to students before classes begin and after school. The operating hours of the media center should be specified in your policy and procedure manual, in a student handbook, and on or near the entrance to the media center.

Additionally, you might be able to decide whether your media center will operate on a fixed, flexible, or mixed schedule. There are advantages and disadvantages for each of these types of schedules. Fixed (or rigid) schedules are sometimes utilized in elementary schools. In this type of schedule each class is given a prescribed time (usually once a week) to visit the media center. In a school that uses fixed scheduling, the visits to the media center are often part of a master schedule that provides classroom teachers with planning time. Music, art, physical education, and computer skills are generally in the same master schedule to provide planning time for classroom teachers. More often than not, in a fixed schedule only one class is allowed into the media center at a time.

Some advantages of a fixed schedule include the following:

- All students have access to the media center resources at least once a week during their scheduled library time.
- The media specialist has the opportunity to teach information literacy skills to all students in the school.
- Teachers are provided with a planning period.

Some disadvantages of a fixed schedule are as follows:

- Information literacy skills are often taught in isolation and may soon be forgotten by the students.
- The media center is treated as a subject, rather than a center for resources and learning.
- Students cannot visit the media center at times when they may have specific needs for media center resources.
- Teachers may not be able to send individual students or small groups of students for check-out or research activities.
- In a large school, a fixed schedule can occupy 80 to 90 percent of a media specialist's day, leaving little time for other management responsibilities.

In flexible (or open) scheduling, classes are scheduled as classroom teachers and the media specialist define a need. For example, in one week a classroom teacher may have the students working on research projects and schedule a forty-minute block of time every day of that week. The classroom teacher accompanies students to the media center and plans cooperatively with the media specialist. The schedule for teaching information literacy skills is based on need and is integrated into research activities; thus the schedule varies each week. With a flexible schedule, individuals and small groups of students use the media center as often as needed.

The many important advantages of flexible scheduling include the following:

- Students have access to resources at the time of need or interest.
- Media center visits and the teaching of information literacy skills are related to classroom activities and assignments.
- The media specialist has time to collaborate with classroom teachers, thus improving communication—the media specialist becomes familiar with the curriculum and the teachers learn what resources are available in the media center.
- Students become more independent users of resources and gain information literacy skills for lifelong learning.

Although the American Association of School Librarians (AASL) strongly recommends flexible scheduling, some media specialists note disadvantages:

- It is possible that some students never or infrequently visit the media center and thus do not get opportunities to check out materials for either research or pleasure.

- Some teachers may send their "problem students" to the media center frequently, simply to get them out of the classroom.

- The media specialist may feel as if there is not sufficient time to take care of other management responsibilities, such as ordering or cataloging, when there are constantly students and teachers using the media center resources and needing assistance.

Some elementary school media centers use mixed scheduling, which is a combination of fixed and flexible scheduling. For instance, the media specialist could have fixed classes in the morning and flexible access during the afternoon. Another frequently used mixed schedule involves having fixed classes for the lower grades and flexible access for the upper elementary grades. If a full-time clerk is available in the media center, the media specialist might teach classes in a fixed schedule, while the clerk assists small groups of students or individuals who come to the media center from other classes. Fixed and flexible scheduling have many possible combinations. Some elementary media specialists consider the mixed scheduling to be the ideal program.

Media centers in secondary schools usually operate on a flexible schedule in which teachers "sign up" with the media specialist for times to bring their classes to the media center. Other times they are allowed to send individual students or small groups of students to the media center. Some middle school media specialists choose to use a mixed schedule, generally scheduling fixed classes through English teachers, with specific times for students to check out books or work on special projects and yet still remaining open for small groups of students or individuals. Regardless of which type of scheduling is used in a media center, students and teachers must be made fully aware of the schedule and how it affects their access to the media center.

The type of scheduling utilized in a school library media center can impact the collection. If you are in a school where flexible or mixed scheduling is present, you will most likely find there is more use of the media center for both personal reading and research activities; thus, you need to develop a collection that includes the materials needed to support such activities. You should become familiar with the curriculum, possible research assignments, and the times of the year there will likely be a demand for particular resources. Additionally, you need to work collaboratively with your classroom teachers to provide integration of the teaching of information skills into the curriculum, and at the same time develop a collection tailored to the needs of the students and teachers.

General Services

What general services are included in a media center program? This may vary according to the number of media center personnel, student body enrollment, grade levels included in the school, and media center facilities. General services provided to students and teachers could include the following:

- Providing orientation sessions for students and teachers
- Providing copy machines so students and teachers can make copies of media center materials
- Providing access to online databases
- Making it possible to print Internet resources
- Assisting with research projects
- Providing reading and viewing guidance for students and teachers
- Providing booktalks for classes
- Preparing bibliographies
- Providing style sheets for students
- Bookmarking Internet sites for classroom assignments
- Providing resources and equipment for students with special needs
- Conducting professional development workshops for teachers

How are these services related to the media center collection? A review of the services listed above reveals that most, if not all of the services, are directly related to the media center collection. The collection is inescapably intertwined with the library media program. Providing the services listed and a collection that reflects the needs of the students and teachers will help create an effective, high-quality library media program.

With the present focus of school library media centers on student learning it is essential that library media programs effectively engage students and provide programs and services that contribute to authentic student learning. This includes providing learning opportunities through technology; thus, it is important to have emerging technologies available to all students. In turn, media specialists need to base their technology-related instruction on student learning, rather than the technologies themselves.

Special Programs

You will have many opportunities to provide special programs in a school library media center. Traditionally a high priority of media center programs has been the promotion of reading. With the recent emphasis in the United States on increasing standardized reading test scores, this priority has become even more of a focus and has functioned to more closely link classrooms and the media center. In some instances special reading programs, such as computer reading programs (Renaissance Learning's *Accelerated Reader* and Scholastic's *Reading Counts*) or the Battle of the Books (a reading competition program) are school-wide and closely connected to the reading curriculum, while in other schools the programs are used as reading motivational tools and are administered only through the media center. These programs are discussed in more depth in Chapter 14, "The Curriculum." Today many media specialists also design their own reading motivation programs and contests, as has been done traditionally since school libraries were first developed.

Although media specialists are not reading teachers, they can collaborate with classroom teachers and reinforce the strategies and techniques used in the classroom to teach reading. This might involve pointing out rhyming words in a poem, defining unfamiliar words, predicting what will happen next in a story, or determining an author's message. Introducing students to various genres and imparting a love for literature will also help students to enjoy reading and become lifelong readers for both pleasure and information.

Other special programs that are sometimes part of a media center program include audiovisual or computer clubs, book discussion groups, and student media center aides. Many media specialists also plan programs for special events held in the media center. These include author visits, book fairs, career days, speakers, storytelling, read-ins (famous local persons or parents are invited to the media center to read a book aloud), and National Library Week or Children's Book Week celebrations.

Evaluation of Programs

Every media program should frequently utilize varied means of evaluation. Initially, a media specialist should perform some type of self-assessment of a program. One way to evaluate a program is to put in written format the mission, goals, and objectives of the media center and then compare the current program to those items.

Using a rubric will provide a more thorough evaluation and present an overall picture of the current status of your program and the areas in which you would like the program to move forward. Several school districts and states have developed program evaluation rubrics that can be used for this purpose. Check with your school district or state department of education to see if such a rubric is available for your use. If there is not already a rubric that you can use for this purpose, you can adapt other rubrics to accommodate the objectives and needs of your media center. At the end of this chapter you will find Web site listings of some program evaluation rubrics that could potentially assist you in developing a self-assessment evaluation for your media center program. In your rubric be sure to include items that will evaluate how well the program is developing critical problem solvers and how the program contributes to student achievement.

You also should provide opportunities for your patrons to evaluate the media center program. You can do this by interviewing students and teachers or by creating surveys in which patrons can indicate their present usage of the media center and provide useful feedback for improvement of a program. Surveys should provide anonymity, be relatively brief (shorter for younger students), and be written in clear, concise language.

Figure 4.1 is an example of a student survey appropriate for a high school media center program. Different questions might need to be used for middle school or elementary students. You can also choose to utilize a different format for student responses.

Classroom teachers can provide valuable information about the media center program, particularly if you are utilizing a flexible schedule and teachers are accompanying their students to the media center. Figure 4.2 is a sample of a survey that could be used for classroom teachers to help evaluate the media center program.

Conclusions

Research has shown that strong media center programs contribute to authentic student learning and student achievement. Effective media

Figure 4.1. Student media center survey

Student Media Center Survey

This survey is being conducted to help us understand how you use the library media center (LMC) and how the LMC program can be improved. When you have completed the survey, please place it in the box provided on the circulation desk. Thank you for taking the time to provide us with this valuable information.

--The LMC Staff

1. How often do you visit the LMC?
   ___ Daily ___ 2-3 times a week ___ 2-3 times a month ___Never

2. When do you visit the LMC (check all that apply)?
   ___ Before school ___ At lunch time ___ With classes ___ After school

Indicate your level of agreement by checking the statement that most closely represents your response. If the item does not apply to your experiences in the LMC, leave it blank.

3. The LMC provides the resources I need to complete school assignments.
   ___Strongly agree ___Agree ___Disagree ___Strongly disagree

4. The LMC provides the resources I need for my special interests.
   ___Strongly agree ___Agree ___Disagree ___Strongly disagree

5. The LMC promotes reading.
   ___Strongly agree ___Agree ___Disagree ___Strongly disagree

6. The LMC Web site is useful.
   ___Strongly agree ___Agree ___Disagree ___Strongly disagree

7. The training I receive in the LMC helps me locate information within the LMC.
   ___Strongly agree ___Agree ___Disagree ___Strongly disagree

8. The skills I learn in the LMC help me to access electronic resources through the Internet.
   ___Strongly agree ___Agree ___Disagree ___Strongly disagree

9. The hours that the LMC are open provide me with adequate opportunities to utilize its resources.
   ___Strongly agree ___Agree ___Disagree ___Strongly disagree

10. The atmosphere in the media center is conducive to learning.
    ___Strongly agree ___Agree ___Disagree ___Strongly disagree

11. Please provide at least one change in the LMC that would help improve the services that the LMC provides to students:

12. Indicate your grade level:
    ___9 ___10 ___11 ___12

Figure 4.2. Faculty media center survey

Faculty Media Center Survey

We are conducting this survey to determine how we can serve the needs of all teachers in the school. We would appreciate it if you would complete the survey and place it in the library media center (LMC) mailbox in the main office. Thank you for taking the time to provide us with valuable input.

--The LMC Staff

Indicate your level of agreement with the following statements by circling the appropriate number.

	Strongly disagree ⟶			Strongly agree	
1. The LMC staff solicits input from me regarding materials to purchase for the LMC.	1	2	3	4	5
2. The print resources in the LMC are adequate to support my subject area.	1	2	3	4	5
3. The nonprint resources in the LMC are adequate to support my subject area.	1	2	3	4	5
4. The LMC staff informs me of new additions to the collection.	1	2	3	4	5
5. The LMC staff assists my students in developing information literacy skills.	1	2	3	4	5
6. The technology resources in the LMC (computers, online subscriptions, software, etc.) are sufficient to meet my needs.	1	2	3	4	5
7. The procedures used to schedule classes in the LMC work well for me.	1	2	3	4	5
8. The LMC has adequate resources to support my professional development.	1	2	3	4	5
9. The LMC staff assists me in the use of LMC resources.	1	2	3	4	5
10. The atmosphere in the LMC is conducive to learning.	1	2	3	4	5
11. The LMC effectively supports our total school program.	1	2	3	4	5
12. The LMC is critical to learning in our school.	1	2	3	4	5

Please add any comments that will help clarify your responses or will help us better serve you and your students:

---

center programs are dependent on a collection that is responsive to the needs of students and teachers and is integrated into the curriculum through resource-based instruction of information literacy skills. A media center program should be frequently evaluated, both through self-assessment by the media specialist and by its users.

References

American Association of School Librarians. (1999). *A position statement on: The value of independent reading in the school library media program.* Chicago: American Association of School Librarians.

Baumbach, D. (2002). *Making the grade: The status of school library media centers in the Sunshine State and how they contribute to student achievement.* Spring, TX: Hi Willow Research and Publishing.

Burgin, R., & Bracy, P. B. (2003). *An essential connection: How quality school library media programs improve student achievement in North Carolina.* Spring, TX: Hi Willow Research and Publishing.

Lance, K. C., Rodney, M. J., & Hamilton-Pennell, C. (2001). *Good schools have school librarians; Oregon school librarians collaborate to improve academic achievement.* Terrebonne, OR: Oregon Educational Media Association.

Loertscher, D. V., & Todd, R. J. (2003). *We boost achievement!* Spring, TX: Hi Willow Research and Publishing.

Rodney, M. J., Lance, K. C., & Hamilton-Pennell, C. (2002). *Make the connection: Quality school library media programs impact academic achievement in Iowa.* Bettendorf, IA: Mississippi Bend Area Education Agency.

Todd, R. J., Kuhlthau, C. C., & OELMA. (2004). *Student learning through Ohio school libraries: The Ohio research study.* Columbus, OH: Ohio Educational Library Media Association.

Helpful Web Sites

Bellingham Public Schools. (n.d.). *Supervisor's resource bank: Standards for library media programs.* Retrieved January 4, 2006, from http://www.bham.wednet.edu/departments/libmedtech/Supervisors/srbstandards.htm

Dow, M., & Willems, H. (2003). *School library media specialist evaluation.* Retrieved January 6, 2006, from http://slim.emporia.edu/kschool/docs/Librarain%20Evaluation.pdf

Jackson, G.G., & Scott, R. (2005). *No library media center left behind: Assessing library media programs.* Retrieved January 6, 2006, from http://www.ala.org/ala/aaslbucket/pittsburgh/NoLMCLeftBehind.pdf

Lamb, A., & Johnson, L. (2005). *Evaluation.* Retrieved January 4, 2006, from http://eduscapes.com/sms/evaluation.html

Massachusetts School Library Media Association. (2002). *Model school rubrics.* Retrieved January 4, 2006, from http://www.mslma.org/whoweare/rubric.pdf

New York State Education Department. (2004). *School library media program evaluation.* Retrieved January 4, 2006, from http://www.emsc.nysed.gov/nyc/Library/RubricsJan2004.doc

Pennsylvania School Librarians Association Professional Development Committee. (2002). *Preemptive action: The busy librarian's guide to program evaluation.* Retrieved January 4, 2006, from http://www.psla.org/pslaworkshops/fall2002_files/psla2002workshop.ppt

5

Policies and Procedures

One of the most important responsibilities of a school library media specialist is to develop or maintain an updated policy and procedures manual. Written policies and procedures are critical to the efficient management of a school media program and collection. Such policies and procedures have numerous purposes:

Introduction Paragraph info.

- ensure a degree of consistency;
- define the scope and coverage of the collection;
- assign selection responsibility;
- facilitate quality selection;
- provide guidance in the acquisition, processing, and cataloging of materials;
- provide for maintenance of materials and equipment;
- aid in weeding or deselection of the collection;
- impart information dealing with the circulation and promotion of the collection;
- guide evaluation of the collection;
- acknowledge the rights of individuals to ask for reconsideration of materials;
- guide staff in handling complaints;
- protect intellectual freedom;
- promote fair use of copyrighted materials;
- ensure student access to materials, including those on the Internet;
- serve as a training tool for new staff or volunteers;
- create a public-relations document to inform the public of the purposes of the program and collection; and
- provide a means of assessing overall performance of the media program.

Having written policies can save time, help avoid confusion, and provide guidance. For instance, if you are absent from your position for a long period of time due to illness or perhaps maternity leave, a policy and procedures manual will be invaluable to the person who is substituting in your position. If you leave your position to take another, your replacement will be able to have background on your program and collection, including a clear understanding of what policies and procedures have been in place. In difficult situations such as a materials complaint being made by an emotional parent, the written procedures for handling a challenge can provide guidance, consistency, and support. Written policies and procedures demonstrate to a reader that the program is run in a professional manner, decisions are not arbitrarily made, and overall planning is taking place.

Policy versus Procedure Statements

Policy statements and procedure statements guide the activities of the collection program and tell why the collection exists. They state goals in general terms, allowing for flexibility and change. Policies establish the basis for all the collection activities by identifying who will use the collection and what will be in the collection. They need to be in place before procedures are developed. Policy documents are known by various terms including *collection policy*, *selection policy*, and *materials policy*.

Procedure statements direct the implementation of policies. They should be concrete and measurable. By defining "what, how, and when" questions, they address the tasks or processes for attaining the policy goals. Procedure statements explain how policies will be put into practice and identify the people responsible for their implementation. Procedures are specific and should be reviewed and updated on a regular basis. Examples of policies and procedures for specific school media centers can be found in the "Helpful Web Sites" listed at the end of this chapter.

As you examine documents, try to determine whether the policies and procedures are clearly distinguished. Questions you can ask yourself include the following: Does the statement

- address the purpose of the collection? (a policy)
- identify the types of materials that will be included? (a policy)
- explain how the collection will be created? (a procedure)
- state who is responsible for the collection? (a policy)
- describe the steps for maintaining the collection? (a procedure)
- explain the basis for adding or withdrawing materials from the collection? (a policy)
- identify who (students, teachers) will be involved in the selection process? (a policy)
- describe how teachers, administrators, and students will be involved in the selection process? (a procedure)
- identify student responsibilities for the use of resources in an ethical and educational manner? (a policy)

Formulating and Adopting Policies

Policies need to reflect the goals and needs of the individual media program and its institution. To be effective and responsive to these specific goals and needs, policy statements should be created at both the district and building levels. For example, usually the school district's stance on intellectual freedom and fair use are developed at the district level; questions dealing with the level of collecting materials on specific subjects would be at the building level.

The diversity of building-level educational programs and the changing needs of users limit the effectiveness of adopting another school's policy statement. However, it is helpful to examine statements from various sources. Doing so can prevent omissions, provide guidance for the outline, and offer suggestions for wording.

You should obtain input from others when writing specific policies for your school media center. A library advisory board comprised of teachers, administrators, parents, and perhaps students can assist with the development, approval, and implementation of both policies and procedures. Each school will have its own process for approving policies. In some schools, the policy is approved only at building level. For instance, in a school utilizing site-based management a school advisory board composed of administrators, classroom teachers, and parents might be the group to whom policies are submitted for approval. In other school districts, there is a defined procedure that terminates with school board approval. Consult your school administrators to plan for the steps to obtain formal approval of your policies.

The following is a sample of the steps that might be followed by a governing body in formally formulating and adopting a policy:

1. Decides to establish and adopt a policy.

2. Appoints an ad hoc committee composed of representatives of the school community.

3. This body may include parents, students, certified media specialists, administrators, people from other libraries and educational institutions, and community members. If the policy is to cover all instructional materials, including textbooks, then the body should also include subject specialists.

4. Determines who will use the policy.

5. Identifies when the statement might be used for evaluating the collection, preparing funding proposals, generating accreditation reports, or guiding cooperative resource-sharing agreements.

6. Charges the committee with the responsibility of developing the policy and establishes a deadline for the presentation of a draft.

7. Distributes general guidelines to the committee to facilitate its work.

8. Studies the draft before discussing it with the committee.

9. Determines whether and how the policy can be easily updated.

10. Solicits discussion and suggestions from legal counsel, personnel within the school (such as department heads or curriculum

committees), and groups such as parent-teacher associations and the teachers' association.

11. Conducts a closing review of the committee's recommendations and the comments expressed by others who studied the draft.

12. Adopts a formal written statement as the approved policy of the issuing agency.

13. Provides for implementation of the newly adopted policy. This involves disseminating the policy to all staff members involved in the evaluation, selection, and use of materials covered in the policy. A meeting or staff development program should familiarize the staff with the policy so they can respond to inquiries about it. Media personnel and teachers are likely to be the ones who receive requests that materials in the collection or used in classrooms be reconsidered.

14. Disseminates the policy to the community.

15. Plans and conducts school and community activities to make people aware of the importance of the freedom to read, speak, view, listen, evaluate, and learn.

16. Establishes periodic evaluation and revision of the policy. Reviews should be scheduled on a regular basis with intervals of one to three years.

17. Formally adopts changes. Dates of the original adoption and sequential revisions recorded on the document are helpful indicators of the document's history.

A graphical representation of this process can be found in Figure 5.1.

Writing a Policies and Procedures Manual

If you take a position in a school media center that does not have written policies and procedures, one of your initial responsibilities should be to begin the development of a manual that includes the policies from the district level, plus any policies and procedures specific to your media center. Policies and procedures can be integrated into one manual or you may choose to separate them into two different manuals.

Your manual should be written in third person, and proper names of persons should not be included. Instead of naming the person who performs a certain task or has a specific responsibility, use terms such as *the media specialist* or *the media clerk* or *the principal*. These terms should not be capitalized. Using such terms will create a more professional manual and will avoid having to make frequent revisions when personnel changes are made. Other helpful hints for creating a professional manual include the following:

- Be concise; use a minimum of verbiage.

- If you use acronyms, spell them out the first time they are utilized.

- Include step-by-step instructions for describing procedures.

Figure 5.1. Process of policy formulation and revision

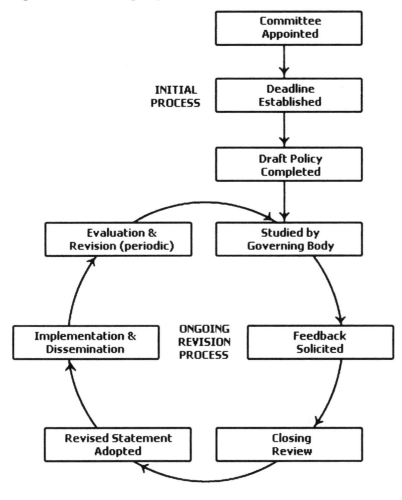

- Do not be too technical; make the manual simple enough to be understood by a lay person or a new employee.

- Make generous use of white space.

- Be factual; double-check for accuracy.

A table of contents should be included in the beginning of the manual; however, the manual pages do not need to be numbered. Putting your manual in a sturdy loose-leaf binder with various topics presented in separate sections (perhaps denoted by labeled tabs or color-coded division pages) will make it easier for you to make revisions or additions when you want to update the manual. If at a later date, you choose to add or delete a few paragraphs printing out a couple of revised pages of a section is much more efficient than having to reprint the entire manual. When you make revisions, it is often helpful to add the date of the revision (e.g.: 11/07) in a footer at the bottom of the page.

You do not need to "recreate the wheel" when you are writing a manual, but if you take a substantial amount of wording from another document, you should provide a citation for the original document. This can easily be done by placing an asterisk after the original wording and putting a citation in a footer at the bottom of the page. You might want to adopt a certain style (MLA, Turabian, etc.) for your citations, but no matter what style you decide to utilize, the citations need to have enough information for the reader to access the original documents. If you are including a district-level policy or procedure in your manual, you might choose to place it in an appendix and cite the item in the text of your manual. You can then add into the text any other information that is specific to your school media center, such as where a complainant can obtain a copy of a form for reconsideration of a challenged material.

If the media center in which you take a position as a media specialist already has written policies and procedures, you need to carefully read and follow them until any revisions are made. Again, it is helpful to include a date for revisions that you make, especially if there are additional copies of the manual in other parts of the school. Ideally, all copies of a manual should contain any new revisions. You definitely need to retain the original in your media center office and date any revisions, just in case confusion arises over differing versions of a policy or accepted procedure.

As a library school educator the author of this book has often required students to write a manual for a hypothetical school media center or work collaboratively with a school media specialist to develop a manual for an actual media center. This assignment can be very time-consuming so often the students complete the assignment in groups, making group decisions about which selection tools will be used, what steps to follow for a challenged book, whether to charge fines for overdue books, and various other topics. This creates some interesting discussions and careful consideration of all the areas that comprise collection development and management. Former students of this educator frequently contact this library school educator to express appreciation for including this assignment in their educational programs.

You will be extremely busy as a new media specialist so having already carefully considered all the aspects of collection development and management and having a model to follow for written policies and procedures will be a huge timesaver in the future.

Contents of a Manual

Numerous topics can be included in a policy and procedures manual. The following are suggested items for all manuals:
Table of Contents

- Community and School Analyses
- Library Philosophy/Mission Statement
- LMC Goals and Objectives
- Description of Programs and Services
- Personnel Job Descriptions
- Formats Collected
- Selection Policies and Procedures

- Acquisition, Processing, and Cataloging of Materials
- Gifts
- Maintaining Materials and Equipment
- Inventory of Materials
- Weeding Materials
- Circulation
- Collection Evaluation
- Internet/Technology (Including an Internet Use Policy)
- Copyright and Fair Use Compliance
- Intellectual Freedom

These items do not need to be in the order listed, but they should be in a logical order. For instance, a community and school analysis should be toward the beginning of the manual since the policies and procedures are supposed to be based on the needs of the users.

Other topics or items which can be helpful to include in the text of a manual or in an appendix are: resource sharing, behavior guidelines and classroom (LMC) management techniques, budget and fundraising, public relations, evaluation of the LMC program, evaluation of personnel, confidentiality of records, a student handbook, a manual for volunteers, and any useful forms or surveys. As you can see there are many policies and procedures to remember when developing a collection and managing a program. You will not want to carry all this information around in your head—and it will not serve others adequately if it is not in a written format.

Conclusions

In order to efficiently develop and manage collection activities, policies and procedures need to be developed by the school library media specialist, with input from others who utilize the materials. District-level policies that relate to the media center must be considered and followed. Additionally, policies should go through an approval process. All policies and procedures should be organized in a written format so that consistency can be maintained and a clear understanding of collection activities and the media center program is available. Policies and procedures should be regularly reviewed for possible revisions to make certain they are meeting the mission and goals of the media center.

Additional Reading

Hoffman, F. W., & Wood, R. J. (2005). *Library collection development policies: Academic, public, and special libraries.* Lanham, MD: Scarecrow Press.

Helpful Web Sites

Bellingham Public Schools. (2004). *Library collection management.* Retrieved June 20, 2006, from http://www.bham.wednet.edu/departments/libmedtech/libcollmanage.htm

Lamb, A., & Johnson, L. (2004). *The school library media specialist: Policies and procedures.* Retrieved April 23, 2006, from http://eduscapes.com/sms/policies. html

Washington Library Association. (1996). *Policies and procedures impacting school library media centers*. Retrieved March 11, 2006, from http://www.wlma.org/ WaLibraries/policyconcepts.htm

6

Selection

As a media specialist you will be involved in updating a selection policy for your school or if one is not in place, you should take the lead in creating a selection policy, including policies and procedures that relate to requests for reconsideration of materials. As discussed in Chapter 5, "Policies and Procedures," policy statements are stronger and more effective when formulated by a group. The media specialist's professional responsibility is to ensure that appropriate policies are in place. Involving teachers, administrators, students, and members of the community is vital to the process. A major benefit to this is the participants' advocacy and support of the principles on which the policy is based. This process presents an opportunity to explain the media center's role in the educational process, to emphasize the importance of a commitment to intellectual freedom, and to discuss the concept of providing access to information.

Some states have mandates for school media center selection policies that include procedures for reconsideration of challenged materials. In other states similar mandates are present at the school district level. You should contact your state department of education or department of public instruction for information about such mandates.

Elements of a Selection Policy

If a selection policy is issued as a separate document, several elements need to be included. The following section discusses each of these elements. If you include the selection policy in a larger manual that deals with all policies and procedures, then some of the initial element that addresses philosophy might be covered in an earlier section of your manual.

Statement of Philosophy

This brief statement presents the school district's values and beliefs. It can refer to the school's mission and goals statement or language from that document. The statement of philosophy should also address how the educational resources help the school achieve its goals.

Other relevant documents can be duplicated in this section. A statement referring to the *Constitution of the United States* First Amendment's protection of students' rights to access information to read, listen, view, and evaluate is important to include. Readers can be directed to copies of documents in an appendix that support these principles. Such documents include the American Library Association's *Library Bill of Rights* and *Freedom to Read Statement*, the National Council of Teachers of English's *Students' Right to Read*, and the American Film and Video's Association's *Freedom to View Statement*.

Sample phrases in this section generally start with "the Board of [school district's name] through its professional staff shall provide," "will provide," or "is committed to facilitating teaching and learning by providing." One or more of the following phrases could be used to complete sentences:

- "library media center collections that meet both the curricular needs and personal needs of students."
- "resources in various formats and varying levels of difficulty."
- "materials that provide a global perspective and promote diversity."
- "resources that reflect the basic humanity of all people and are free of stereotypes."
- "library materials that present different points of view in an objective manner."
- "materials that will help students develop critical thinking skills and aesthetic appreciation."

Selection Objectives

This element of the policy translates the school district's philosophy and goals into collection objectives. The statements show how the collection helps the school meet its goals. Objectives identify the materials that will be in the collection, present a rationale for using a variety of resources in the school, and describe the basis for judging the educational suitability of the materials for use by students and teachers. Examples of main objective statements are:

- To make available to faculty and students a collection of materials that will support, supplement, and enrich the curriculum
- To provide a wide range of the best materials available on appropriate levels of difficulty
- To enhance the curriculum with a variety of materials that are representative of the points of view of the religious, cultural, ethnic, and social groupings within the community
- To select materials that present various sides of controversial issues so that students have an opportunity to develop skills in critical analysis and in making informed judgments in their daily lives
- To place principle above personal opinion or prejudice in order to assure a comprehensive collection that is appropriate to the school community
- To provide materials in a variety of formats, including both print and electronic materials, to support the students' learning needs

- To select materials that stimulate growth in factual knowledge, literary appreciation, aesthetic values, and societal standards

Responsibility for Selection

An important element of the selection policy is stating who is responsible for selection decisions. If the policy applies to all instructional materials, this statement should distinguish between those who are responsible for text materials and those responsible for media program materials.

These statements usually acknowledge that the school board is legally responsible and delegates to media specialists the authority to select. The term *media specialist* can be defined as "professional, certified personnel employed by the district."

A statement that identifies who participates in the selection process should also be included. This statement indicates the role and level of involvement of teachers, students, administrators, staff, and community members in the selection process. Some questions that might be addressed include the following: Does a committee make selection decisions? Do media specialists work independently? Is a combination of committee selections and media specialist selections utilized? How is responsibility delegated? How is input for selection gathered from teachers and students?

Selection Criteria

Selection criteria generally consist of two or more parts. The first is a list of general criteria that apply to all materials and relate to the district or school goals. A statement that these criteria apply to all materials, including gifts and loans, can eliminate the need to write a separate section about such items.

General criteria commonly utilized include literary qualities, technical qualities, qualifications of authors or producers, and appropriateness for audience. You can obtain additional assistance for this section by consulting Chapter 7, "General Selection Criteria." Criteria that are often used for general selection indicate that the materials should do the following:

- Contribute to the instructional program's objectives.
- Be consistent with and support the general educational goals of the state and district.
- Help students gain an awareness of our pluralistic society.
- Be relevant to today's world.
- Reflect the problems, aspirations, attitudes, and ideals of society.
- Be appropriate for the age, ability level, learning style, and social and emotional development of the intended user.
- Be appropriate for the subject area.
- Meet quality standards in terms of content, format, and presentation.
- Be selected for their strengths, rather than rejected for their weaknesses.
- Reflect value commensurate with cost and/or need.

- Not represent a personal bias.

- Represent artistic, historic, and literary qualities.

- Have a high degree of potential user appeal.

- Motivate students to examine their own attitudes; to understand their rights, duties, and responsibilities as citizens; and to make informed judgments in their daily lives.

In selecting all formats for possible purchase the media specialist should consider the following general criteria:

- Reputation of the author, illustrator, publisher, and producer

- Overall quality and accuracy

- Currency and appropriateness of the content

- Value in relation to cost and need

- Value to the collection

The second part of selection criteria can address criteria for specific formats of materials, including electronic formats and equipment. If you want to address the criteria for specific formats, the content of Chapter 8, "Criteria by Format," will be especially helpful.

Some policies identify selection sources to consult and then specify that two or more favorable reviews must appear in the selection tools before an item can be considered for selection. This practice has several disadvantages that may prove to be restrictive. First, reviewing journals and selection tools often do not review the same titles. Second, a dearth of reviews exists for many formats. Third, a specific list of selection tools may not be comprehensive or may not identify sources actually used. This policy creates a problem if none of the cited sources has reviewed a particular item. The requirement of having two reviews in particular selection tools limits selections made by media specialists and should not be included in policies.

While selection aids can be helpful in identifying titles to be considered for purchase, using reviews as a criterion for selection focuses on the review, rather than the professional judgment of the media specialist. However, if you choose to include procedures relating to selection of materials, you might want to list the selection tools that are recommended as consultation aids. Possible wording could be: "The following recommended lists can be consulted in the selection of materials, but selection is not limited to their listing." An annotated listing of some selection aids that could be included in such a list can be found in Appendix "Resources".

Gifts

If the acceptance of gifts is not included in the general criteria section of your selection policy, statements addressing criteria used for the acceptance or rejection of gifts need to be included in a separate section. Most schools apply the same criteria for acceptance of gifts as they do for purchases. However, you might want to also consider how you will handle items that are donated by businesses or commercial concerns. Noting that no advertising beyond the name of the contributing company and including a statement that such donations must relate to the curriculum can be useful. You might also wish to include a statement relating to the currency of donated materials. This may eliminate the need of having to deal with boxes of donated *National Geographic* magazines from the 1960s and 1970s. While some of the articles in those magazines might have interesting information, most of the information will be quite outdated, and your available space to put them on your shelves will most likely be quite limited.

Some school media centers also include a statement relating to the fact that all gifts become the property of the school district and when declared surplus can be dispensed as deemed appropriate by the media specialist. This might include transferring the surplus items to another school or weeding them from the collection. A statement could read: "The media center does not accept gifts with restrictions or conditions relating to their final use, disposition, or location."

Policies relating to the acceptance of monetary gifts to purchase materials should also be addressed. If accepting monetary gifts, specific procedures should be written and carefully followed.

You might also want to include some procedures relating to gifts to the media center. Providing letters and/or receipts to acknowledge gifts to a media center should be part of such procedures. This letter or receipt should note the number and types of materials donated, but should not specify a dollar amount, unless the gift was monetary. Other procedures might include whether notations of donated resources are included in the catalog entry and whether a bookplate or notation is added to the material itself.

Policies on Controversial Materials

You should include a section in your policy that deals with intellectual freedom and the handling of controversial materials. Most school districts have written policies that address this topic not only in regard to materials present in the media center, but also for books or other formats used in classroom lessons. Thus, it is important for you to include in your selection policy any school district policies that relate to controversial materials in a media center. This can be done in the text of your selection policy, or the school district policy can be placed in an appendix and referred to from the text.

You need to include a statement that your school media center supports the principle of intellectual freedom and explain why it is important to maintain. If you have not already referred to the First Amendment to the *United States Constitution* or to other documents that address intellectual freedom, you should do so in this section. Wording in this section might read as follows: "The Lincoln School Media Center supports the principles of intellectual freedom inherent in the First Amendment to the *United States Constitution* as expressed in official statements of professional associations. These include [identify statement(s)] and form a part of this policy."

Request for Reconsideration of Materials

Most selection policies also include procedures for handling complaints and for focusing the complainant's attention on the principles of intellectual freedom, rather than on the material itself. A school district may have specific procedures for dealing with challenged materials. In such a case, you will need to place these procedures in your policies and procedures document and make certain they are implemented correctly.

If the steps to follow for challenged materials are not specified by the school district, then you should meet with an advisory board at your school, develop the procedures, and put them through an approval process.

Possible steps to consider in your reconsideration of materials in your media center include:

1. Listen calmly and with courtesy to the complainant.

2. Explain to the complainant the selection criteria used for materials that are in the media center and try to resolve the issue informally by discussing the educational uses of the material in question and noting relevant sections of the American Library Association's *Access to Resources and Services in the School Library Program: An Interpretation of the Library Bill of Rights*.

3. If the complainant wants to proceed with a formal request for reconsideration of a material, provide a copy of the policies and procedures related to the handling of challenged materials, as well as a copy of the school's *Request for Reconsideration of Library Resources* form.

4. Instruct the complainant that the form must be completed before a formal complaint proceeds.

5. Inform the principal of the challenge and the identity of the complainant (if the complaint is resolved informally, keep the identity of the complainant confidential).

6. When the complainant returns the completed form, the principal will inform the superintendent of schools of a request for formal reconsideration.

7. Form a reconsideration committee to include a building administrator, a classroom teacher from the appropriate grade level or subject area, the school library media specialist, an objective member of the community, and a student (if the challenged material is in a secondary school).

8. Appoint a chairperson for the committee.

9. Have the chairperson arrange a meeting of the committee to be held within ten working days after the form is returned to the school by the complainant.

10. At the first meeting, instruct all members of the committee to read the completed *Request for Reconsideration of Library Resources* form and to read, view, or listen to the material in question. The media specialist may need to obtain additional copies of the resource (book, video, or audiocassette) through interlibrary loan or through informal means before a time for the next meeting can be set.

11. At a second meeting when all committee members have had ample opportunity to examine and evaluate the challenged resource, discuss the material that has been questioned.

12. Instruct the committee members to form opinions on the resource as a whole, not on specific passages or selections.

13. Have the committee reach a decision, using majority rules, to retain or remove the item.

14. Have the chairperson complete a report of the committee's procedures and their decision regarding the challenged material and submit the report to the principal.

15. Instruct the principal to send a copy of the report to the complainant and discuss it with the complainant if so requested. Remind the principal to also submit a copy of the report to the superintendent of schools.

16. If the complainant continues to be dissatisfied with the process, inform that person that he or she has the right to appeal the decision of the committee to the superintendent of schools and the district school board.

17. Keep challenged materials in circulation until the process is complete.

Figure 6.1 is a sample of a form for requesting the reconsideration of a library resource. You should make certain that the form that you utilize meets the needs of your particular school setting and has been approved. In some schools the same form is used for challenging materials in a classroom setting as for the reconsideration of materials in a library media center; thus, in those cases some adaptation of this sample form would be needed.

Generally speaking, procedures are written for internal use and are not necessarily available for public use; however, in the case of challenged materials, a single document for the public's use should combine both the policies and procedures for handling the challenge. This document should be readily available to the public, with a copy kept at the circulation desk. Sharing this information in a forthright manner can alleviate some of the tension that can occur in situations where materials are challenged.

In this author's experience with challenged materials, she found most challenges are settled informally if one takes the time to calmly listen to the complainant's concerns and then explain the media center's criteria for selection, emphasizing the principle of intellectual freedom. Assuring parents that you respect the interest that they have in their own child's reading or viewing can often satisfy the needs of parents to voice their concerns.

Challenges to materials are to be expected in most schools. The challenges may come from parents, community members, teachers, principals, or organized groups. Having a written procedure to follow and knowing how to respond to a challenge will alleviate the emotional upset that sometimes is experienced by media specialists when faced with an irate parent or an outspoken member of an organized group that challenges library materials. To ensure that all queries, whether internal or external, are treated in the same manner, each individual's complaint should be treated according to the written procedures.

Selection Procedures

In choosing materials, a media specialist plans and carries out certain activities that culminate in selection decisions. These activities include identifying and assessing evaluative information about materials,

Figure 6.1. Sample request form

Request for reconsideration of library resources

Before a request can be acted upon, the following form must be completed. You should read, view, or listen to the material in its entirety.

Type of Resource (book, magazine, video, audiocassette, software):

Title of the Resource:

Author or Producer:

Publisher/Distributor: Copyright Date:

Person Initiating the Request: Date of Request:

Address:

Home Telephone: Work Telephone:

Please answer the following questions:

1. Are you making this request on your own behalf?

2. Are you representing an organization with your request?
If so, identify the organization:

3. Have you received a copy of the school's policies and procedures in regard to selection of library resources and the handling of resources that are challenged by an individual or an organization?

4. Have you read, viewed, or listened to the entire resource?

5. What are your concerns about the resource? Be specific.

6. What are some positive aspects of this resource?

7. Can you recommend other resources that could serve similar educational purposes?

8. Do you want to make an oral presentation to the Reconsideration of Library Resources Committee in regard to this material?

Please return this form to the principal of the school who will contact you regarding your request after the Committee has made its decision about whether to retain the material or remove it from the school library media center collection.

arranging for examining materials either through visiting exhibits or examination centers, and providing ways to involve others in the process. These steps lead to the direct acquisition of materials or obtaining materials and information through resource sharing and electronic means. For a listing of resources that can assist in the selection process, see Appendix, "Resources."

Overview of the Selection Process

Selection is the process of deciding what materials to add to the collection. Media specialists can identify potential materials through many sources. For example, administrators, teachers, and students request specific items or types of materials. The media specialist learns about new materials by reading reviews, viewing the announcements of publishers and producers, and previewing materials.

You need to keep a record of suggestions and requests to purchase materials. This can be done in a computer file, a card file, or simply by keeping written notes; this record is called a *consideration file*. You should record as much bibliographic and purchasing information about the item as you can obtain, including the identifying source and the person who requested the item. The next step is to determine whether the item is already in the collection or on order. Some media specialists enter the information in the online catalog so users will be aware that the item is being considered or on order.

Once an item is fully identified, the media specialist must decide to include or exclude it from the collection. The media specialist bases this selection decision on several considerations, including collection policy, budget, content, format, use, and immediacy of need. After the media specialist has decided to purchase the item, the status of the record for the item is changed from "consideration file" to "order file." The actions following this step compose the acquisition process.

Sources of Information about Resources

Bibliographic tools provide information about the availability of materials, their cost, and whether they are recommended. Trade bibliographies, such as *Books in Print* (R. R. Bowker) and *Canadian Books in Print* (University of Toronto Press), provide information about the existence of materials, but do not evaluate them. They are available in print and electronic versions. Selection tools, such as *Senior High School Library Catalog* (H.W. Wilson), *Middle and Junior High School Library Catalog* (H.W. Wilson), and *Children's Catalog* (H. W. Wilson), evaluate materials and may include purchasing information. They are also available electronically and are especially useful for core collections if you are developing a library collection from scratch.

When considering a bibliography or selection tool for use or purchase, read the introduction and examine several entries. This will help answer the following questions about the work:

- *Purpose of the bibliography*: Does it meet your need?

- *Directions for use*: Are they clear? Does the work give sample entries with explanations?

- *Format*: Is the bibliography available in print, CD-ROM, or online?

- *Extent of coverage*: Does the resource include information about a variety of formats? Does it provide information for many items, or is coverage limited? Does it include materials for a wide range of audiences, preschool through adult? What periods of publication and production does the work include?

- *Method for collecting the information and designated responsibility*: Who wrote the entries? What are the writers' qualifications? Are reviews signed?

- *Criteria for inclusion*: On what basis are items included? Are the criteria stated? Is the selection policy provided?

- *Form and content of entry*: Does the work present information clearly? Does it use symbols and abbreviations? Symbols may indicate levels of recommendation, reviewing sources, interest level, readability, and type of media. What ordering and bibliographic information does the work give? Are the annotations descriptive, evaluative, or both? Are all items recommended equally? Are items recommended for specific situations, uses, or audiences? Are there comparisons with other titles or formats? Does the work include only materials that have received favorable reviews in other tools?

- *Organization of entries*: Are the indexes necessary to locate an item? Do cross-references direct the user to related items? Do indexes provide access by author, title, series titles, audience, reading level, and subject? Does the index include analytical entries? For example, the selection tools by H. W. Wilson Company include analytical entries for individual folktales in anthologies, biographical sketches (not limited to collective biographies), subjects, and short stories in collections. This information is helpful in locating these materials for students and teachers.

- *Date of publication*: Does the work provide the compiler's closing date? How often is the bibliography revised or cumulated? Does it provide supplements? What time lag exists between compiling the information and the issuing of the bibliography?

- *Special features*: Does the bibliography include directories for sources of materials? Does the work include appendices? If so, what is included?

- *Cost*: Does the tool provide sufficient information for a variety of users to merit the expenditure for it?

Selection Tools

Selection tools exist in a variety of formats: books, reviewing periodicals, and bibliographic essays. These tools can be in print or electronic format.

Books

Commonly used general selection tools that appear in book format are the H. W. Wilson series (*Children's Catalog, Middle and Junior High School Library Catalog,* and *Senior High School Library Catalog*). The lead time required to produce these books creates a time gap between the publication of the last item reviewed and the publication date of the bibliography. As a result, books, even if available in electronic format, are not as current as reviewing journals.

Other book-formatted selection tools list recommended materials for specific subjects, audiences, or formats. See Appendix, "Resources," for titles of these books.

Reviewing Journals

Reviewing journals evaluate currently published and produced materials. You will find a wide range of these journals, each with unique and valuable features. Commercial firms, professional associations, education agencies, and other publishers produce reviewing journals. Generally they are written for a specific audience, such as media specialists or classroom teachers. The coverage of materials that journals review is often limited by format, potential users, subjects, or particular perspectives.

The reviews are written by journal staff members or by professionals in the field. Signed reviews sometimes provide information about the reviewer's position or background.

The content of some journals such as *Booklist* are primarily reviews of materials. However, many reviewing journals, such as *Library Media Connection* and *School Library Journal*, also include articles or columns of interest to media specialists. Some professional journals, such as the American Association of School Librarians' *Knowledge Quest*, limit their reviews to materials that could be a part of a professional collection.

Journals might not review a specific title for legitimate reasons. Some journals do not review a work unless it can be reviewed within a specific time after its publication. Some titles may be outside a journal's scope, or they might simply fail to meet other criteria set up by the journal. A huge number of juvenile resources are produced each year so it is impossible for a journal to review all of them.

Locating reviews for audiovisual materials, computer software, electronic materials, and online databases can be more challenging than finding book reviews. However, more review journals are including these formats than in past years. Cumulated indexes that appear in the back pages of some journals can be helpful in the search for reviews, but a more comprehensive approach to review indexing can be found in tools such as *Book Review Index, Book Review Digest*, and *Media Review Digest*. These tools are available in print format and online. The cost of such tools may require that all media centers in the district share them.

Bibliographic Essays

Bibliographic essays that describe and recommend materials about a subject, a theme, a specific use, or an audience can be found in journals such as *Teacher Librarian* and *Book Links*. These essays can be very helpful, but they require careful analysis. Readers do not know whether the writer simply overlooked an omitted item or whether the writer deliberately omitted that item. Usually, bibliographic essays focus on a specific topic and do not provide overall assessments of the resources.

Relying on Reviewing Media

Media specialists use reviewing media on a regular basis. If no selection committee exists, the entire burden of selection rests with the media specialist. To examine every item published or produced within a given year would be an impossible task.

What do media specialists look for in reviews? Janie Schomberg (1993) writes,

> I need and expect a lot from reviews. First, book reviews should be descriptive, objective statements about plot, characters, theme, and illustrations. Second, I expect book reviews to have an evaluative statement including comparison of the title being reviewed to similar titles and literature in general. Third, the potential appeal, curricular use, and possible controversial aspects of the title need to be addressed to fully inform me as a potential selector. (p. 41)

You need to remember that reviews reflect the writer's opinion, based on her or his knowledge of materials and students.

A variety of sources provide reviews. In addition to the ones noted earlier in this chapter, reviews can be found on Web sites of individuals, professional groups, and commercial organizations, such as Amazon.com. As with other review sources, you should try to determine the authority and background of the reviewer and whether there are guidelines for the reviewers.

You should evaluate reviews by examining the following:

- Bibliographic information
- Purchasing information
- Cataloging information
- Description, and evaluation of literary characteristics: plot, character, theme, setting, point of view, and style
- Description and evaluation of usability: authority, appropriateness, scope, accuracy, arrangement, and organization
- Description and evaluation of visual characteristics: shape, line, edge, color, proportion, detail, composition, and medium style
- Description and evaluation of comparison: author, illustrator, and other works
- Description and evaluation of sociological factors: controversial or popular
- Description and evaluation of other considerations: total artistic appearance, book design, use, and audience

Kay Bishop and Phyllis Van Orden (1998) in a comprehensive study dealing with journal reviewing of children's books noted that school media specialists need to have access to more than one reviewing journal and they should select reviewing journals that most closely suit the specific needs of their media centers. Table 6.1 displays some of the journals frequently utilized by school media specialists. All of these journals include reviews of more than one format. Some of the journals are available both in print format and online.

Personal Examination

The ideal way to select resources for your media center is by personal examination. Depending on your school district's policies, you may be able to personally examine materials. The most practical ways include visits by

Table 6.1. Reviewing journals' coverage of formats

Title	Book	Graphic Novel	Electronic Online	Audio-cassette	CD	Video-cassette	DVD	Web Site
Booklist	X	X	X	X	X	X	X	X
Canadian Review of Materials	X			X	X	X	X	
Kliatt	X	X		X	X			
Library Journal	X	X	X	X	X	X	X	X
Library Media Connection	X	X	X		X	X	X	X
Resource Links (Canadian)	X	X			X	X	X	X
School Library Journal	X	X		X	X	X	X	X
Teacher Librarian	X	X	X			X	X	X
VOYA	X	X	X	X		X	X	X

sales representatives, formal previewing arrangements, visiting examination centers, and attending conferences.

Previewing is one of the most efficient ways to examine materials prior to purchasing. This is the practice of borrowing materials from an examination center, a producer, a distributor, or a jobber for a specific time for the purpose of evaluation. Previewing is an effective way to involve students and teachers in the selection process. Previewing is not a free way to supplement the collection, nor should several teachers within one building request the same item for examination at different times. The media specialist is responsible for returning previewing materials in good condition within the specified time. Some companies will not allow preview of certain formats, such as videocassettes or computer software. Also, some school districts do not allow the request of materials for preview. Requesting materials you are seriously considering for purchase and planning for their systematic evaluation, however, is an excellent way to make informed selection decisions.

When attending conferences you should always set aside ample time to examine the materials in the exhibit areas. This is an excellent opportunity to not only view the materials but to also ask company representatives questions or to provide them with suggestions. Vendors are interested in the opinions of school media specialists and welcome their input into ways to improve their products.

Some school districts arrange for exhibits of materials in a central location during the pre-opening school activities. These exhibits allow media specialists and teachers to compare a wide range of materials, including software, on the same subject. If your school district sponsors such exhibits, invite teachers to examine the materials with you.

Another way to personally evaluate materials is to visit an examination or preview center. These centers may serve district, regional, or state levels. They can be housed in the district media center, at a university, or in a state agency. Often the materials in a preview center cannot be checked out, but can be examined only within the center.

Whether your evaluation involves personal examination of items or relies on reviews, some materials will, for one reason or another, remain unused or prove to be inappropriate. You should consider these situations as learning experiences. Schomberg (1993) observes, "There seems to be no way to avoid the occasional 'lemon.' . . . Selection of materials based upon reviews cannot be expected to be successful 100% of the time" (p. 42).

Other Sources of Information

Information about materials can also be obtained from publishers, producers, distributors, vendors, and wholesalers. The information appears in catalogs, on flyers, on television, and on the Internet. However, you should always be cautious about making selections from only these types of sources since their main objective is to sell their products.

Involving Others in Selection

The idea that teachers, students, and administrators should participate in making selection decisions is not new, but its practice is not always utilized. Common ways to involve others in the process include:

- Routing bibliographies and reviewing journals to teachers and administrators
- Attending faculty, departmental, or grade-level meetings to learn about curriculum changes and to discuss future purchases
- Conducting interest inventories with students
- Sending out forms to teachers and administrators to ask them what materials they would like purchased
- Providing a materials suggestion box at the circulation desk

Media center advisory committees are another way to involve others. Teachers, community members, and students can be members of the advisory committee. In some districts, the advisory committee's responsibilities are limited to policy issues and to establishing priorities for acquisition. In other districts, the advisory committee may be involved in the selection process or in making decisions about which materials to remove or replace.

Sources of Assistance

Information regarding selection of materials is available from a variety of sources, including professional colleagues and professional associations. Several school districts and individual schools have placed their selection policies online. A selected list of such policies can be found at the end of this chapter under "Helpful Web Sites." The American Library Association site, which includes a workbook for selection policy writing, will be particularly helpful to you if you are creating a new selection policy for a school.

A list of suggested readings dealing with selection policies, intellectual freedom, censorship, handling challenges, and book reviewing can be found at the end of this chapter. Additional discussion of intellectual freedom appears in Chapter 13, "Ethical Issues and the Collection."

Other organizations, besides the American Library Association, offer valuable assistance in handling censorship disputes. These include the American Association of School Administrators, American Association of University Women, American Booksellers Foundation for Freedom of Expression, American Civil Liberties Union, American Federation of Teachers, Association of American Publishers, Electronic Frontier Foundation, Electronic Privacy Information Center, Free Expression Network, Freedom Forum, Freedom to Read Foundation, International Reading Association, Media Coalition, National Coalition Against Censorship, National Conference for Community and Justice, National Congress of Parents and Teachers, National Council of Teachers of English, National Education Association, National School Boards Association, and People for the American Way Foundation. Contact information for these groups can be located easily by using the title of the organization in an online search on the Internet.

Conclusions

Written selection policies for materials can be a separate document or part of a larger policies and procedures manual. Many school districts have selection policies for school media materials, as well as for textbooks. It is important to include in an individual school media center's policies and procedures manual any portions of the school district's policies that relate to school media materials. Selection policies should include who is responsible for selection, criteria for selecting materials, and how to handle controversial materials. Having written policies and procedures for challenged materials can ease tensions for a media specialist, as well as provide an objective process for those persons who register concerns about specific materials in a collection.

The ideal way to make selections of materials is to personally examine the resources. This can be done at conferences, special exhibits, examination centers, and by requesting materials for preview. Reading reviews of items and referring to bibliographies and special selection aids are other valuable means of selecting materials for a media center. Teachers, administrators, and students should also be involved in the selection process.

References

Bishop, K., & Van Orden, P. (1998). Reviewing children's books: A content analysis. *Library Quarterly, 68,* 145–182.

Schomberg, J. (1993). Tools of the trade: School library media specialists, reviews, and collection development. In B. Hearne & R. Sutton (Eds.), *Evaluating children's books: A critical look: Aesthetic, social, and political aspects of analyzing and using children's books* (pp. 37–46). Champaign-Urbana: University of Illinois, Graduate School of Library and Information Science.

Additional Readings

Bartow, D. (2002). The teachers' lounge. *The Education Digest, 68*(2), 62–65.

Brisco, S. Online material selection. *Teacher Librarian, 32*(2), 35.

Broman, J. (2001). Too many journals, too little time: A busy librarian offers some tips for learning to read through reviews. *School Library Journal, 47*(9), 46–47.

Coley, K. P. (2002). Moving toward a method to test for self-censorship by school library media specialists *School Library Media Research,* 5. Retrieved March 11, 2006, from http://www.ala.org/ala/aasl/aaslpubsandjournals/slmrb/slmrcontents/volume52002/coley.htm.

Credaro, A. (2004). Walking through the valley of the shadow of happy talk. *Library Media Collection, 23*(3), 51.

Hopkins, D. M. (2003). The value of support during a library media challenge. *Knowledge Quest, 31*(4), 32–36.

Jenkins, D. (2002). Selection and censorship: It's simple arithmetic. *School Libraries in Canada, 22*(4), 22–23.

Johnson, D. (2003). Foiling the language police. *Library Media Connection, 22*(3), 98.

Kelley, P. (2003). "When I was a Puerto Rican" by Esmeralda Santiago [Responding to a censorship challenge]. *Ohio Media Spectrum, 55*(1), 19–26.

Leffingwell, S. L. (2003). Banned and challenged books in Texas Public Schools 2002-2003. *Texas Library Journal, 79*(3), 110, 112–114.

Miltner, L. (2003). A challenge is just around the corner: Is your library ready? *Ohio Media Spectrum, 55*(1).

Minkel, W. (2001). Policy discussion: Add Web sites to your materials selection policy. *School Library Journal*, *47*(3), 41.

Mires, D. (2003). Censorship and the freedom to read. *PNLA Quarterly*, *67*(3), 15–17.

Sanacore, J. (2006). Teacher-librarians, teachers, and children as cobuilders of school library collections. *Teacher Librarian*, *33*(5), 24–29.

Shirley, L. J. (2001). Intellectual freedom in school libraries. *Louisiana Libraries*, *64*(2), 17–19.

Wilson, M., & Bishop, K. (1999). Criteria for reviewing children's books: A content analysis. *Library Resources & Technical Services*, *43*(1), 3–13.

Helpful Web Sites

American Library Association. (1998). *Workbook for selection policy writing.* Retrieved March 11, 2006, from http://www.ala.org/Template.cfm?Section= dealing&Template=/ContentManagement/ContentDisplay.cfm&ContentID= 57020

Baltimore County Public Schools. (n.d.). *Selection criteria for school library media center collections.* Retrieved March 11, 2006, from http://www.bcps.org/offices/ lis/office/admin/selection.html

Falk Lab School (2003). *Library selection policy.* Retrieved March 11, 2006, from http://tc.education.pitt.edu/library/SelectionPolicy.htm

Foothills Elementary School. (n.d). *School media center selection policy.* Retrieved March 11, 2006, from http://www.arches.uga.edu/~ahitchco/selectionpolicy.htm

Hawaii Department of Education. (1994). *Materials selection policy for school library instructional technology centers.* Retrieved March 11, 2006, from http://sls.k12. hi.us/selection.html

Hearn Elementary School. (2002). *Library media center selection policy.* Retrieved March 11, 2006, from http://www.kysma.org/Selection.htm

Hopkins, D. M. (n.d.). *School library media centers and intellectual freedom.* Retrieved March 11, 2006, from http://www.ala.org/ala/oif/iftoolkits/ifmanual/ fifthedition/schoollibrary.htm

Hopkinton High School and Hopkinton Middle School Library. (2005). *Selection policy and guidelines.* Retrieved March 11, 2006, from http://www.hopkintonschools. org/hhs/library/selpol.html

Iowa Association of School Librarians. (n.d.). *Selection policies.* Retrieved March 11, 2006, from http://www.hopkintonschools.org/hhs/library/selpol.html

Lanier, G. D. (n.d.) *Conducting a challenge hearing.* Retrieved March 11, 2006, from http://www.ala.org/Template.cfm?Section=dealing&Template=/Content Management/ContentDisplay.cfm&ContentID=11087

Montana State Library. (n.d.). *Collection development policy guidelines for school library media programs.* Retrieved March 11, 2006, from http://msl.state.mt. us/slr/cmpolsch.html

School District of Philadelphia. (2002). *Selection policy for school library materials.* Retrieved March 11, 2006, from http://libraries,phila.k12.pa.us/misc/selection-policy.html

University at Buffalo Libraries. (2005). *Educational media reviews online.* Retrieved November 7, 2006, from http://libweb.lib.buffalo.edu/emro/search.asp

7

General Selection Criteria

Selection is a complex decision-making process, not a simple, gut-level "I like this" response. Responsible collection development requires that broad considerations govern the evaluation and choice of a single item. A media specialist is responsible for the collection as an entity, as well as for individual items. You must base your choice on your evaluation of an item and its relationship to the collection. You should also justify your choice of an item by assessing its contribution to the policies and goals of the collection program.

When making selection decisions, the basic criterion is quality. Two fundamental questions must be considered. Is the format appropriate for the content? Does the presentation effectively address the users' needs? When evaluating an item's presentation, consider these questions: What is the idea (intellectual content)? How is it presented? Does the medium provide the most suitable treatment for the idea? The criteria that are provided in this chapter are guides, not absolutes. The collection, the users, resource-sharing plans, and outside resources influence the applicability of each criterion to specific items.

Selection decisions require the evaluator to judge materials within the framework of given criteria. These criteria can help one evaluate the content, physical form, or potential value of materials to users or to programs. In the final selection of whether to add an item to a collection, a media specialist must consider all the criteria.

The first part of this chapter describes general criteria that one may apply to all types of materials in a media center. The second portion of the chapter discusses criteria that can be utilized for equipment selections. For assistance in selecting specific formats of resources, see Chapter 8, "Criteria by Format."

Intellectual Content and Its Presentation

How can one evaluate the idea, or intellectual content, of a work? Criteria to help one do so include the following: (1) authority, (2) appropriateness of content to users, (3) scope, (4) authenticity, (5) treatment, (6) arrangement and organization, (7) instructional design, (8) special features, (9) materials available on the subject, and (10) value to the collection.

Authority

The basis for the criterion of authority addresses the qualifications and credibility of the people who created the work. This includes authors, illustrators, editors, directors, publishers, producers, and anyone else involved in the creation of a work. You can judge authority by considering the qualifications of the author, illustrator, or director; the quality and acceptance of other works by the same person; and the dependability and reputation of the publisher or producer.

Appropriateness of Content to Users

Appropriateness of content focuses on the intellectual content of a resource in relation to its intended use and audience. The concept must be appropriate to the users' developmental level. In other words, the presentation should be geared to the maturity and interest level of the intended users. Whether the content is factual or imaginative, it should not be presented in a condescending manner, nor should it supersede the users' capacity to understand. An item should be appropriate for the students who will use it and not for some arbitrary standard established by adults.

Scope

Scope refers to the content's overall purpose and depth of coverage. You can examine the introduction, teacher's guide, or other documentation for an item to learn the intended purpose and coverage. You should then evaluate whether the stated purpose meets a need of the collection and, if so, then decide whether the resource itself actually fulfills the stated purpose. When the content of the item you are considering duplicates content in other materials in a collection, you should consider whether the item presents content from a unique perspective. If it does, it may be a valuable addition that broadens the scope of the collection.

Authenticity

Information presented in materials should be valid, reliable, complete and current. Opinions need to be distinguished from facts and, as much as possible, impartially presented. Accuracy is often linked to timeliness, or how recently an item was published or produced, especially in technological subjects where changes occur rapidly. Check with a subject area specialist, if necessary, to be sure the information is timely. Remember, however, that a recent publication date does not necessarily show that the material itself is current or accurate.

Treatment

The treatment or presentation style can affect an item's potential value. It must be appropriate for the subject and use. In the best items, the presentation catches and holds the users' attention, draws on a typical experience, and stimulates further learning or creativity. Asking the following questions can help you evaluate the presentation of an item:

- Are the material's signs (pictures, visuals) and symbols (words, abstractions) necessary to the content and helpful to the user?

- Are the graphics, color, and sound well integrated into the presentation?
- Is the presentation free of bias and stereotyping?
- Does the material reflect our multicultural society?
- Is the information accessible to those who have physical limitations?
- Does the user control the rate and sequence of the content presentation?
- With electronic information, can the user easily enter, use, and exit the program?

The treatment of an item must be appropriate to the situation in which it will be used. Some materials require an adult to guide the student's use of material; other materials require use of a teacher's guide to present the information fully. Treatment may present very practical limitations. For example, consider whether the length is appropriate to class periods as generally scheduled. The use of a sixty-minute video may be problematic if the longest possible viewing period is fifty-five minutes.

Arrangement and Organization

Presentation of the material in terms of sequences and development of ideas influences comprehension. Content should be presented clearly and develop logically, flowing from one section to another and emphasizing important elements. The arrangement of information needs to facilitate its use. Content should be divided by headings, and information should be easy to locate. The presence of a summary or review of major points enhances effectiveness and helps users understand the work.

Instructional Design

Some materials are intended to meet certain instructional objectives. This is particularly true of textbooks, but can also apply to other books and formats, such as videocassettes or computer software. These materials need to meet the expectations of the learner or teacher. The following general questions can be asked to help evaluate such resources:

- Does the material encourage problem solving and creativity?
- Does the resource promote the understanding of ideas?
- Will users have the necessary capabilities (reading ability, vocabulary level, or computational skills) to learn from the material?
- Will the presentation arouse and motivate interest?
- With electronic materials, is direct access to specific parts of the program possible?
- Does the presentation simulate interaction?
- Are instructions clear?
- Is there effective use of color, text, sound, and graphics?
- Are there suitable instructional support resources provided?

Special Features

Some works have special or unique features that are absent from other resources on the same topic and thus they could have value to a collection. Some of these features may be peripheral to the main content of a work but still add to the collection. Distinctive characteristics, such as maps, charts, graphs, other illustrations, and glossaries, could serve particular reference needs in a media center. A teacher's guide to a videocassette might offer suggestions for follow-up activities or contain a bibliography of related materials. These special features can be a decisive factor in selection decisions that are not clear-cut.

Materials Available on the Subject

In selecting materials to fill a need for a particular subject, program, or user, availability may outweigh other criteria. This occurs frequently with current events, such as the election of a new U.S. President. Biographical information may be needed immediately and yet little may be available for young users. By the end of a President's first four-year term, there is most likely a wide range of titles and formats from which to select, but at this time the attention to the information may be on the wane. Other examples of information that may have initially limited availability of materials for young people include new scientific discoveries, creation of new nations from former countries, and diseases that suddenly become a threat. The author of this book can remember having difficulty finding quality materials for elementary and middle school students on the subject of AIDS when it first became a frequent news item in the popular media. Availability of any materials for young people on the subject was extremely limited, and yet today there is much material on AIDS that is produced with young readers or viewers in mind.

Value to the Collection

After evaluating the specific qualities of the item, the media specialist needs to consider it in relation to the collection by asking some of the following questions:

- Does the item meet the needs of the school program or the users?
- Can the resource serve more than one purpose?
- Who are the likely users? How often would they use the item?
- Could a teacher in an instructional situation use the item for informational or recreational purposes?
- Is the item readily available through interlibrary loan?

Other Considerations
Series

Deciding whether to select items in a series can sometimes be problematic. It may be tempting to order an entire series produced by a company, but a media specialist should judge each item within a series independently in terms of its value and known needs. Several authors may write books in a series, but not all the authors may be equally skilled. Even if one author writes the entire series, you should consider whether that person is knowledgeable about all the subjects presented in the series. Authors of fiction may not be able to sustain the readers' interest throughout a series. Thus, you need to consider whether the works function independently of each other, or whether sequential use is required. In the case of nonfiction series, your users may not need all the topics that are covered in the series. You may have sufficient coverage in other materials for some of those topics.

Sponsored Materials

Particular organizations may produce and distribute materials often referred to as "free or inexpensive." They include books, computer programs, games, maps, multimedia kits, posters, videocassettes, DVDs, and realia. The materials may provide more up-to-date and in-depth information than you will find in other materials. Sponsors include local, state, national, and international groups, such as government agencies, community groups, private businesses, and trade and professional associations. For example, you can obtain posters from foreign countries from airline and cruise ship companies. Embassies can provide information about their country. The U.S. Government Printing Office and the National Audiovisual Center identifies free and inexpensive materials that are available on a wide range of subjects.

In addition to applying general selection criteria and format-related criteria when evaluating these materials, one needs to also assess whether the information presents a one-sided or biased view of the topic. Advertising and references to the company or organization should be extremely limited and not dominate the content.

Physical Form

Although content is one basis on which to evaluate an item, you also need to evaluate the packaging of the information, or its physical form. The quality of the content can be weakened if it is not presented through the appropriate medium. Criteria to consider in this area are (1) technical quality, (2) aesthetic quality, (3) durability, and (4) safety and health considerations.

Technical Quality

In order to judge the technical qualities of items, some of the following questions may need to be considered:

- Are illustrations and photographs clear and eye catching?
- Is the balance of illustrations to text appropriate to the content and prospective user?
- Do colors express the theme or message?
- Are line, shape, and texture used effectively?

- Does the use of sound, visual materials, and narrative help focus attention?
- Is there a balance of music, narration, and dialogue?
- Are sound elements synchronized?
- Is the speech clear and effectively paced?
- Is the sound clearly audible?
- Is closed captioning available?
- Are the mobility of subjects, expressiveness of presenters, camera work, resolution, and clarity used effectively?

Aesthetic Quality

Aesthetics refer to a resource's appeal to the intellect, senses, and imagination. Both the external design of an item and the presentation of the content need to be aesthetically pleasing. Book jackets and CD or DVD covers should appeal to the potential user, but they also need to be appropriate. For instance, book jackets for teen romance novels should have illustrations that are vibrant and interesting, but they should not be "racy" or depict characters that are much older than the main characters in the story. All aspects of an item should integrate to create an aesthetically pleasing whole.

Durability

It is important to consider the quality of a resource in relation to its durability—how long an item will remain in usable condition with frequent use. Unfortunately many resources produced today do not compare in durability to materials that were produced many years ago. For instance, the paper and binding in many books today are far inferior to those produced in the early and mid-twentieth century. The types of bindings used to make book covers, and the quality of materials used to make CDs or videocassettes can all affect durability. Items that are going to be frequently used, such as those in a reference collection, should be especially durable. Print encyclopedia sets and books in elementary schools can often be ordered in special library binding which will help them stay in good condition through heavy usage. Since most items in a media center collection circulate and leave the media center itself, you want your resources to be as durable as possible.

Safety and Health Considerations

While safety and health features are particularly important when selecting tactile materials, you should consider these issues for all materials. When dealing with items in a kit, such as puppets or stuffed animals, you need to consider whether the items are constructed with nonflammable materials and whether they can be cleaned. Some real objects present a special challenge in terms of cleanliness. What can you do with a piece of salt from the Great Salt Lake that probably will be licked by most of the 1,000 students in an elementary school? Materials with movable parts can also pose problems, possibly with loss of integral parts. Models and kits may have parts that can cut fingers or be swallowed, while architectural models may collapse.

Cost

Cost is an item that must be analyzed in relationship to both intellectual content and technical qualities. Once the criteria discussed previously have been sufficiently applied to an item that you are considering adding to a collection, you must then decide whether the price of the item is commensurate with the intellectual content and technical qualities of the item, the value to the collection, and the monies available in your budget. These factors, of course, are important and will greatly affect your decision on whether to purchase an item. If you determine that the contemplated item for purchase is of high quality and you are in need of the resource for your particular collection, but you do not have sufficient funds in your budget, then you should consider some other options for obtaining the item—interlibrary loan, shared collection development with another library, or fundraising projects. These options will be discussed in more detail in later chapters.

Equipment

Most media specialists also have some responsibility for selecting equipment for the media center. Additionally, you may be asked to select equipment that is housed in the media center, but circulates to classrooms. Examples of such equipment are overhead projectors or visual presenters. If a school is not able to purchase this type of equipment for all classrooms, then teachers check out the equipment on the days that it is needed. The author of this book remembers well when video players first became popular for use in classrooms and she had only four video players on carts that circulated to over 30 teachers in a school. Just keeping a schedule of circulation by period and delivering the carts to the appropriate classrooms took much time and organization. Fortunately today video players and video recorders have come down in cost and many classrooms have their own; however, as new electronic equipment is introduced into schools, similar situations could occur. This will probably occur less often than in the past since many schools are acquiring network systems that make it possible to transmit audiovisual programs to classrooms.

If you are responsible for selecting equipment, it is important to remember that many school districts put the purchase of equipment above a certain cost (usually $100) through a bid process in which they generally accept the lowest bid for each type of equipment. If this is the case in your school district, someone at the administrative office of the school district can provide you with a listing of the equipment and the companies from which you are allowed to purchase certain types of equipment. In your policy and procedure manual, you should include the selection criteria and procedure for obtaining equipment, noting whether certain types of equipment are put through a bid process.

Criteria that should be considered when selecting equipment include (1) quality and durability, (2) performance, compatibility, and versatility, (3) ease of operation, (4) safety, (5) maintenance and service, (6) reputation of manufacturer and dealer, and (7) cost.

Quality and Durability

Quality and durability are very important criteria to consider when selecting equipment. You should choose equipment that is constructed of strong materials and will remain intact through heavy and sometimes fairly abusive use. Some types of equipment, such as video recorders, may have both home and commercial versions. It is always to your advantage to select equipment designed for commercial use when selecting equipment that may have many users. Selecting the equipment designed for home use is cheaper initially, but most likely will be more costly in the long run.

If a piece of equipment will circulate outside of a building, it needs to have a weatherproof carrying case. Straps and handles used to aid in moving the equipment should be strong enough to withstand the weight of the item when carried any distance.

Performance, Compatibility, and Versatility

Equipment should operate efficiently and consistently at a high level of performance. Poor-quality projection or sound reproduction can negate the technical quality of materials so carefully sought during selection. The noise or light from the equipment should not interfere with its use, nor should the equipment be easily subject to overheating.

Equipment needs to be compatible with other equipment and materials in the collection. This is especially true when selecting computers. You should not purchase equipment whose use is limited to materials produced by the manufacturer.

Equipment that can be utilized in a variety of ways may be desirable. You might also want to consider whether the equipment can be used by one individual and by a group. Also, some equipment can be used for more than one medium, such as a computer that can handle both disks and CD-ROMs.

Ease of Use

If equipment is too complex, it will discourage use; thus, it is wise to select equipment that has only the features that are needed and have clearly written directions that are easy to follow. If possible, try to examine the equipment that you are considering for purchase. The following questions will help you determine how easy it is to operate the equipment:

- What level of manual dexterity must one have to operate the equipment?
- How many steps must one follow to run the equipment?
- Does the equipment have many controls?
- Does the equipment operate efficiently with minimum delay?
- Are there parts that can be easily removed and possibly misplaced?
- Are automatic operations dependable?
- Is there an option for manual or remote control?

- Are shut-off or cooling-down features automatic?

- Does the size, weight, or design of the equipment require that you use and store it in one location?

- Can one easily move the equipment to a cart?

- How much time will be needed to teach students and faculty to use the equipment?

Safety

Safety features demand consideration, especially when young children will use equipment. The media specialist should choose equipment that has no rough or protruding edges that could injure the user. Equipment should be balanced so that it will not topple easily. Also, it should not be easy for users to come into contact with potentially dangerous components, such as a fan or a heated element.

Equipment needs to meet established safety regulations. You can look for seals from the Underwriters Laboratory (UL) or the Canadian Standards Association (CSA) to help determine whether equipment meets safety standards.

Maintenance and Service

Although you want the equipment you select to be built to withstand hard use, you also need to plan for regular maintenance and service. You may be able to perform some of the easy maintenance, such as cleaning the equipment on a regular basis.

You should examine warranties and guarantees to see what conditions are covered. Also, try to determine how easily it will be for minor repairs to be made or for parts to be replaced quickly and easily. You might want to inquire as to whether the distributor or manufacturer offers inservice training on operating or repairing the equipment. Some distributors and manufacturers provide on-the-spot repairs, whereas others require that the purchasers send the item to a factory. Thus, it might be important to ask whether the manufacturer, vendor, or repair center provides replacement or rental equipment while they are servicing the equipment that needs repair. Finally, if the district or school has a staff person assigned to do repairs, you should consult the person regarding whether they will service the equipment that you are considering for purchase.

Reputation of Manufacturer and Dealer

If you are a new media specialist and are not familiar with the manufacturers or distributors of equipment for schools, you should consider asking other media specialists who they regard as the most reputable manufacturers and distributors with whom to deal. The following are some questions you could ask:

- Does the manufacturer have a reputation for honoring warranties?

- Is delivery prompt?

- Does the manufacturer handle requests for assistance pleasantly and efficiently?

- Does the dealer have outlets near the school?
- Does the manufacturer provide support service through e-mail, telephone hotlines, toll-free numbers, backups, preview opportunities, updates, refunds, and replacements?
- Is the support assistance readily available?
- Are the service hours convenient?

Cost

When selecting equipment, a media specialist should weigh quality over cost, but also consider budget constraints. You should try to determine whether a competitor offers a similar item at less cost. You can also ask if trade-ins are allowed. When purchasing a very expensive item, such as a large copy machine for the media center, you will need to decide whether to purchase or lease the equipment. The answer to this question may depend on how much use the copy machine will have, whether monies are being taken in for copies, and from where the financial support for items such as paper and ink cartridges will come.

Conclusions

There are several general criteria that can be addressed when selecting items for a school media center. For print and electronic resources, the intellectual content and its presentation, as well as the physical form of an item should be considered. When selecting equipment for the media center, specific criteria need to be addressed, but one needs also to be aware of any school district policies that deal with equipment selection and maintenance. For all purchases that are being considered, a media specialist should strive to get the best quality within the constraints of the media center budget.

8

Criteria by Format

It is widely accepted knowledge that people gather information through their senses (seeing, hearing, touching, tasting, and smelling) and have different learning styles depending on how they utilize those senses. Excluding persons with particular physical disabilities, such as deafness or blindness, most students learn through a combination of all their senses. However, they usually have a predominant learning style—visual, auditory, or kinetic. Students learn better from media formats that incorporate their predominant learning style. Thus, a variety of media need to be included in a school media center collection in order to meet the learning styles of all students.

In your media center's policy and procedures manual, there should a listing of all the media formats that are in your collection. This can be a separate listing or it can be included in your circulation section with a possible indication of which formats can be checked out by students and/or by faculty.

This chapter focuses on the characteristics of different formats and how media specialists should consider them in selection decisions. The formats are arranged in alphabetical order. Each description includes physical characteristics, advantages, disadvantages, selection criteria, implications for collection development, and copyright considerations. Even though some of the formats are being phased out of most school library media centers, if they are still available for purchase, they are included to accommodate all types of media centers, regardless of their technology capabilities or budgets. In addition to the selection criteria listed for each format, you should consider whether the item has received awards or favorable reviews. The general selection criteria from Chapter 7 should also be applied.

You can refer to the Appendix "Resources" to locate materials that will provide reviews or other guidance for selection of particular formats. The additional readings and Web sites listed at the end of this chapter are primarily those that relate to the newer formats that are being collected in school library media centers.

Art Prints *See* Graphic Materials

Audiocassettes

Although not a new technology, audiocassettes remain popular in school libraries today. Combination kits of books and audiocassettes are frequently found in elementary school libraries, while middle school and high school students enjoy "books on tape" (audiobooks). They are also extremely appealing to students who are visually impaired. Audiocassettes require tape recorders; thus, if teachers check out audiocassettes for classroom use, you should also provide quality tape recorders that make it possible for large groups of students to easily listen to the audiocassettes.

Advantages

- Tapes are portable and easy to use.
- A wide range of content is available.
- Equipment is easy to use and inexpensive.
- Information is locked into a fixed sequence, and specific sections can be easily located through use of counters on tape recorders.
- Most students are familiar with the equipment.

Disadvantages

- Listening for an extended period of time may induce boredom with some students.
- Use with large groups requires high-quality tape recorders, with adequate amplification.
- Cassettes must be rewound before circulating if a previous user did not rewind them.
- Cassettes are small and can easily be stolen.
- Cassette cases break easily; thus a supply of empty cases may need to be purchased.

Selection Criteria

- Is the sound free of distortion?
- Are the length and quality of the performance appropriate to the intended audience?
- Do labels provide enough information to distinguish one item from another (cassette #1, cassette #2, etc.)?
- Do labels provide the time required to listen to the tape?
- If the recording is based on a book, is the recording true to the original?
- Does the recording engage the listener's attention?

- Does narration begin with attention-getting words to capture the listener's interest? Are keywords or key statements emphasized to help the listener?
- Are accompanying materials, such as a teacher's guide, appropriate and useful?

Implications for Collection Development

The items should provide for individual and group use of narrative presentations, as well as for music and documentaries. For music, other formats, such as compact discs, are better choices and more appealing to most users. Cassette tapes can be fairly easily damaged in circulation, particularly with young children.

Copyright Considerations

Although it is easy to do, it is not legal to make copies of audiocassette tapes. Converting cassette tapes to another format requires written permission from the copyright holder.

Books

Most school media centers contain more books than any other format, although they are not always the most popular format among students, particularly in high school settings. Hardback and paperback books share similar characteristics, but often fulfill different needs. Hardback books with special library bindings are frequently purchased for very young patrons, while paperback books are especially appealing to teenagers. E-books, which are becoming more popular, are discussed in a separate section.

Advantages

- Books are usually designed for individual users.
- The user can set his/her own pace and stop in the process to recheck information or reread a section.
- The table of contents and index can provide ready access to information.
- Books are portable.
- A wide range of subjects and genres are available in books.
- Books do not require equipment.
- They are relatively inexpensive.

Disadvantages

- Use of colored artwork or photography, although adding to appeal or clarity of text, increases the cost.
- Movement is difficult to illustrate on the printed page.
- Large-group viewing of the same material is difficult, except with "big books" (oversized paperback books).

- Contact with books is a personal, internal experience; interaction and feedback for students is difficult to achieve except in programmed texts.
- Students must have the appropriate reading- and comprehension-level skills.
- It usually takes several months to get a book published; thus, the information may not be as current as that in electronic formats.

Selection Criteria

- Are the shape and weight of the book appropriate for the intended audience?
- How opaque is the paper? Print that shows through the page may be confusing to a young or disadvantaged reader.
- Is the typeface suitable for the intended audience?
- Is the spacing between words and between lines adequate for the young or reluctant reader?
- Is the book jacket attractive? Does it reflect the content of the book?
- Are the illustrations placed within the text where readers can use them easily, or are they placed all together in an inconvenient location?
- Is the medium used for illustrations (for example, pen-and-ink drawings, block prints, or oil paints) appropriate to the setting and mood of the story?
- Do the page layouts and color add appeal and clarity to the book?
- When a readability formula, such as Fry or Spache, is applied, is the text appropriate for the intended audience?
- Is the content accurate and current?

Additional Criteria for Hardbacks

- Are the bindings durable and covers attractive and easy to clean?
- Are reinforced bindings available for titles that very young children will use or titles that will circulate frequently?
- Will the hardcover books lie flat when open?

Implications for Collection Development

Even though selections should cover a wide range of subjects and genres, one should also consider the reading and maturity levels of students. You should order additional copies of popular books; paperbacks are an inexpensive way to meet these demands. A paperback book may appeal to some users more than would the same title in hardback. Policies should address questions such as what foreign languages to purchase and whether there is a need for large-print books.

Copyright Considerations

Copyright law defines print materials as books, periodicals, pamphlets, newspapers, and similar items. A teacher may make a single copy of a chapter in a book, a short story, short essay, short poem, chart, graph, diagram, cartoon, or picture to use in teaching. Multiple copies are limited by specific guidelines:

- If a poem is less than 250 words and is not on more than two pages, the entire poem can be copied. For poems longer than 250 words, only 250 words can be copied.

- An article, story, or essay can be copied in its entirety if it is less than 2,500 words. Other types of prose are limited to 1,000 words or 10 percent of the whole, whichever is less.

- Creation of anthologies, compilations, and collective works is prohibited.

Cartoons *See* Graphic Materials

Cassette Tapes *See* Audiocassettes

CDs

A compact disc (or CD) is an optical disc used to store digital data. The disc is covered with a transparent coating and is read by a laser beam. Compact discs reached library markets in the mid-1980s. Originally they were developed as music formats, but they grew to encompass other applications. Compact discs are available in different sizes, but the most common size is 120 mm in diameter.

Advantages

- CDs take up little storage space.
- CDs are small, lightweight, and portable.
- Equipment used to play CDs is inexpensive.
- CD players are easy to use, and many students are familiar with them.
- Sound on CDs is generally superior to that on audiocassettes.
- Because a track system is used on CDs, it is possible to access certain parts of a CD.
- Since nothing touches the encoding on the disc, CDs are not worn out in the playing process.
- Compact discs retain superb sounds for hundreds of hours.

Disadvantages

- It is relatively easy to scratch a CD, thus ruining parts of the CD. The topside (label side) is particularly vulnerable and is difficult to repair.
- If using a CD with a large group, the CD player must have adequate amplification.

- Capacity is fairly limited compared to other formats.
- CDs are small and therefore easy to steal.
- As with audiocassettes, cases are easily broken; thus, it is wise to have extra cases on hand.

Selection Criteria

- Is the sound of high quality?
- Is the content appropriate for the intended audience?
- Will the content be appealing for more than just a few months?
- Are there accompanying materials, such as the words to the songs or the time to play each track?
- Does the label provide information on the time required for playback?

Implications for Collection Development

You need to consider whether you wish to collect and circulate CDs that contain music. Although they are popular items with teenagers, they can be easily damaged and copied (thus violating copyright). Some lyrics of songs, especially in the rap music category, may not be appropriate for a school setting. Musical CDs for preschool and elementary level students are also becoming increasingly popular. If you have a generous media center budget, CDs will undoubtedly be a popular format. So many selections are available that it may be difficult to decide which items to purchase. Also, some of the musical CDs (particularly pop music) may be popular for only short periods of time.

Copyright Considerations

It is illegal to make copies of any sound recordings; even archival copies may not be made. Converting CDs to another format requires written permission from the copyright owner. It is a good idea to place appropriate copyright warning stickers on CDs that circulate.

CD-ROMs

Soon after the introduction of audio CDs, CD-ROMs (compact disc read only memory) were developed. A CD-ROM is a form of a compact disc that is read by using a CD-ROM drive on a computer. CD-ROMs can provide access to very large quantities of digitally encoded information at relatively low cost. Graphics, sound, and other non-text items can mix with text. This format is used for encyclopedias, reference sources, databases, multimedia products, interactive books, games, music, online public access catalogs (OPACs), computer software, clip art, and graphics.

Advantages

- A single CD-ROM can store the equivalent of 1,000 short books.
- A single disc can hold more than 650 megabytes of text, graphics, and sound.

- With a good index, information retrieval is flexible.
- Use of CD-ROMs helps students learn search strategies before going online.
- The quality of images is high, and they do not fade as photographic images do. The images take less storage space than if they were individual slides or photographs.
- CD-ROM discs are small, lightweight, and portable.
- The discs are durable and resistant to fingerprints.
- The laser-beam reader does not come into direct contact with the disc so the disc does not wear out with play.
- Text downloaded from a CD-ROM is ready for word processing or other manipulation.
- The format is very appealing to students.

Disadvantages

- A CD-ROM player is required.
- To read the screen, one must turn on the computer and CD-ROM player.
- Some CD-ROM discs require specific methods of retrieval.
- Access is slower than on hard drives.
- Capacity is limited compared to online databases.
- Information cannot be updated or changed.
- Use of a single CD-ROM is limited to one student or a small group, creating scheduling and teacher planning difficulties. Networking CD-ROMs can alleviate these problems.

Selection Criteria

Criteria for CD-ROMs and software are similar (see the discussion in the Computer Software section). Additional questions to consider are the following:

- How frequently is the CD-ROM updated?
- Does the cost of a subscription include the update?
- Is there an annual fee?
- Are on-screen tutorials provided? Are they simple and easy to understand?
- Is the menu system easy to use?
- How fast is access to the information?
- What is the quality of the video and audio production?
- What is the technical quality of the underlying program, the manual, and the support personnel?

- Does the CD-ROM contain a large amount of high-quality information?
- Are the advertisement and promotional materials accurate about the number of minutes or hours of full-motion video, high-fidelity audio, number of photographic images, and amount of text?
- Is the CD-ROM truly interactive in the sense that users can explore options?
- Will a bundled package of applications, rather than an individual CD-ROM, serve your needs?

Implications for Collection Development

You should plan procedures to establish (1) time limits for individual student use of a CD-ROM workstation, (2) number of printouts allowed, (3) fee if applicable, (4) security for discs, and (5) whether to have a dedicated machine for each disc. Plans should also include how to obtain appropriate licenses and how to insure adherence to copyright issues. These plans must be flexible and are best designed in conjunction with teachers. Administrators may be involved in setting fees, if students are to be charged for printouts.

When you find recommended titles you want to consider, find out whether you can obtain a copy of the CD-ROM for a trial period on your equipment. During the trial, evaluate the technical support found in the documentation, user manuals, and telephone or online help lines. It is important to remember that free demos can supply you with a look at the content of the CD-ROM, but the demos may be technically different from the CD-ROM itself. Use of previews (often with slide shows making a marketing pitch) can give you a sense of the possible interest to your users.

Copyright Considerations

Unlike books, audiocassettes, maps, and some other formats, the physical medium (CD-ROM) is purchased, but the content is licensed for use. For multiple users or multiple copies of the disc at multiple workstations, you will need to obtain a site or network license.

Charts *See* Graphic Materials

Comics

Comic books, or the shortened form *comics*, tell a narrative by depicting sequential art. Although sometimes humorous, the subject matter varies. Popular genres include super-heroes, fantasy, horror/supernatural, action/adventure, science fiction, and manga (Japanese comics). The majority of comic books are marketed to teenagers, with the two largest U.S. publishers being Marvel and DC (Diamond Comics).

Advantages

- Comics are particularly appealing to teens and will attract students to the media center.
- Reluctant readers of books will often read comic books.

- Visual learners like the art format, which can assist them in understanding a narrative.
- Comic books can lead readers to explore other literature.
- Comics can help students develop an appreciation for art and different artistic styles.
- Many comic books address themes that are important to teens and pre-teens, including acceptance, prejudice, social issues, and triumph over adversity.
- Comic books are inexpensive.

Disadvantages

- Comic books are not very durable.
- Media specialists may not be very familiar with comic books and might need assistance in selecting the best ones for a collection.
- Some teachers, administrators, and parents may think that comic books should not be included in a school library media collection.

Selection Criteria

- Can you obtain sample copies to help you in selection?
- Is the content appropriate for the intended audience?
- What is the reputation of the publisher?
- Is the quality of the writing and the art good?
- Have the comics won any awards?
- Will the selected titles be popular with students?
- Are the comic books available as trade paperback collections?

Implications for Collection Development

Comic books are particularly appealing to pre-teens and teenagers and will attract them to the media center. Since they are not very durable, it is wise to treat comics similarly to magazine subscriptions where use is generally limited to the media center and the materials are often placed in magazine protective covers. If you wish to circulate comics, you can purchase trade comics (stories collected in paperback format). Specialized comic book subscription agents and mail-order services offer subscription plans for comic books. Subscriptions can also sometimes be arranged through local comic book stores. Subscriptions are not available from the major subscription agencies like EBSCO or Faxon. You should preview materials before placing them on the shelves and be prepared to address possible censorship issues.

Copyright Considerations

Although not specifically addressed in fair use guidelines, comic books would most likely be similar to picture books. Two pages of picture books may be copied as long as the two pages do not make up more than 10 percent of the book.

Computer Software

Computer software is available through educational institutes and consortia, commercial vendors, software companies, and textbook publishers. Shareware (courseware available at no cost or more often on a trial basis) is available from the educational agency or other body that produced it. After the software has been evaluated and retained, the user is expected to register the program and pay a voluntary fee. Public domain software is a computer program that the author has released and can be copied by anyone. Such software is often on Internet Web sites dedicated to public domain use. The title screen of the program indicates that the program is in public domain.

Most computer software is currently produced on CD-ROM discs, rather than floppy disks. See the selection criteria under CD-ROMs in addition to the following section, which emphasizes instructional software.

Advantages

- Software can be used for creative problem solving, drill and practice, testing, recreation, and guidance.
- Individual and self-paced interactions are special instructional features of computer software.
- Programs can provide the reinforcement and stimulation needed by students who have learning disabilities.
- Programs with branching allow the student with correct answers to move into more difficult questions, while allowing those who need to review and repeat responses opportunities to do so.
- Rapid information retrieval is possible.
- Use of computer software can be highly motivating for many students.
- Desktop publishing allows students to design and enhance their presentations.
- Teachers can use record-keeping programs to monitor students' progress.

Disadvantages

- Teachers who are not trained to use computers may be reluctant to use them in teaching.
- Incompatibility of software and equipment can limit use.
- Poor computer software programming can lead to improper use of the medium to teach material that could be taught more effectively using other techniques.
- More software programs are designed to appeal to boys than to girls.
- Students and teachers may have unreasonably high expectations of how quickly learning will happen.
- Many programs will not accept creative or original student responses.
- A high level of student use can limit the amount of interaction between teachers and students.

Selection Criteria

- Are the software and equipment compatible?
- Is content more appropriate for presentation on a computer than on other instructional media?
- Is the program designed to run on the user's computer? The computer's brand, model, memory size, operating system, storage format, display technology (monitor and graphics system), and accessories (mouse, game paddles, etc.) must be compatible.
- Is the computer's disk operating system compatible with the software program?
- Does the user control the rate and sequences of the content presentation (unless timing is an integral part of the program)?
- Is the student able to enter, use, and exit the program with relative ease and independence?
- Are the responses or feedback to answers (both correct and incorrect) appropriate?
- Will the software design lead students to correct answers or to remedial instruction when they need assistance?
- Are on-screen instructions clear and easy to understand?
- Are the student guides and worksheets, the teacher guide, and the technical information adequate and comprehensive?
- Does the program require students to be familiar with special terms or symbols related to computers?

Implications for Collection Development

As mentioned previously most computer software programs are now available on CD-ROM format. You will need to consider the scope of the software collection and whether it will circulate, and to whom it will circulate (only teachers or to both teachers and students). It is wise to obtain teachers' opinions in deciding purchases.

Copyright Consideration

One archival or backup copy of each program is permitted. It may not be used at the same time as the original. For use at more than one computer (such as on a LAN [local area network] or WAN [wide area network]), a site license agreement must be obtained. Any computer software programs that circulate should have copyright warning stickers placed on them.

DVDs

DVDs (digital versatile discs) are compact optical discs read by laser beams. DVD discs are the same diameter and thickness as compact discs, but are capable of storing up to thirteen times the data contained on one side of a CD. Both sides of a DVD can be utilized for storage data; thus it offers twenty-six times the power of a compact disc. Movies, documentaries, and music are all available in DVD format. DVDs are rapidly replacing videos and laser discs. Many experts feel that they will also soon replace CDs and CD-ROMs.

Advantages

- DVDs can deliver near-studio-quality video and better-than-CD-quality audio. The pictures are characterized by more color detail and color resolution than videos.
- Content can be easily searched and specific sections can be quickly accessed.
- Interactive menus are available.
- Many DVDs have "extra's," such as additional footage, interviews, commentaries, links to online resources, and biographical materials.
- Some DVDs have additional materials, such as accompanying booklets or viewers' guides.
- The compact size is easy to store, and portable players are available.
- Discs are durable.
- Wear does not occur from playing, only from physical damage.
- DVDs do not deteriorate in quality over time.
- Unlike videos, DVD discs are not affected by magnetic fields.
- DVDs can be played on a computer that has a DVD drive.
- DVDs are inexpensive—as cheap as or cheaper than videos.

Disadvantages

- Careless production can create visible artifacts (anything that was not originally present in the picture), such as banding, blurriness, fuzzy dots, and missing details.
- The production of materials has centered on those for the home-entertainment center, rather than those designed for educational and instructional purposes.
- Most DVD players must be connected to a television set.
- Some television sets need to have the controls adjusted to take advantage of the DVD's capabilities.
- Wide-screen televisions and multi-channel digital surround sound capabilities are needed to get the most enjoyment of DVDs.

Selection Criteria

Criteria applied to video, audiocassettes, and computer software should be applied to materials on DVDs. As with other developing technology, there are additional questions to consider:

- Is the content connected to the curriculum?

- Is the standard used to judge the content the same as for other materials in the collection?
- Do users have convenient access to a player?
- Would purchase of the item duplicate something easily available in public libraries or local video stores?
- Is a DVD the best format for the message?

Implications for Collection Development

You should monitor the production of materials, which currently centers on presentations for the home-entertainment center, such as movies, rather than materials designed for educational or instructional purposes. Development and availability of DVDs should also be monitored for its anticipated replacement of audiocassettes, CDs, videotapes, laser discs, and CD-ROMs. When you add DVD drives to your systems, look for those that are designed to play CD-ROM titles, as well as DVDs.

Copyright Considerations

A number of copy-protection schemes are used with DVDs. One is the SCMS ("serial" copy generation-management system), which is designed to prevent copying. The copy generation-management system (CGMS) is embedded in the outgoing video signal, and one must use equipment that recognizes the CGMS. The U.S. Digital Millennium Copyright Act (DMCA), in which "don't copy" flags are incorporated by the producers, became law in October 1998. Although perfect reproductions can be made of a DVD, copyright restrictions do not allow archival copies to be made of DVDs. DVDs bought in stores are protected by the copyright law and are not intended for use outside the home. However, fair use guidelines permit the use of the DVDs in face-to-face instruction if they are part of the curriculum. Any movies that are to be shown in a school for entertainment purposes require a Movie Copyright Compliance Site License.

E-Books

Many different types of electronic books (e-books) are available. Some can be accessed electronically and are meant to be printed out for reading; others are distributed electronically but are intended to be read on a computer or on e-book readers. Unfortunately there is no standardized format for e-books, and some of the books require special software or hardware to use. Librarians have been fairly reluctant to purchase e-books, but this will most likely change as younger library users are more comfortable with accessing all types of information through electronic formats.

Advantages

- Books are available twenty-four hours of the day.
- If allowed by the licensing agreement, several students can access an electronic book at the same time.
- Since some e-books also include sound files and moving images, they are particularly interesting to reluctant readers.

- E-books save shelf space in a library and do not have to be transported.
- The books cannot be lost or damaged by users.
- Search functions can be used to locate specific parts of the book.
- In some e-book formats, notes can be inserted right into the text, thus providing instructional features for a classroom teacher.
- Students who are into technology may be more apt to read e-books than the print versions.

Disadvantages

- The format for e-books is not standardized.
- Special software and hardware are required to access and read e-books.
- Some book titles are not available in the e-book format.
- A fair number of distributors of e-books have gone out of business and their resources are no longer available.
- Annual licensing fees are required.

Selection Criteria

When evaluating e-books, media specialists should apply traditional criteria and also consider both the licensing arrangement and the equipment necessary for using them. As with other developing technology, basic questions are whether the media center will circulate the materials and whether the media center will provide the equipment needed to use the material. Some additional questions that should be asked are as follows:

- What titles are available in e-book format?
- Will the students and teachers use the e-books?
- How much will the books cost in comparison to purchasing print versions of the titles?

Implications for Collection Development

Many book titles are already in public domain and available for free. The Project Gutenberg Web site has a large collection of public domain e-books as does the University of Virginia Web site and the Internet Public Library. The International Children's Digital Library, which was developed by a team at the University of Maryland, provides free access to children's books from around the world. Before purchasing e-books, a media specialist should promote the use of these sites and then determine whether teachers and students want or need access to additional titles.

Copyright Considerations

Copyright restrictions introduced by the Digital Millennium Copyright Act (DCMA) in 1978 apply to e-books, as well as to other digital technologies. It is necessary to sign a licensing agreement for e-books that are purchased and abide by the copyright restrictions of the agreement.

E-Journals

E-journals or electronic journals are serial publications that are in digital format. Some e-journals are free of charge and are published only on the Internet. Such journals are generally referred to as open access journals. Other journals appear only in electronic format and are available by subscription, while still others appear in both electronic format (on Internet or on a CD-ROM) and also have print versions. Some electronic journals are peer-reviewed, scholarly journals, while others are not quality-controlled. Thus, the term *e-journal* is not always specific. There are even more e-journals (many thousands) than e-zines. Some academic libraries attempt to maintain lists of e-journals, but it requires too much time for school media specialists to provide this collection service.

Advantages

- E-journals can be read around the clock from any location that has Internet access.
- They can be delivered to one's computer desktop.
- More than one person can read an e-journal at a time.
- They can be published much more quickly than print versions of journals.
- E-journals can be searched.
- They can be retrieved directly through links when accessed through an indexing database.
- Hyperlinks to information can be inserted into articles.
- E-journals do not take up space on the media center shelves.

Disadvantages

- The main disadvantage is that one must have a computer to access e-journals.
- Unless the e-journal also has a print version, one must sit at a computer to read it.
- Some journals do not include illustrations, and if they do, the illustrations may not be in color or as clear as the print version.

Selection Criteria

The selection criteria for e-journals are similar to those of print periodicals (see Periodicals). Additional selection questions include the following:

- How does the cost compare to the print version of the periodical?

- Can you negotiate the cost of the e-journal according to the number of students in your school or the number of users who will access the e-journal?

- Is the journal title included in vendor databases, such as ProQuest or EBSCO?

- Is the journal easily available to students in informational databases provided by the state or by a public library?

- Will enough students use the journal to make the cost of its electronic access feasible?

- Are back issues of the journals available?

Implications for Collection Development

One must carefully consider whether to purchase periodicals in print version or electronically. Few media centers purchase the same title in both formats. Students in secondary schools enjoy reading print versions of popular periodicals such as *Sports Illustrated* or *Seventeen* so you should consider having these types of periodicals available on shelves in the media center. Electronic access to periodicals can be provided for those journals that are used primarily for research purposes. This will save enormous amounts of shelf space in a middle or high school media center. Generally elementary schools provide their periodicals in print format.

Copyright Considerations

Students can make one copy of an article for research purposes. Teachers should not make multiple copies of an article for classroom use unless they obtain copyright permission from the publisher of the journal or the need meets the spontaneity guideline (not enough time to get a timely reply to a request for permission to copy).

E-Zines

E-zines are publications (magazines or newsletters) that are distributed by e-mail or posted on a Web site. They usually focus on a particular subject and are free. Often one person or a small group of people who have special interest in a topic publish e-zines on the Web. Some e-zines are updated constantly so they do not have regular distribution, while others are periodically updated. Far too many e-zines are available (thousands) to try to include them in OPACs, but if you want to help students locate e-zines, the following sites are helpful: http://e-zinedirectory.com/ and http://www.ezine-dir.com/. The University of Oregon Libraries maintains an e-zine entitled *New Breed Librarian*, which is intended to foster a sense of community for those new to librarianship. As a new media specialist, you may want to check out their Web site. Access to their e-zine can be found at <http://scholarsbank.uoregon.edu/dspace/handle/1794/1071>.

Games

Games are recreational or educational activities involving one or more persons. They involve either reaching some type of goal or following a set of rules. Games can be categorized by those that involve skill, those that require strategy, and those that rely on chance. Many games involve a combination of skill, strategy, and chance. Some games require using a computer or other special equipment.

Advantages

- Participants become involved in solving problems.
- Some games simulate realistic environments.
- Participation usually generates a high degree of interest.
- Students receive immediate feedback.
- Some games contribute to effective learning by motivating and supporting learning and attitudinal changes.

Disadvantages

- Games can be very time-consuming.
- The limited number of players can create problems if others want to participate.
- Some games have parts that can be easily lost or damaged.
- Some teachers may not be aware of the learning value of games, and thus may not understand why they are included in a collection.

Selection Criteria

- Is the packaging designed to store and quickly identify missing parts?
- Can lost pieces be easily replaced?
- Are the items durable?
- Are the directions clear?
- Are the content, reading level, time requirements, and required dexterity appropriate for the intended audience?
- Does the game require a computer? Will it run on the media center's equipment?
- Is the game too costly or elaborate for its intended use?

Implications for Collection Development

Games can serve many purposes, but it is wise to get input from teachers and administrators on the inclusion of games in the collection and whether to make them available for use in a media center. You should also carefully consider whether to circulate games to students, particularly if the games have many parts that can be easily lost. More elementary media centers than secondary school media centers tend to have games available for student use. However, some secondary media centers have chess or checker sets available.

Copyright Considerations

Copyright considerations are generally not involved with games, unless the games are in a different format, such as on computer software. In those cases, the same copyright considerations apply as to computer software (see Computer Software and CD-ROMs).

Graphic Materials

Graphics are nonmoving, opaque, visual materials that provide information. In a media center these materials include posters, graphs, charts, tables, diagrams, cartoons, art prints, study prints, drawings, and photographs.

Advantages

- Graphic materials are inexpensive and widely available.
- Carefully selected graphics can help prevent or correct students' misconceptions.
- Graphic materials are easy to use.

Disadvantages

- Sizes and distances are sometimes distorted.
- Lack of color or poor quality may limit proper interpretation.
- The size of the material must be large enough for all members of a group to see the same detail.
- Motion cannot be simulated, only suggested.
- Today's students are technologically aware enough to prefer presentations in more recently developed formats.

Selection Criteria

- Is the information presented in a precise manner?
- Are less important elements de-emphasized or omitted?
- Is the presentation unified? Are the basic artistic principles of balance and harmony observed?
- Is lettering clear and legible?
- Is the size appropriate for the intended audience?
- Does an art print give an accurate reproduction of the original work's color and detail?
- Is the item durable?

Implications for Collection Development

Many graphics are now available electronically on the Internet. Some search engines make it easy to locate specific graphics. Many media specialists and teachers are projecting these images onto large screens. Thus, there are fewer needs for purchasing graphic materials. If, however, you anticipate purchasing prints for group lessons, look for ones that provide information on the back of story prints or study prints. If you circulate graphics, consider either laminating them or protecting them in some manner. Special storage units may be needed.

Copyright Considerations

Graphics such as study prints or art prints are usually copyrighted and cannot be duplicated. Graphic materials in periodicals can be copied provided they meet the copyright test for illustrations: one chart, graph, diagram, drawing, cartoon, or picture per periodical. If you have questions about whether a graphic is copyrighted, you should check with the publisher.

Graphic Novels

Although some librarians have considered graphic novels as a fad, their popularity with young people has certainly earned them a place in secondary school libraries. They are also becoming somewhat popular in elementary settings. It is important to remember that graphic novels are not a genre, but rather a separate format. They are "stand-alone" stories in a comic form that are published as books. Storylines in graphic novels are longer than those found in comic books and are often more complex and serious. The modern types of graphic novels began in the 1970s, but in recent years they have become extremely popular and many libraries are including them in their collections. The majority of the titles come in trade paperback versions.

Advantages

- Visual learners are able to connect with graphic novels.
- Graphic novels can lead students to explore other types of literature.
- Boys who are reluctant readers are often attracted to graphic novels.
- They are useful for ESL students or students who read below grade level.
- Having graphic novels in a collection will attract young people to a media center.

Disadvantages

- Some teachers and parents may think that graphic novels do not belong in a media center collection.
- Some titles are not available through jobbers.
- The content of some graphic novels is not appropriate for young people.
- Many media specialists are not familiar with the format and may need assistance in selecting titles for the collection.

Selection Criteria

- Is the content appropriate for the intended audience?
- Are students able to follow the art format?
- Is the title one that will be popular with students?

- What are the reputations of the author, illustrator, and publisher?
- How relevant is the content to existing coverage in the collection?
- Are you able to locate a review of the title?

Copyright Considerations

Graphic novels were not invented when the fair use guidelines were written; however, they most likely would be considered as picture books. Two pages of picture books can be copied as long as the two pages do not comprise more than 10 percent of the book.

Kits

A kit contains a variety of formats in one package. In some kits the materials are pre-selected to present information in a fixed sequence. Other kits and packages are less structured, such as a collection of related materials that can be used singly or in any combination by an individual or a group.

Advantages

- Various formats relating to a specific subject are combined in one package.
- The various formats can meet different student learning styles.
- Kits that include sound recordings of accompanying text materials can help the learner who has difficulty reading.

Disadvantages

- One kit may include material designed for several grade levels.
- Some kits may include materials that duplicate items in the collection.
- Kits can be expensive.
- Lost non-replaceable parts may render a kit unusable.

Selection Criteria

- Does the kit create a unified whole? Is there a relationship among its parts?
- Is special equipment needed to use the materials in the kit?
- Does each item in the kit meet the criteria for that particular format?
- Is the kit easy to use?
- Are the directions clear?
- Is adult guidance needed?
- Does the kit fulfill a unique purpose that other materials in the collection do not meet?
- Is there sufficient space to store the kit?

Implications for Collection Development

Select kits on the basis of their potential use and appeal. Students and teachers may prefer to create kits using materials from the collection.

Magazines *See* Periodicals

Maps and Globes

Materials included are flat maps, wall maps, and globes. When a map is published in a book, evaluate it in light of the criteria listed under "Books."

Advantages

- Maps can provide a wide range of information: place locations and spellings; significant surface features; distances between places; and scientific, social, cultural, political, historical, literary, and economic data.
- Several people can simultaneously study wall maps.
- Unlabeled outline maps or globes encourage children to learn the names, shapes, and locations of political and topographical features.
- Maps are readily available at a wide range of prices.

Disadvantages

- If a group of students need to examine the same detail in a map, multiple copies or a transparency may be needed.
- Cartographic details, especially those on geographic, scientific, or political topics, quickly become outdated.
- Wall maps take up wall space that might be needed for book shelves or displays.

Selection Criteria

- Is the map aesthetically pleasing?
- Does the color code help the user interpret the information?
- Is the depth of detail suitable for the intended audience?
- Are symbols representational and clearly designed?
- Is the item durable?
- Is a laminated surface that allows erasable writing for instruction available on large wall maps?

Implications for Collection Development

The collection should include maps of various sizes to meet the different needs of individuals and groups. Maps and globes should be easily accessible. Because geographic names of countries tend to change fairly frequently, you should set aside monies in your budget to replace maps and globes on a regular basis.

Copyright Considerations

Wall maps, globes, and flat maps are usually copyrighted by the company that produces them. Simple flat outline maps are not eligible for copyright and may be copied. More complex maps require the same criteria as graphics.

Models

Models and dioramas are representations of real things. A model is a three-dimensional representation of an object and may be smaller or larger than the real object. Cut-away models show the inside of an object. Dioramas provide an impression of depth, with three-dimensional foreground against a flat background.

Advantages

- These formats offer a sense of depth, thickness, height, and width.
- They can reduce or enlarge objects to an observable size.
- They can simplify complex objects.
- The model can be disassembled and reassembled to show relationships among parts.

Disadvantages

- The size of models may limit their use with a group.
- Some models are difficult to reassemble.
- Loose parts are easy to misplace or lose.
- Specially designed shelving and storage units may be needed.

Selection Criteria

- Are size relationships of the part to the whole accurately portrayed?
- Are parts clearly labeled?
- Are color and composition used to stress important features?
- Will the construction withstand handling?

Implications for Collection Development

The size of many of these materials creates storage and distribution problems. Packaging models for circulation may also be difficult. Materials produced by staff and students may lack the durability needed for permanent inclusion in the collection.

Newspapers

Newspapers are commonly found in media center collections in secondary schools. You may also want to subscribe to a local newspaper if you are in an elementary school setting. Today many newspapers, such as the

New York Times, are available online and can be utilized for current events, as well as for research purposes.

Advantages

- Newspapers are a familiar format as a source of information to students.
- Having print copies of newspapers in a media center frequently draws students and teachers into the media center.
- The information in newspapers is current.
- Some newspapers, such as *USA Today*, pictorially display data, making them accessible to those comfortable with figures and graphs.
- More than one user can simultaneously access online formats of newspapers.

Disadvantages

- Storage of print newspapers can be difficult.
- Only one person at a time can read a print newspaper, unless the newspaper is separated into sections.
- Many users tend to not leave the print newspaper in its original order and condition.
- Online subscriptions to some newspapers may be costly.

Selection Criteria

- Is the content of interest to students and teachers?
- Are subjects treated clearly in a well-organized manner?
- Are illustrations pertinent and adequately reproduced?
- Do the strengths of the newspaper fulfill a need within the school?
- Is the paper directed to a local, regional, national, or an international audience?
- Does the newspaper feature visual materials with attention-getting pictorial information and clear graphics?
- In which formats (print, CD-ROM, or online) are the newspapers available?
- Is the content the same in all formats?
- How frequently is information updated?
- How easily can one retrieve back issues?

Implications for Collection Development

In secondary schools, local, state, and national newspapers should be represented in the collection through print subscriptions or through access on the Internet. Elementary schools should have at least a local newspaper available in the media center. If classes subscribe to instructional newspapers, the media specialist may find it useful to have a copy of the teacher's edition in the media center.

Copyright Considerations

A teacher can copy a chart, graph, diagram, cartoon, picture, or an article from a newspaper for instructional use. Word limits for multiple copies for classroom use are 250 words for poetry and 2,500 words for articles. A copyright warning notice should appear on each copy. Online newspapers that require subscriptions are subject to licensing agreements.

Online Databases

Online databases provide electronic access to organized collections of data through the use of a computer that is connected to the Internet. Numerous databases are available to libraries. Some contain data of special formats, such as indexes to periodicals, and others provide information from more than one format. Some vendors provide "bundled" databases or aggregators. Aggregator databases are databases selected by a vendor and put together as a package to which you can subscribe. Thomson Gale, ProQuest, and EBSCO are examples of vendors who provide bundled databases to libraries. Types of databases are the following:

1. Full text: includes all the information available for a certain record. Examples are encyclopedias, journal articles, and entire newspapers.
2. Bibliographic: provides citations and may include abstracts. An example is a magazine index or *Books in Print*.
3. Directory: provides a list of information. An example is a faculty and staff directory.
4. Numeric: contains numbers. Examples are population and census figures provided by the government.
5. Mixed: includes a mixture of the other types of databases.

Advantages

- Information is current.
- Users can easily and quickly locate information.
- Users can modify searches during the process.
- Immediate feedback lets users know whether information is available and whether their search strategy was too narrow or too broad.
- The information provides complete citations.
- Bibliographies are easy to generate.
- Users can save search strategies.
- Many students prefer to access information electronically, rather than use print formats.

Disadvantages

- Not all the subjects in the curriculum may be included.

- Users may need training in developing search strategies.

- Students need training in evaluating and selecting information.

- Users may need training in interpreting bibliographic information.

- Teachers and media specialists may be unable to quickly determine whether students are downloading information without analyzing it, evaluating it, or synthesizing information from several sources.

- Teachers may need assistance in designing assignments that call for evaluation of information, rather than merely locating a predetermined number of sources on a topic.

- Materials cited may not be available locally, and interlibrary loan requests may increase.

- Information generated before 1970 might not be included, limiting historical searches.

- Full-text information might not include graphics from the original work.

- Monographs are not covered as adequately as periodical articles and newspapers.

- Downtime and malfunctions that occur on a network may frustrate users.

Selection Criteria

- Are the intellectual level and the reading level appropriate for the intended users?

- Will students use the disciplines covered in the database?

- How is the database indexed?

- Can students conduct searches using title, author, and keywords?

- Can searchers use Boolean logic, connecting search terms with *and*, *or*, and *not*?

- Are cross-references provided?

- How frequently is the database updated? Is this appropriate for the curriculum needs?

- How accurate is the information?

- What years does the database cover?

- What services does the vendor offer?

- How clear is the written documentation? Does it include sample screens and other aids?

- If there is a print version, is the online search time less than that required for searching the print version?

- Is the screen easy to read and are directions clear?

- What criteria or standards were used in creating the database?
- Can the users access the database from home after school hours?
- Is the vendor willing to negotiate cost and having the database available during after-school hours?
- If the databases are bundled, can you search simultaneously through more than one database?

Implications for Collection Development

Important questions arise when making a decision on whether to subscribe to online databases. Costs for subscriptions can usually be negotiated with a vendor. The costs may vary depending on a school's enrollment, number of persons able to simultaneously access the database, and whether the students have around-the-clock access to the databases. These are all parts of the licensing agreement that you will sign when subscribing to a database or to bundled databases. Agreements with such vendors can affect use. The number of interlibrary loan requests may increase as searchers identify resources not available in the media center and not available in full text in the databases. Future funding concerns may necessitate the formation of resource-sharing plans to accommodate the increase in requests for resources the media center does not own.

Copyright Considerations

License agreements usually define what the publisher considers to be fair use of the product. Limitations may include the amount of information that users can download or the number of users who may access the service at the same time.

Pamphlets

Pamphlets are multiple-page, printed materials that are frequently housed in the vertical file, rather than shelved as books. Local, state, and national governments, as well as associations or businesses, publish them. Pamphlets and other vertical file materials can provide a wealth of current information and special treatment of timely subjects. Government documents frequently provide concise and up-to-date information about a topic, although the vocabulary may be beyond the elementary school pupil's comprehension.

Advantages

- Pamphlets are inexpensive or free; media specialists can readily obtain duplicate copies for topics of high interest.
- Often information found in pamphlets is more current than that in other print media, except magazines and newspapers.
- Pamphlets can provide a variety of viewpoints on a subject.
- Pamphlets often discuss subjects unavailable elsewhere in the collection. Their treatment is usually brief, focusing on a specific subject.

Disadvantages

- Because of their size and format, pamphlets are easily misfiled.

- The flimsy construction of pamphlets limits repeated use.
- Free pamphlets issued by organizations or corporations may take a specific position on issues or contain a great deal of advertising.
- It takes much time to set up and maintain a vertical file containing pamphlets.

Selection Criteria

- Because groups or businesses sponsor many pamphlets, media specialists must consider the extent of advertising. Does advertising dominate the presentation and distract from or distort the information?
- Regardless of whether the item contains advertising, is the message presented without bias and propaganda?
- Is the information provided elsewhere in the collection?

Implications for Collection Development

Since much of the information that is contained in pamphlets is now available through Internet access, many school media specialists have eliminated collecting pamphlets and setting up vertical files. However, if you decide to collect pamphlets, they are an inexpensive way to provide balanced information on controversial issues. Materials should be readily accessible, and media specialists should review them periodically for timeliness. Because many pamphlets are undated, media specialists find it helpful to date them as they file them. This simplifies the re-evaluation process. As new versions of pamphlets arrive, the old ones should be removed.

Copyright Considerations

Some pamphlets have copyright limitations. Others, particularly those that government agencies produce, frequently have no copyright restrictions. The user needs to examine each pamphlet for copyright information.

Periodicals. *See also* E-Journals and Newspapers

A periodical is a magazine or other publication which is issued on a regular basis. The following section deals only with magazines. Hundreds of magazines can be included in a school media center collection. Some popular magazines that are read primarily for entertainment are *Ranger Rick*, *Rolling Stone*, and *People*. Others, such as *Scientific American*, *U.S. News and World Report*, and *American Heritage*, are used heavily for research. Many of the professional magazines are referred to as journals. Examples of ones that you might have in your professional library are *Reading Teacher*, *School Library Journal*, and *Journal of Science Education and Technology*.

Advantages

- Periodicals offer short stories, participatory activities for young users, and extensive illustrations.

- Some magazines solicit contributions of writing or illustrations from students.
- Many periodicals suggest activities that adults can use with students.
- Reluctant book readers often enjoy reading magazines.
- Having a collection of popular magazines will attract teen users to the media center.

Disadvantages

- Circulation controls are difficult to establish.
- Periodicals lend themselves to theft and mutilation.
- When a large number of children are involved, reader participation activities (such as fill in the blanks, connect the dots, or puzzles) need to be copied or laminated so they can be used more than once. Copying is subject to copyright restrictions.
- Storage space that provides easy access to several volumes of a journal may be difficult or expensive to provide.
- If foldouts and cutouts are removed from periodicals, portions of the text may be eliminated.
- The number of advertisements in journals may detract from their usefulness.

Selection Criteria

- Is the content of interest to students and teachers?
- Are subjects treated clearly in a well-organized manner?
- Are the illustrations pertinent and adequately reproduced?
- Is the format appropriate for the purpose of the magazine and the intended audience?
- Do any users need large-print items?
- Is the journal indexed?
- Does the electronic version have the same coverage as the print version?
- How easy is it to access back issues?
- How is the electronic version updated?
- Does the electronic version provide links to other electronic sources?
- How easy is it to download articles?

Implications for Collection Development

The length of time one keeps print versions of periodicals depends on their use and the availability of storage facilities. Anticipated use plus cost are key factors in deciding whether to obtain periodicals in print, online, or in CD-ROM formats.

Copyright Considerations

A teacher can copy a chart, graph, diagram, cartoon, picture, or article from a periodical or newspaper for instructional use. Word limits for multiple copies for classroom use are 250 words for poetry and 2,500 words for articles. A copyright warning notice should appear on each copy. Creation of anthologies, compilations, and collective works are prohibited.

Posters *See* Graphic Materials

Realia *See also* Games; Models; and Toys

Realia are three-dimensional objects from real life that can be used for classroom instruction. Coins, tools, stamps, postcards, and fossils are examples of realia. They bring the real world into the hands of inquisitive users.

Advantages

- Students can handle and closely examine real objects.
- One can inexpensively acquire some objects, such as stamps and postcards, from a wide range of sources, including the students themselves.
- Teachers can check out realia and use them in classroom lessons.

Disadvantages

- Students can easily drop and break some realia.
- Some items may be too fragile or too small for more than one person to use at a time.
- Other items, such as an abandoned bird's nest, are hard to keep clean or to retain the original shape.

Selection Criteria

- Does the item serve an instructional purpose?
- Is the item durable?
- Is there a display area where several students can observe one item at the same time?
- Are items safe to handle?

Implications for Collection Development

You should avoid duplicating specimens found in other departments of the school, such as the science laboratory. Items should not be put in the collection unless they can potentially serve an instructional purpose. Realia may require special storage facilities.

Slides

Two types of slides are (1) two-by-two-inch slides used with projectors with trays, carousels, or cartridges, on slide sorters, or in individual viewers and (2) microslides of biological specimens used with a microprojector.

Advantages

- Color slides are economical to produce.
- The size of slides permits compact packaging and storage, with ease of distribution and circulation.
- Instructors can adapt sequencing and can edit according to their needs.
- With proper equipment, sound can be added.
- Microslides permit an entire class to view microscopic materials, rather than requiring each student to have a microscope.
- Slides can be projected for an indefinite time to accommodate discussion.

Disadvantages

- Single slides are difficult to access rapidly.
- Although slides are inexpensive to process or duplicate, this takes time and depends on the quality and speed of local laboratory services. Copyright restrictions apply to duplication.

Selection Criteria

- Are art slides faithful to the original?
- Are mountings durable?
- Is there continuity to the set of slides?
- Are content and length of presentation appropriate for the intended purpose and audience?

Implications for Collection Development

Effective group use of slides requires projectors with remote-control features and lenses of appropriate focal length. Student-produced and teacher-produced slides should meet the same criteria as purchased items. Newer technologies, such as digital photos, have replaced most of the use of slides in schools. Students and teachers are now able to access photographs of art and science specimens via the Internet. They can also develop their own slide presentations through the use of digital photos and *PowerPoint* slides.

Copyright Considerations

Copying slide sets in their entirety, altering a program, or transferring a program to another format requires written permission.

Software *See* Computer Software

Study Prints *See* Graphic Materials

Textbooks and Related Materials

Materials include textbooks (basic and supplementary), workbooks, and multimedia items. Commercial companies and educational agencies develop these materials. Textbooks may be used as chief sources of information or as supplementary information sources.

Advantages

- Instruction is in a fixed sequence but is usually flexible enough for the instructor to reorganize.
- The table of contents and index facilitate rapid access to information.
- Each student can have a copy.
- The teacher's editions offer suggestions for related materials and activities.
- Textbooks are field tested, and one may request and evaluate the results of those tests.
- Users can move at their individual pace.

Disadvantages

- Textbooks can limit a teacher's creativity.
- Textbooks can encourage rote learning rather than stimulate exploration.
- A textbook's bibliographies may cite out-of-print materials or fail to reflect appropriate resources in the collection.
- Textbooks take up much shelf space if they have to be housed in the media center.
- Adoption of textbooks often implies they will be used over a number of years.

Selection Criteria

Teachers, in consultation with media specialists, usually select the textbooks or other instructional systems. In some situations, the media specialist may not participate, but the criteria presented here provides basic information necessary to consider in making selection decisions. A media specialist may want to buy a single copy of a particular text for its informational content, even though it is not used in a classroom.

- Is the content accurate and objective?
- Does the content represent a broad spectrum of viewpoints on a given topic?
- Are the visual materials keyed to the text?

- Are bibliographies up to date? Do they include a wide range of formats?
- Is the treatment appropriate for the intended purpose and audience?
- Is the arrangement chronological or systematic?
- Is the presentation free of racial or sexual stereotyping?
- Is the type clear, and are the pages uncrowded?

Implications for Collection Development

In some schools, media specialists are responsible for the organization, storage, distribution, and inventory of textbooks. Regardless of whether you have this responsibility, you need to be aware of the content, the materials recommended in the bibliographies, and the potential use of textbooks as information sources. Individual titles may be useful as information works or for anthologies of short stories or poetry. You may want to include textbooks in the professional collection.

Copyright Considerations

Users may not copy workbooks, exercises, test booklets, and other consumable works.

Toys

Toys (dolls, stuffed animals, puppets, cars, etc.) allow students opportunities to develop coordination and to learn through touch, manipulation, and sight.

Advantages

- Play is a way of exploring natural laws and relationships.
- Toys can help develop perceptual motor skills.
- Dolls and stuffed animals can help develop affective skills.
- Toys are inexpensive.

Disadvantages

- Parts can be lost.
- The various shapes of toys can create storage problems.
- Germs and lice can be spread through the use of toys. Toys need to be cleaned and sanitized.
- Safety requirements must be observed.
- Toys can be used by a limited number of people.

Selection Criteria

- Can a student play with the toy independently, or is adult guidance needed?

- Has the user's developmental stage been considered in the selection of the toy?
- Is the toy durable?
- Will the toy withstand use by children?
- Can one buy replacement parts or make them in-house?
- Is the material nonflammable?
- Can one wash or clean the toy?
- Are the parts of the toy safe for children to use without injuring themselves?

Implications for Collection Development

Selection should be based on knowledge of the children's developmental needs. You may need to provide duplicate items so more than one student can use the same toy or so that the toy can be used in the media center and also circulated. You will need to consider whether you want to collect and circulate toys.

Videocassettes

Videocassettes contain magnetic tapes on which both audio and video can be recorded simultaneously. They were first developed in the 1970s so movement in addition to sound could be recorded. The two major standards for videocassettes were Sony's Betamax (Beta) and JVC's VHS format. The VHS format eventually squeezed Betamax out of the consumer market. Videocassettes can still be purchased today, but in recent years the DVD format overcame VHS as the most popular for playback of recorded video.

Advantages

- The videocassette can be stopped or replayed.
- Videocassettes are easy to store, maintain, and use without damage.
- The format is familiar to users.
- Several people can view a video at the same time.
- Showing videos over closed-circuit televisions can make a presentation accessible to a large number of viewers in different locations.

Disadvantages

- Small monitors limit the size of the audience, unless one can provide multiple monitors or video projector systems.
- Compatible equipment is necessary.
- DVDs produce a clearer image than videocassettes, and many producers are moving to DVDs, rather than videos.

Selection Criteria

- Is the content of the video appropriate for the intended audience?
- Are there reviews available for the video?
- Is it possible to preview the video before purchase?
- Is the case protective?

Implications for Collection Development

This format became popular because of its ease of use and range of selections. If possible, you should preview video media before making a purchase. If they meet the selection criteria, videos produced by students, teachers, and staff can be placed in the collection. Video recordings of teleconferences and educational television programs can also be added to the collection.

Copyright Considerations

Copying or altering an entire video requires written permission. Off-air recordings may be retained for no more than forty-five calendar days; then they must be erased. They may be shown to a class twice within ten teaching days. If further use of the video is sought, then one needs to obtain a license.

Web Sites

Web site refers to a collection of pages of documents accessible on the World Wide Web (WWW or the Web). This environment on the global computer network allows access to documents that can include text, data, sound, and video. The user can move from one location to another within the Web site or use *links* to move to related Web sites. Access is by the Web site's address or by the *uniform resource locator* (URL). The URL identifies the name of the host computer, the server, the name of the directory, the domain, the directory or server, and the Web page, or the actual filename. The domain is identified by three letters describing the sponsoring organization: .com for commercial site, .edu for educational, .k12 for a school, .org for a non-profit organization, .gov for a government agency, and .net for an Internet Service Provider, among others. The tilde symbol (∼) designates a personal Web page. These letters and symbols give a clue as to the author (and authority) of the information.

Advantages

- The Web provides access to information on a global basis.
- The information is generally current.
- The process is quick, cheap, and efficient.
- The links connect related sources of information.
- The information may be presented through text, sound, graphics, animation, video, and downloadable software.
- Users can interact with the Web site at their own pace.

Disadvantages

- Searching for information takes place without the guidance of an index or a classification scheme.
- The content of some Web sites, including the identified links, are not updated on a regular basis.
- The advertising on some Web sites can be distracting.
- Content may not be age appropriate.
- Students can easily get lost or lose focus when accessing numerous links.
- Students can download a file, alter it, and (illegally) claim it is their own work.

Selection Criteria

- Is the following information provided: name of sponsoring organization or individual, their qualifications, the full mailing address, the e-mail address, the date the page was created, the date the information was updated, and copyright information?
- Is the content and vocabulary appropriate for the intended audience?
- Is the purpose clearly stated?
- Does the Web site fulfill its purpose?
- How long does it take to access the Web site?
- Is it easy to navigate through the various pages of the Web site?
- Are the links updated so that one does not get an error message indicating that the link no longer exists?
- Does the design add to the appeal for the intended audience?
- Does the type and background make the pages readable?
- Is there a link back to the home page on each page?
- Is a table of contents or outline provided for longer documents?
- Does the Web site have its own search engine for searching all the pages?
- Has the site been reviewed? If so, what did the reviewer say?
- If the Web site offers a fee-based service, is it a justified and reasonable price?

Implications for Collection Development

Selection of Web sites for assignments should be the media specialist's responsibility, rather than having users rely solely on search tools. The media center's Web site can be one way that users learn of links to selected sites related to their needs and interests. The media center's own Web site should be updated on a regular basis. If you are subscribing to a fee-based Web site, you may be able to negotiate the cost.

Copyright Considerations

All Web pages are copyrighted. The design of the page, the HTML code, the graphics, and the collections of links are copyrightable. A notice will inform users if they may copy the materials. If you do not find a notice that you can reproduce the material, you must obtain permission to make more than one copy for personal use. If you are subscribing to a Web site, you will need to adhere to the licensing agreement.

Conclusions

It is important to include a variety of formats in a school media center in order to meet the needs of all users. When selecting materials, media specialists should consider who will use the materials, what formats they prefer, how they will use the materials, and whether appropriate equipment is available. Few collections will include every format described. Some materials may be outside the scope of a school's collection policy; others may not be suitable for a particular group of users. Each format has advantages, disadvantages, and selection criteria that may be specific to that particular media format. Media specialists should also be familiar with copyright laws and fair use guidelines and how they relate to each format. Advances in technology will continue to bring new formats to the market. As new materials and formats appear, media specialists need to consider their relevance to the collection.

Additional Readings

Agee, J. (2003). Exciting e-books: A new path to literature. *TechTrends, 47*(4), 5–8.

Bell, M. A. (2005). State-funded informational databases: You may lose them even if you use them! *Teacher Librarian, 32*(3), 8–11.

Bilton, K. (2004). Kids love comics, too! *School Library Journal, 50*(7), 30–31.

Brown, J. B. (2004). S.O.S.: Save online services! *Library Media Connection, 23*(2), 50–51.

Chelton, M. K. (2006). Perspectives on practice: Young adult collections are more than just young adult literature. *Young Adult Library Services, 4*(2), 10–11.

Ching, A. (2005). Holy reading revolution, Batman!: Developing a graphic novel collection for young adults, *Young Adult Library Services, 3*(4), 19–21.

Clyde, L. A. (2005). Electronic books. *Teacher Librarian, 32*(5), 45–47.

Crawford, P. (2003). *Graphic novels 101: A resource guide for school librarians and educators.* Salt Lake City, UT: Hi Willow Research & Publishing.

Crawford, P. (2004). Graphic novels for elementary schools libraries. *Knowledge Quest, 32*(3), 35–37.

Ganesh, T. G. (2003). Ejournals in education: Just generating excitement or living up to the promise? *Education Libraries, 26*(1), 5–15.

Ireland, K. (2004). Built and they will come: Graphic novels for your collection. *School Libraries in Canada* (Online), *23*(1).

Johnson, D. (2004). Turning the page. *School Library Journal, 50*(11), 44–46.

Larson, J. (2006). Listen up! What's new in audiobooks. *Library Media Connection, 24*(7), 24–27.

Lyga, A. A. W. (2006). Graphic novels for (really) young readers. *School Library Journal, 52*(3), 56–61.

Pawuk, M. (2002). Creating a graphic novel collection @ your library. *Young Adult Library Services, 1*(1), 30–35.

Robinson, L. (2003). For the love of books: Expanding e-books and audio books in school libraries. *Media & Methods, 40*(2), 6–8.

Schultz, C. D. (2006). Timing is everything: Using videos. *Library Media Connection, 24*(4), 14–17.

Tal, N. (2006). Which one to choose?: A comparison between three aggregators. *Knowledge Quest, 34*(3), 24–29.

Walliser, K. (2005). Graphic novels as part of your collection. *School Libraries in Canada* (Online), *25*(1).

Helpful Web Sites

Beck, S.E. (2006). *The good, the bad & the ugly: Or, why it's a good idea to evaluate web sources.* Retrieved April 20, 2006, from http://lib.nmsu.edu/instruction/eval.html

Brenner, R. (2004). *More than words: Graphic novels in Kentucky's libraries.* Retrieved April 20, 2006, from http://kdla.ky.gov/onlinepubs/selectionotes?AprJune2004/gn_wheretostart.htm

Copyright Website. (2005). Retrieved April 20, 2006, from http://www.benedict.com

Kannenberg, G. (2006). *ComicsResearch.org.* Retrieved April 20, 2006, from http://www.comicsresearch.org

Lavin, M. R. (2000). *Comic books for young adults.* Retrieved April 20, 2006, from http://ublib.buffalo.edu/lml/comics/oages/ourchasing.html

Miller, S. (2005). *Graphic novels in libraries: Hundreds of librarians can't be wrong.* Retrieved April 20, 2006, from http://www.angelfire.com/comics/gnlib/resources.html

North Carolina Department of Public Instruction. (1997). *Copyright in an electronic environment.* Retrieved April 20, 2006, from http://www.dpi.state.nc.us/copyright1.html

Raiteri, S. (2003). *Recommended graphic novels for public libraries.* Retrieved April 20, 2006, from http://my.voyager.net/~sraiteri/graphicnovels.htm

Schrock, K. (2006). *Teacher helpers: Critical evaluation information.* Retrieved April 20, 2006, from http://school.discovery.com/schrockguide/eval.html

9

Acquisitions and Processing

Acquisition is the process of obtaining materials. This involves confirming that materials are available, verifying order information, identifying and selecting sources of materials, arranging for orders to be sent, allocating funds, keeping records, and producing reports on expenditures of funds. Obtaining electronic products, reviewing license agreements, and negotiating for leases are also included in the acquisition procedures. Speed, accuracy, and thrift are common goals of the acquisition process.

The media center may acquire materials through purchase, lease, solicitation of free materials, gifts, or exchanges. Schools participating in resource-sharing programs also borrow and lend materials that are available through interlibrary loan.

This chapter focuses on the components of the acquisition process that are most likely to involve the building-level person directly. It also reviews the relationship of acquisition procedures to acquisition policy, identifies the distribution systems for materials, describes procedures for acquiring materials (including electronic materials), discusses the relationship between media professionals and vendors, and describes possible processing and cataloging procedures. Obtaining materials through resource sharing is also discussed.

Policies and Procedures

Policies establish procedures to follow and rationale for such procedures. Procedures describe how a process will take place and who will be responsible for implementing the steps in the process. An acquisition policy might state that materials will be purchased from the least expensive and most efficient source, for instance—a jobber. The policy might also indicate that a media specialist may buy an item locally if the need is immediate. In a high school, a policy could state that a paperback format is preferable to buying fiction books in hardback format.

In many school districts acquisition policies are uniform throughout the schools. The school district might also dictate the acquisition procedures. For example, the district's purchasing agent may specify the order forms that one should use. Some school districts may have agreements to utilize a particular jobber or to order their materials from an online catalog. Procedures for accounting and record keeping are frequently established at the district level. As a new media specialist you should ask the director of the district media program or a school administrator for a copy of district policies and procedures that affect the media center. In some school districts you can find this information online.

In order to obtain input from teachers, administrators, and students, you may want to create an acquisitions form. An example of such a form can be found in Figure 9.1. This form can be printed out and made available to library users, perhaps at the circulation desk or at faculty meetings. Ideally, the form should be available electronically through the school library Web site so users can access the form from classrooms or homes.

Distribution Systems

Choosing the best source for ordering materials or equipment is an important decision in the acquisition process. Chief distributors of materials include jobbers, distributors, publishers, producers, subscription agencies, dealers, and local sources such as bookstores and video stores. Any for-profit organization that markets a product or service to libraries can be considered a *vendor*. Other possible sources for materials include museums, online businesses, and garage sales. Remainders (publishers' overstocks) and out of print materials can sometimes be obtained from online vendors and from both new and used bookstores. Web sites that can help you identify some of these sources are found at the end of the chapter under the heading "Helpful Web Sites."

Utilizing Jobbers

Jobbers, wholesalers, and distributors are intermediaries between publishers or producers and the buyer—the media specialist. The term *jobber* is used interchangeably with the word *wholesaler*. Jobbers buy materials from publishers and producers and sell them to bookstores and libraries. For example, one can buy books and videocassettes directly from the publisher or producer, but the same items are often available at a lower price from a jobber or distributor. The word *distributor* is often used for audiovisual materials. Distributors may serve a region of the country or the entire country. Some jobbers and distributors provide newsletters, product hotlines, and Web sites.

Dealing with jobbers has many advantages:

- You avoid the cost and paperwork of ordering through many publishers or producers.
- You have only one source to contact for follow-up on orders.
- Libraries receive better discounts from jobbers than from publishers or producers.
- You obtain indirect access to publishers who refuse to deal directly with libraries or give poor service to small orders.
- Most jobbers provide full processing, cataloging services, security devices, and plastic jackets for materials.

Figure 9.1. Acquisition form

Acquisition Form
Suggested Materials for Purchase

Requestor:

Name:

E-mail: Phone:

Status (please check one):

___ Teacher

___ Administrator

___ Student

Source of Citation (where you found information about the material):

_____

Book (complete as much information as possible):

Author or Editor:

Title:

Publisher: Year of Publication:

ISBN#:   Price:

Magazine or Journal (complete as much information as possible):

Title:

Publisher:

ISSN#:   Price:

Audio-Visual Material (complete as much information as possible):

Type of Material (audiocassette, video, CD, DVD, etc.):

Producer: Distributor:

Price:

- Pre-selection plans (approval plans in which the media specialist examines new titles at the usual discount rate, with full return privileges) are frequently available.
- Some jobbers offer online ordering services.

Utilizing the services of jobbers also has disadvantages:

- It sometimes takes a month for jobbers to fill orders, whereas publishers can deliver in one to two weeks.
- The availability of older titles depends on the wholesaler's inventory.
- No wholesaler can supply every available title. Some titles, such as materials that professional organizations produce, can be purchased only through direct order.
- Policies on the return of defective or damaged copies may say that credit or replacement is not granted until the wholesaler has received the returns.

Libraries can expect jobbers or wholesalers to have a large inventory of titles, to fill orders promptly and accurately at a reasonable cost, and to report on items not in stock. If you receive an order and do not obtain satisfactory information about whether a book is out of print (OP), out of stock indefinitely (OSI), or temporarily out of stock (TOS), you should contact the publisher or producer to inquire about why an item was not received.

If a media center has a standing order with a publisher, it is not necessary to initiate orders for titles that the publisher delivers under the conditions of the standing order. A *standing order* is an agreement that is made to purchase all items that match certain terms, such as Caldecott Medal Award-winning books or materials on a particular subject. Many media centers have standing orders to renew their magazine subscriptions with vendors, such as EBSCO or Faxon. In such a case, the vendor sends the media specialist a list of all the subscriptions that are to be renewed, and the media specialist can delete items or add items to the list. As a new media specialist you need to check to see if your media center has any standing order agreements in effect.

Selecting Jobbers

Selecting jobbers who meet the needs of your media center can be critical. Thus, you should "do your homework" in choosing jobbers. You can ask a jobber to provide you a list of schools in your state that use their services and then inquire with other media specialists about their satisfaction with the use of that jobber. This can also be done on school library listservs. The following are some questions that you might want to ask:

- What types of discounts does the jobber offer?
- Does the jobber change prices of items without prior notice?
- On the average what percent of an order gets filled?
- How long does it take to get an order filled?
- Does the jobber provide information about items that are not received?
- If the jobber is a magazine vendor, is there a claim procedure in place and how long does it take to obtain missed issues?
- Does the jobber follow your specifications for processing and cataloging?

- Is the cataloging information accurate?
- Are the items packaged well and in good condition when you receive them?
- Are you able to return items?

Some Web sites that will help you identify possible jobbers, distributors, and publishers who deal with library materials, supplies, and equipment are listed under "Helpful Web Sites" at the end of this chapter. These companies can also be found by looking for advertisements in professional school media and library journals. Some jobbers that are frequently used by school media specialists include Baker & Taylor, Brodart, Follett, Mackin, and PermaBound. When you obtain your first school media position, you will also find that you automatically begin to receive catalogs and advertising brochures from companies that deal with library items. It is wise to keep these catalogs in an organized file and replace old catalogs as you receive newer versions.

Establishing and maintaining good working relationships with jobbers and distributors is partially your responsibility. You need to make certain that your requests are reasonable, that you keep jobbers informed about your collection needs, and that invoices are processed promptly. To stay in business and provide quality services to libraries, vendors need to have large volumes of sales and to have good cash flow. Thus, any way that you can contribute to these goals will be appreciated by the vendors with whom you do business.

Acquisition Activities

An initial goal of acquisitions is to avoid duplication, both of effort and of the item itself. Thus, the first step that should be performed when receiving a material request from a teacher or student is to check to see if the media center already owns the item or whether it is on order. The media center's online public access computer (OPAC) can provide information about current holdings, as well as materials that are on order (as long as this information has been entered into the OPAC). If on-order materials are not entered into the OPAC, then you will need to refer to all orders that you have made to check for duplicates.

Bibliographic Verification

When teachers or students request that you purchase an item for the media center, they often do not include the full information needed for ordering or they may even provide some inaccurate information (the title might not be exactly correct or they do not remember the publisher correctly). Thus, it is necessary to verify the bibliographic information needed to order the item. The verification procedure consists of two steps. The first is to establish the existence of a particular item. The second is to identify the correct author, title, publisher/producer, and other necessary ordering data, such as ISBN (International Standard Book Number) or ISSN (International Standard Serial Number).

To learn whether an item is available, one can start with a special type of bibliography called a *trade bibliography*. These tools provide ordering information for materials that are currently in print or otherwise available. Bibliographic tools that indicate availability may also state additional information such as whether the item is available through purchase, rent, or loan and the purchase or rental price, whether one must order the item directly from a publisher or producer or whether it is available through a jobber, distributor, or vender, and if there are postage or delivery charges.

The information included for each item may vary from one tool to another. For print formats, the bibliographic entry usually includes the author, title, editor, publisher, date of publication, series title and number, available bindings, price, and ISBN or ISSN. For audiovisual items, the bibliographic entry usually includes the title; production and release dates; producer or distributor; physical characteristics (for example, color or black and white, captioned or sound, audiocassette or videocassette, length or running time, and special equipment needed); number of pieces included (for example, four study prints and one teacher's guide); languages; price; and special conditions of availability.

Many bibliographies can be used for the verification process. *Books in Print* (Bowker), *Books in Print Supplement* (Bowker), and *Children's Books in Print* (Bowker) are frequently used to verify information for books. These resources are available in book format. *Books in Print* and *Children's Books in Print* are also available online. Bowker also recently introduced *Large Print Books and Serials*. Other fairly recent products produced by Bowker include *Bowker's Complete Video Directory* and *Books Out Loud: Bowker's Guide to Audiobooks*. *Ulrich's Periodicals Directory* (Bowker) is useful for periodical titles and is available in book format and online. You should use the latest edition of these tools for the most current information on price and availability.

If you do not have access to these tools that need to be purchased or subscribed to online, other options are available. One place to find out whether titles are correct and whether a work is in print is through commercial online bookstores. A word of caution, however, is that the bibliographic information in these online bookstores is not always completely accurate. Another option is to look on the publisher's or producer's Web sites. The bibliographic information for ordering will be available, as well as frequent listings of forthcoming titles.

Publishers and jobbers catalogs can also assist in bibliographic verification. Catalogs provide price and availability information, but they should not be used for reviews. Remember that catalogs exist to sell materials, not to offer evaluative reviews. When catalogs do quote reviews, full citations to the reviews are usually not given, so the media specialist needs to consider the limitations of incomplete reviews, words taken out of context, and the absence of more critical comments that reviews offer.

Ordering

After a jobber or other vendor is selected, materials then need to be ordered. Each school or school district has a procedure that must be followed in order to purchase items. This consists of filling out standardized purchase orders. Some jobbers and publishers provide online access to ordering. Follett's *Titlewave* is an example of an ordering tool that can save you much time. You can find the Web site information for *Titlewave* under "Helpful Web Sites" at the end of this chapter. You should contact financial personnel at your school to determine whether you are able to utilize online ordering opportunities and how that should be coordinated with the school's purchasing process.

Common information that vendors need to provide materials include shipping address, author or editor, title, publisher, date of publication, price, number of copies, order number, instructions regarding processing and shipping, invoicing, and method of payment. Vendors may also request ISBN or ISSN numbers.

Receiving

Care must be taken when unpacking shipments of materials. Special training might be necessary for clerical personnel and student assistants. The first item to locate is the packing slip or invoice (itemized list). This may be attached to the outside of the package or buried underneath the materials. If you do not find the packing slip, you should keep all the items in that shipment separate from those in other shipments.

As each item is received, check it against the packing slip or invoice for title match. In the case of audiovisual or computer materials, this step must take place before you remove the shrink wrap because many jobbers and distributors will not accept returns of unwrapped electronic materials. Check the item for damage or missing parts. Know the jobber's or vendor's policy on returns and whether they will give credit for damage that occurred in shipping.

Common problems include wrong editions, items added to or deleted from the list, wrong number of copies, and damaged or incomplete items. After all items have been checked, stamp the school library mark on them. Then enter the barcode into the database. Finally, approve the invoice for payment.

Record Keeping

Acquisition activities involve large amounts of detail work. You can handle the tracing of orders either manually or electronically. Manual systems often consist of keeping binders or files for purchase orders (POs) by categories such as "outstanding," "completed," or "to be paid." Another possible organizational category is using budget account numbers.

Computer software can simplify accessing information and generating records. Consideration files (the record of desired items) can be organized with a database management program, enabling one to print, in priority order, a list of items to be ordered from a single vendor. As materials are ordered and received, you can update these records. Some systems allow you to transfer the information to a different file, such as outstanding orders or new arrivals. Some systems also allow the administrator to create categories, such as a subject area, a specific format, back orders, or specified jobbers. You can use word-processing programs to create a template to print specific information on preprinted continuous forms, including purchase orders. You can also use a spreadsheet program to keep track of budget reports and projections.

If your school district is not using computer programs for management activities, consider the following questions: What jobs can best be handled through the use of computer programs? What equipment resources are available? What are the implications for staffing? What is the capability of existing software programs? Does your automated program permit online ordering, electronic invoicing, and credit-card payments?

Online Subscriptions

Most school media centers are purchasing databases through online subscriptions, rather than purchasing many materials in print or CD-ROM formats. Thus, while ownership through purchase used to be the traditional method, that is now being replaced by access to materials through license. It then becomes necessary to negotiate licenses with vendors. Such a license is a legal agreement of acceptable understandings and commitments that is often negotiated between the vendor and the school media specialist.

Both the cost and the terms of a license can usually be negotiated with a vendor. The cost often depends on the enrollment of your school, the number of users who can simultaneously access the materials, and whether you want remote access to the materials from classrooms and users' homes. It is important that you read through any license agreement and understand the terms. If you do not understand the terminology used in an agreement, you should ask the vendor to define the terms in vocabulary that is appropriate to school library media use.

If the quoted cost for access is more than your budget allows, you should not automatically give up on the idea of subscribing to online materials. Rather, you should explain your situation to the vendor representative and ask how the cost can be reduced. The online subscriptions are well worth obtaining since it makes access to materials much easier and also saves valuable space in the media center.

Equipment

In most school districts or schools, equipment that costs over a certain amount (often $100) must be put out for bid. In such instances, specifications for the bids must be drawn up. It is important to include every characteristic that you wish to have for the piece of equipment—for instance the amount of memory needed in a computer, the size of the monitor, the size of the processor, and any other specifications you require. You should instruct bidders not to include taxes in their bids since schools are usually tax-exempt institutions. The business office of the school district or a regional center will handle the bidding process and the awarding of bids. You will be provided with the name or names of vendors from whom you must order the equipment. If for any reason you know that a vendor does not provide quality products or service, you should share this information with the business office so the vendor is not included in the bids that are considered.

For equipment that costs less than those requiring bids you should check with your business office to see if there are any requirements regarding vendors. For instance in some schools you may not be able to purchase from local dealers but must order from catalogs. In other instances you may not be able to order from online vendors. Regardless of the way you order equipment, you will need to keep records of your purchases.

In most instances materials in a media center are either purchased outright or obtained through licensing agreements. Although equipment is usually purchased, large, costly equipment, such as a copy machine, are sometimes leased from a commercial vendor. In these cases the media specialist must read the leasing agreement carefully and keep track of the cost effectiveness of leasing the equipment in comparison to purchasing the item.

Processing Activities

The final stage in the acquisition process is preparing the materials for use. This involves cataloging and classifying each item, identifying the media center as owner, adding security strips and circulation barcodes, putting needed labels on the materials, and providing protective cases or other packaging for circulation of the materials. You should place copyright warnings on audiovisual and computer materials.

Some school districts have their own central processing of materials, particularly of books. In these cases, the books are sent directly to the central processing office where they are cataloged, have barcodes placed on them, and have the name of the school stamped on the items. If there are no such central processing services, then you should definitely have the vendor provide as much processing as you want—particularly the cataloging, which is a very time-consuming process. All major vendors of library books and many who deal with audiovisual materials offer commercial processing for reasonable costs (often from $1.00–$2.00 per item). This is a bargain when you consider the amount of time that it takes to fully process a book (generally between thirty minutes to an hour, depending on the difficulty of cataloging and classifying the item). You will need to fill out a specification form that indicates your processing requests so that the items match your current cataloging and you receive all the processing services that you need.

Some school media specialists order their materials processed, but ask that the school library stamp not be added to the item. This makes it much easier to return materials that are not wanted after examining the items.

If you are employed in a school that is required to do its own processing of materials, it is possible for you to purchase software to help with the cataloging. Many of the vendors of library automation systems provide software for this purpose.

Almost all school media centers use the Dewey Decimal Classification System (DDC) for classifying materials. The *Abridged Dewey Decimal System Classification* (OCLC) will usually fill the needs of a school media specialist who needs to do original cataloging. Other tools that will assist in original cataloging are: *Anglo-American Cataloging Rules* (American Library Association & Canadian Library Association), *Sears List of Subject Headings* (H.W. Wilson) or *Sears List of Subject Headings, Canadian Companion* (H.W. Wilson), and *Standard Cataloging for School and Public Libraries* (Libraries Unlimited). Since some of these materials are expensive they can sometimes be shared by more than one school or the school district can negotiate for licenses to access the resources online.

Resource Sharing

Another way in which materials can be acquired (temporarily) is by borrowing them from another library. This is generally referred to as *interlibrary loan*. Some types of interlibrary loan are formalized with networks to which libraries belong. A school that belongs to such a network has access to a plethora of resources and possibly to some additional services. However, participation carries responsibilities and perhaps financial obligations. Some school media specialists also utilize informal methods of interlibrary loan by e-mailing or phoning media specialists in local schools to see if particular items can be borrowed. This is very helpful when multiple copies of an item are needed or when an item is requested very infrequently. It is important to remember, however, that interlibrary loan should not be used in place of purchasing books or other materials that are frequently requested.

Conclusions

Acquisition activities consume time and energy. Much of the work involved is detailed and should not be performed in haste. Although clerical assistants can perform some of the acquisition activities, they need to receive training in which accuracy is emphasized. A media specialist's organizational abilities, mathematical skills, and business sense frequently come into play during acquisition activities. Errors or misjudgments can be costly. Using computer-management systems can simplify procedures, while controlling the information in a timely manner.

Additional Readings

Baule, S. (2002). Developing bid specifications for facilities projects. *Knowledge Quest, 31*(1), 14–17.

Baumbach, D. (2000). Celebrate success! Celebrate SUNLINK. *Florida Media Quarterly, 26*(1), 35–40.

Bosch, S., Promis, P., & Sugnet, C. (2005). *Guide to licensing and acquiring electronic information.* Lanham, MD: Scarecrow Press.

Langston, D. (2002). Collection development: Use a wholesaler! *School Libraries in Canada, 21*(4), 30–31.

Langston, D. & Whyte, H. (2001). Publishers, agents, wholesalers & jobbers: Book purchasing for school libraries in Canada. *School Libraries in Canada, 21*(1), 30–31.

McCroskey, M., & Turvey, M. R. (2003). What is CIP and how does it benefit the school library media specialist? *Knowledge Quest, 32*(2), 45–46.

Schrader, S. (2003). Thinking big in Iowa: Collaboration and technology in school library media centers. *Tech Trends, 47*(1), 25–26.

Stretch your budget! How to select Web-based subscription resources. (2003). *Computers in Libraries, 23*(2), 20–24.

Helpful Web Sites

AcqWeb. (2001). *Children's literature publishers.* Retrieved April 26, 2006, from http://acqweb.library.vanderbilt.edu/pubr/child.html

AcqWeb. (2001). *Video publishers and vendors.* Retrieved April 26, 2006, from http://acqweb.library.vanderbilt.edu/pubr/video.html

Block M. (2004). *Book bytes: How to find out-of-print books.* Retrieved April 26, 2006, from http://marylaine.com/bookbyte/getbooks.html

Follett Library Resources. (2006). *Welcome to Follett.* Retrieved April 26, 2006, from http://www.titlewave.com

Franklin-Essex-Hamilton School Library System. (1999). *Coordinated cooperative collection development plan.* Retrieved July 7, 2006, from http://www.fehb.org/slscccdp.htm

PMA, the Independent Book Publishers Association. (n.d.). *Remainders book expo.* Retrieved April 26, 2006, from http://www.pma-online.org/remaindr/remain.cfm

Yahoo. (2006). *Small business: Library services>supplies and equipment.* Retrieved April 26, 2006, from http://dir.yahoo.com/Business_and_Economy/Business_to_Business/Information/Library_Services/Supplies_and_Equipment?o=a

10
Maintenance and Preservation

An effective collection maintenance program serves two purposes. First, materials and equipment should be readily available for use. Second, policies and procedures for preventive maintenance help ensure economical and efficient management of the collection. Maintenance activities include keeping accurate records of what is in the collection (an inventory); inspecting materials; and repairing, replacing, or removing items.

Policies and procedures of the maintenance program are the focus of this chapter. The "Additional Readings" and "Helpful Web Sites" listings at the end of this chapter identify works with more specific information about the preservation and maintenance of items in the collection.

Maintenance Policies

Maintenance policies, particularly those relating to equipment, sometimes exist at the district, rather than at the building level. However, if such policies are not present, you need to create them at the school level.

The overall policy should specify who repairs materials and equipment, whether the media staff does any troubleshooting with equipment, who replaces equipment bulbs and conducts preventative computer maintenance, what preventative measures are taken to maintain equipment, who is responsible for weeding the collection, the criteria used to weed the collection, what is done with discarded materials, whether an inventory is taken of the collection, and who is responsible for the inventory.

In preparing the budget, developmental items (those increasing the size of the collection) can be distinguished from replacement items (those maintaining the current level of service). The media specialist can base the replacement of materials and equipment on the rates at which the items become unusable because of wear or dated content.

Another factor to consider is loss. A loss rate greater than 2 percent suggests that a replacement or loss factor must be a budget item. *Information Power: Guidelines for School Library Media Programs* (American Association of School Librarians & Association for Educational Communications and Technology, 1988) offers two budget formulas for materials and equipment. For example, to replace lost, damaged, and out-of-date books, one formula multiplies by 5 percent the number of books in the collection times the average price of a book. The example uses the following illustration: For a collection with 6,000 volumes, 5 percent of the volumes (300 books) should be replaced. If the average cost of a book is $15.00, then 300 times $15.00 means $4,500 is needed to cover the replacement costs (p. 128). Although this formula can be helpful, it is important to remember that the average cost of a hardback book has risen significantly from the figure used in the example from *Information Power: Guidelines for School Library Programs.* In 2005 the average cost for children and young adult hardback books was $20.52, a gain of $1.21 over the 2004 average (St. Lifer, 2005).

Information Power: Guidelines for School Library Media Programs (AASL &AECT, 1988) also provides a formula for replacing equipment. These formulas, along with other valuable information in the appendices of the book, are in themselves good reasons to purchase or locate a copy of this book, despite its copyright date. The second edition of *Information Power* (AASL & AECT, 1998) unfortunately did not include these valuable appendices.

Equipment

Policies related to equipment maintenance address the following issues:

- When and why equipment will be traded in or discarded
- The type of repairs and maintenance that will be handled at the building level, at the district level, and through repair contracts
- The records to be kept on equipment usage, repair, and maintenance
- The quantity and type of usable pieces of equipment to be provided, including a replacement schedule
- How media specialists will handle the transfer or disposal of equipment

Materials

With tight budgets in most school media centers, it is essential to make efforts to preserve materials that are in the collection. Maintenance policies for materials should include who is responsible for the maintenance of materials, as well as addressing the weeding and inventory of materials. *Weeding* of materials refers to the removal of the resources from the collection. Often this is referred to as de-selection or re-evaluation of the existing collection.

Responsibility

Generally the media specialist, along with the media center staff, has primary responsibility for preservation and maintenance of materials and equipment in the collection. Emphasis on educating students on the proper handling of library materials should be part of the policy. Also addressing what types of materials will be repaired and by whom can be included.

Weeding

The process of carefully weeding a media center to remove outdated and unused materials is as important as the process of selection. A weeding policy should include who is responsible for weeding the collection, the criteria for weeding materials, and what is done with weeded materials.

A media specialist is responsible for weeding a collection, but the expertise of faculty from various fields or grade levels should be enlisted. Classroom teachers can provide information relating to the curriculum that can assist a media specialist in making professional judgments about which materials can be discarded without affecting curriculum needs.

Physical qualities of a material, suitability of the content, recentness of the material, and accuracy of the information are all factors to be considered when making decisions to withdraw resources from a collection.

In general materials should be weeded from the collection for the following reasons:

- Poor physical condition
- Unattractive appearance
- Poor circulation record
- Old copyright date, with outdated or inaccurate information
- Duplicates of titles no longer in demand
- Subject matter unsuitable for users
- Topics no longer of interest
- Biased or stereotypical portrayals
- Inappropriate reading levels
- No longer needed because of a change in the curriculum

Having guidelines for materials also assists in adhering to the weeding criteria that you establish for your media center. Table 10.1 provides some suggested guidelines. You may want to alter the table to fit the needs of your school.

The policy can also identify materials that are not to be discarded. Examples include local and state history materials; major publications of the school, such as yearbooks or school newspapers; classics (unless newer versions are available); and items incorrectly classified or poorly promoted that might circulate under changed circumstances.

The policy might recommend continuous, intermittent, or periodical weeding. The continuous plan, which takes place on a daily basis, may be difficult to handle without disrupting established routine. The intermittent plan calls for designating specific times of the academic calendar for re-evaluating and weeding specific areas or types of media. The periodic plan makes use of days when the media center is not scheduled for use. Careful planning can and should avoid disrupting services to students and teachers.

Inventory

Some school districts have policies that require a complete, annual inventory of media center materials and equipment. You need to inquire

Table 10.1. Age and circulation guidelines

Class	Subject or Format	Age	Last Circulated (Years)	Comments
000	General Works	5	2	Replace one set each year; do not put old sets in classrooms
030	Encyclopedias	5	NA	Self-help books should be current
100	Philosophy/Psychology	10	3–5	Retain basic titles
200	Religion	5–10	3–5	
290	Mythology	10–15	3–5	Retain balance on controversial topics
300	Social Science	5–10	3–5	Have latest edition; may circulate year-old editions
310	Almanacs/Yearbooks	1	NA	Retain standard works
398	Folklore	10–15	5	Retain basics
400	Language	10	3–5	Retain basics, such as Darwin; examine any item
500	Pure Sciences	5	3–5	over 5 years old, except botany and natural history
600	Applied Sciences/Technology	5	3–5	Monitor changes in health materials
700	The Arts	NA	NA	Retain all basic items, especially art history
745	Crafts	NA	5	Retain well-illustrated materials
770	Photography	5	3	Discard dated techniques and equipment
800	Literature	NA	NA	Retain all basic materials, especially criticism; discard minor writers
900	Geography and History	10–15	5	Monitor geopolitical changes; retain local History
920	Biography	NA	3–5	Keep until demand wanes
E	Easy/Everyone	NA	2–5	Keep high-demand materials
F	Fiction	NA	2–5	Keep high-demand materials; evaluate literary merit; replace classics with newer, more attractive editions
Ref	Reference			
	Indexes	3–5	NA	As newer editions appear, discard old copies
	Atlases	5	NA	
	Maps and Globes	10	NA	Check for accuracy
	Newspapers	1 week	NA	Retain 1 week; access older editions online
	College Catalogs	2	NA	
	Periodicals	5	NA	Discard non-indexed titles after circulation
A-V	Audiovisual materials		NA	Discard worn or out-of-date items

about district policies related to this topic. If there is not a district-level policy in place, you should create written policies to address when and by whom inventory of materials and equipment will take place. Usually the media specialist, with assistance by media center staff, supervises inventory. New technologies, which include portable scanners capable of reading barcodes that have been placed on materials and equipment, makes it possible to use responsible students or adult volunteers to assist in the process.

You may also want to include in your policy a requirement that the media specialist submits a report of each inventory to the school principal. Discussing an inventory report with a principal is also a wise idea as it will help an administrator understand the process and possible problems, such as large numbers of lost items. Future budget needs for replacement of books or a security system are more apt to be met if a principal is kept aware of inventory results. A copy of each inventory report should be filed in the media center.

Maintenance Procedures

Working within parameters of the district policies, the media specialist is responsible for establishing collection maintenance procedures for systematic inspection of all materials and equipment. While technicians and aides can repair and clean materials and equipment, the media specialist identifies maintenance problems, diagnoses causes, establishes corrective measures, and monitors the quality of the work completed by media center staff or an outside contractor.

Routine internal maintenance procedures include the following:

Books and Print Materials: Replacing protective jackets, repairing torn pages, reinserting separated pages, eliminating minor scribbling, taping and labeling spines, and purchasing heavily used books in library bindings.

A-V Materials: Splicing tapes, wiping CDs and DVDs, storing discs and videos upright (book style) in plastic cases, returning materials to storage cases immediately after use, and storing materials in cool, dry environments.

Equipment: Cleaning areas of heavy use such as playback heads and lenses, using anti-static wipes on monitors and screens, keeping warranties, manuals, and repair records in an accessible file, training media staff and students in the proper operation and care of equipment (including replacement of bulbs), covering machines when they are not in use, fastening televisions and VCRs to designated carts, not allowing students to transport equipment, maintaining an area or workspace with basic tools for minor repairs, replacing, and properly disposing items such as light bulbs and printer cartridges, preventative computer maintenance such as defragmentation, data backup, and virus scans, and keeping equipment in climate-controlled areas. (Streiff, 1992)

You and your media center staff should also educate students and teachers about the proper care of media center materials and equipment. You can offer professional development workshops to teachers on the proper use of equipment, especially if new equipment is purchased.

When students first begin to use the media center, they should be taught to handle books carefully by turning pages only by the corners, keeping books in safe locations out of the reach of young siblings and dogs, not writing in books or placing objects in books, and refraining from reading books while eating or drinking beverages. Older students should be instructed on how to properly copy pages of materials on a copy machine, emphasizing not pressing down forcefully on the spines of books. If students are using CDs or DVDs, they should be shown how to handle these items properly, holding the discs carefully by the edges and making certain they do not get scratched.

Providing bookmarks at the circulation desk will alleviate the use of inappropriate items being used to mark places in a book or "dog earring" pages for the same purpose. Media specialists have reported finding gum, chewing tobacco, pickles, and numerous other strange items in books returned to their media centers. Additionally, keeping a supply of plastic bags near the exits of the media center can reduce damage to books caused by rain or snow.

Having access to a copy machine in the media center, with reasonable charges for copying pages, will cut down dramatically on damage to books when students tear out pages that they want for research. Installing security systems, particularly in secondary schools, will also help maintain the collection by reducing the loss of materials through theft.

Ensuring appropriate temperature and humidity in the media center to preserve materials and equipment is also one of your maintenance responsibilities. This is particularly important during the summer in hot, humid climates. In such environments, custodial personnel should be instructed to operate air conditioning systems for a part of every day. Not doing so, can result in mold and mildew damage and possibly leave equipment inoperable.

Weeding

Psychologically one of the most difficult tasks of beginning media specialists is weeding a collection. You, like most media specialists, are probably a lover of books and other materials that are found in libraries. Librarians give many reasons and excuses for avoiding weeding. Typical attitudes are these:

- Books are sacred objects; only vandals destroy books.
- Someone may need this in the future.
- I don't have enough time to examine every item in the collection.
- There will be a scene if teacher X wants this item.
- I don't have time to remove the bibliographic and holding records for all these items.
- Our policy doesn't justify the removal of materials bought with public funds.
- I cannot decide when a fiction title is out of date.
- Kits are expensive to replace, and this one has at least half of the original items.
- This software package has gone through several revisions, adding features we could learn to use, but many of us already know how to use this version.

Many benefits come from weeding a collection, including the creation of more space, ensuring accurate materials, avoiding the cost of maintaining unwanted items, obtaining and keeping a reputation as a source of reliable information, and saving time in locating items. After weeding a collection of dull or drab materials, you will also find that you have created a more attractive collection and an orderly, neat environment.

In your policy and procedures manual, you should make a step-by-step listing of how to remove weeded items from the collection. This can vary somewhat from one media center to another, but generally it involves removing the school identification marks from each item, writing with a permanent marker "Discard" on the items (generally in large letters on the front end pages of a book), removing the items from the OPAC, and finally discarding the items. In some cases the items can be recycled or there may be usable materials that can be transferred to another school or given to an organization. Some states do not allow you to sell the items since they were purchased with tax monies, but you might be able to donate useable items to a non-profit organization, such as Boys Club or Girls Club. Most media specialists have found that it is not a good idea to put library materials into a media center trash can since parents and teachers often do not understand why the items are being "thrown away," and it may create the impression that the media center is not in need of funds for materials. It is better to box the items, tape up the boxes, and have them placed directly into a dumpster or arrange for them to be picked up for recycling. For report purposes, you will need to keep a listing of the number of items that you have discarded, and in some school districts you also need to maintain the title and barcode number of each item.

As in other aspects of collection management, media specialists should involve teachers and others in the decisions about what items to remove. Teachers and their students can provide subject area expertise. For example, high school science students can help spot inaccurate information in science materials. Teachers can be encouraged to bring to your attention materials that are no longer useful. Different techniques can be used to involve users in the decision-making process about which items to remove. One technique is to display materials with tags on them on which the faculty can check off "retain," "discard," or "don't know" and then initial the item. Another technique is to use the *book slip* method. In that approach, you put a colored label on duplicate or low-use titles. The call number, the date, and a notice of the intent to remove the item from the collection should be clearly visible. Users are asked to remove the slip and turn it in at the circulation desk if they think the item should be kept. Six months or a year later, the staff checks for materials with slips and removes those materials from the collection, following the procedures written in the policy and procedures manual.

Inventory

The importance of establishing and holding to a designated time for inventory cannot be overemphasized. *Inventory* is the process of verifying holding records. During the process the media specialist assesses the physical condition of each item. In this context, inventory is more than mere matching of barcodes with records to obtain a count of the holdings. Inventory, as described here, is the process of examining each item physically and also checking the records for accuracy. A videotape may be in the wrong container, or a teacher's guide for a DVD may be missing. A detailed examination of materials can uncover problems overlooked during the routine checking of items at the circulation desk.

Some schools close collections for inventory, thus freeing the staff from other duties so they can review the collection in depth. However, closing the collection during the school year is in direct conflict with efforts to work collaboratively with school personnel. Some school districts recognize this conflict and hire media personnel for a period when schools are not in session. In one school district a team is appointed to inventory and weed various collections throughout the summer months. This practice can help prevent the emotional strain on school media specialists that removing items often entails. The disadvantage of this practice is losing the insight of the person who knows the needs of the school.

Other districts rotate sections of the collection for inventory, including re-evaluation, over a three-year period. Inventory can take place when items are in circulation. Through notations on the holdings and circulation records, media specialists can determine whether unexamined materials are on the shelves or still circulating. The size of the staff, the size of the collection, available time, and user demands influence the decision whether to evaluate the entire collection at once or one section at a time.

Again, in your policies and procedures manual there should be a listing of the steps to conduct an inventory. This procedure usually includes putting the books or other materials in proper order on the shelves, passing a scanner over the barcodes on each item, running a report of the inventory to show which items are missing, attempting to locate the missing items (checking circulation records, items on display, or items in an area for repair), removing from the report any items that are successfully located, and printing out a final report. It is a good idea to share the record of missing items with teachers in case some of the materials can be located in classrooms. Also, one can check student lockers when students "clean them out" at the end of a school year. Providing boxes near the lockers with labels that ask students to place library materials in the boxes can also help retrieve missing items.

Today most school media centers have automated circulation and card catalogs, which makes inventory and weeding much easier. If you are in a school that is not automated, the inventory process will be much lengthier as each item must be manually matched to the shelf list of the print card catalog. The weeding process will also take more time as all catalog cards (author, title, and subject) will need to be removed when an item is discarded.

Emergency Planning and Security

Although hopefully you will never need to use them, you should have procedures in place for emergencies, such as fires, floods, hurricanes, or break-ins. It is important to find out if the school district has such plans and to make copies of those plans. It is wise to keep copies of the plans at home, as well as in a file in the media center. Emergency telephone numbers of people who can give advice on how to deal with fire-or water-damaged materials should be in the plan. The plan should also include which school personnel have a copy of insurance policies, and what evidence is needed to make a claim. Holding records of materials and equipment in the media center should be kept in a location outside the school or in a school safe. Most media center automation systems can produce holding records, although they will take a long time to print if your collection is large. These holding records need to be updated periodically to include new materials and to exclude discarded items.

Conclusions

Policies and procedures need to be created for the maintenance of media center equipment and materials. Educating students and teachers on the proper handling of materials and operation of equipment will help preserve these items. Weeding the collection will improve the appearance and use of the collection, as well as ensure that the information in media center materials is accurate and up-to-date. An inventory of the collection is needed to verify that the records in the OPAC are accurate and to help media specialists plan for replacement and security needs. Teachers and students can assist in both the weeding and inventory of a collection, but a media specialist should supervise these procedures. Emergency plans should also be available to assist media specialists in case of disasters such as fires, floods, hurricanes, or major thefts.

References

American Association of School Librarians & Association for Educational Communications and Technology. (1988). *Information power: Guidelines for school library media programs.* Chicago: American Library Association.

American Association of School Librarians & Association for Educational Communications and Technology. (1998). *Information power: Building partnerships for learning.* Chicago: American Library Association.

St. Lifer, E. (2005). 2005 book prices. *School Library Journal, 51*(3), 11.

Streiff, J. E. (1992). *The school librarians' book of lists.* West Nyack, NY: Center for Applied Research in Education.

Additional Readings

Baumbach, D .J., & Miller, L. L. (2006). *Less is more: A practical guide to weeding school library collections.* Chicago: American Library Association.

Braxton, B. (2005). Inventory: 26 reasons for doing one. *Teacher Librarian, 32*(4), 52–53.

Deegan, M., & Tanner, S. (2004). *Digital preservation.* New York: Neal-Schuman.

DePew, J. N. (1991). *A library, media and archival preservation handbook.* Santa Barbara, CA: ABC-Clio.

Fortson, J. (1992). *Disaster planning and recovery: A how-to-do-it manual for librarians and archivists.* New York: Neal-Schuman.

Guidelines for collection renewal in school library resource centres. (2002). *School Libraries in Canada, 21*(4), 35–36.

How does your garden grow? Pruning vs. weeding. (2001). *The School Librarians' Workshop, 21*(5), 4–5.

Lavender, K. (2001). *Book repair: A how-to-do-it manual for librarians* (2nd ed.). New York: Neal-Schuman.

Lincoln, M. (2004). Weeded books inspire student art projects. *Library Media Connection, 23*(3), 20–23.

Lindsay, K. (2004). An ode to a teacher-librarian: Making your poetry section come alive. *School Libraries in Canada, 23*(3), 1.

Oliver, M. (2006). A librarian copes with disaster in New Orleans. *Library Media Connection, 24*(7), 18–21.

Helpful Web Sites

American Library Association. (2006). *Weeding library collections: A selected annotated library collection evaluation.* Retrieved May 23, 2006, from http://www.ala.org/ala/alalibrary/libraryfactsheet/fact15.htm

California Department of Education. (2005). *School library policies: Weeding.* Retrieved May 26, 2006, from http://www.cde.ca.gov/ci/cr/lb/policies.asp

Dartmouth College Library. (2003). *A simple book repair manual.* Retrieved May 26, 2006, from http://www.dartmouth.edu/~preserve/repair/repairindex.htm

Lamb, A., & Johnson, L. (2005). *The school library media specialist: Collection maintenance & weeding.* Retrieved May 23, 2006, from http://eduscapes.com/sms/weeding.html

Library of Congress. (2006). *Preservation.* Retrieved May 26, 2006, from http://www.loc.gov/preserve/

National Center for Education Statistics. (n.d.). *Technology in schools: Chapter 5 : Maintenance and support.* Retrieved May 23, 2006, from http://nces.ed.gov/pubs2003/tech_schools/chapter5_2.asp

State of Iowa Department of Education. (1994). *Weeding the library media center collections.* Retrieved May 23, 2006, from http://www.iema-ia.org/IEMA209.html

Sunlink weed of the month—archive. (2006). Retrieved May 23, 2006, from http://www.sunlink.ucf.edu/weed/

11

Circulation and Promotion of the Collection

Although perhaps not always included in the concept of collection development, the circulation and promotion of collections are primary considerations in the management of collections. Policies and procedures related to them are essential to an effective collection program. The best school media collection is of little use unless the materials in the collection are promoted and circulated to students and teachers.

Circulating the Collection

Circulation Policies

Circulation policies that require consideration include which items should circulate, to whom the materials should circulate, whether there should be limitations on the number of items that circulate to an individual, and how long the materials should circulate. There are no "right" answers to these questions since circumstances in your media center will affect how you respond to these questions. Such circumstances include the population make-up of your school, the number of items in the collection, curriculum needs, access to online information, and your budget (particularly funds for replacement of items).

Formats

Generally books, with the exception of reference books, circulate to students, teachers, and administrators. Most libraries do not check out reference books to patrons since the concept of reference books is that the materials be available and "referred to" as needed by persons using the library. However, in some school media centers teachers are allowed to check out reference materials to classrooms for short periods of time (perhaps during the time that a class is working on a particular assignment). Some media centers, particularly in secondary schools, also have a policy that allows overnight check-out of reference materials.

Audiocassettes, especially if they are "books on tape" or parts of book/audiocassette kits, are also usually circulated to teachers, administrators, and students. Other differences occur regarding circulation of formats other than audiocassettes and books. For instance, some media centers allow students to check out videocassettes, while other policies limit video checkout to teachers. Sometimes teachers request that students not be allowed to check out videocassettes since the teachers use the videos in their classroom instruction. Such a request was made by the teachers in the high school in which this author was a media specialist for eight years. Students who were absent on the day that a video was viewed in a classroom, however, were allowed an overnight check-out of the video. If a school has a large collection of videos and teachers do not object to student check-out, then students should definitely be allowed to check out videocassettes. Students at all grade levels are especially fond of videos and will appreciate a circulation policy that allows videocassette circulation. Undoubtedly it is an effective means of attracting reluctant readers to a media center.

Differences in policies are related to the circulation of periodicals. Often elementary school media centers have fairly generous policies, allowing students to check out back issues of magazines. In secondary schools, the periodical titles are usually indexed, and back issues are kept in the media center for research purposes. In both elementary and secondary schools, current issues of periodicals are available for use in the media center and do not circulate.

Policies relating to the circulation of CD-ROMs, CDs, and DVDs vary from one media center to another. The circumstances previously mentioned, as well as the content (whether it is instructional), will affect decisions on whether and to whom these formats circulate. Although equipment generally circulates only to teachers and administrators in most schools, there are school media centers that circulate digital cameras, video cameras, and even computer laptops to students.

In some schools parents are allowed to check out materials, usually books or videos. Often this policy exists in schools that collect materials that are aimed at parents, and the items are placed in a special, labeled section of the media center. Allowing parents to check out materials, however, can complicate automated circulation by requiring parents to have patron barcodes or identification cards similar to those used by the students. In order to avoid this added task, parents can be allowed to check out materials on the students' cards, but if there are limitations on the number of items that a student can check out, this may affect a student's use of materials.

Number of Items

Unless you have a large collection in comparison to your enrollment, you will most likely need to have a limitation on the number of items that students check out. Sometimes a limitation is set to help students keep track of the materials checked out and to be responsible for them. In elementary media centers the lower grades often are allowed fewer books than the upper grades.

In secondary media centers, policies usually allow for a larger number of items to be checked out by students. Some high school media centers have no limitations on the number of items, unless there is high demand for many of the books that are being checked out.

Teachers at all levels are generally not limited in the number of items they can check out from a media center. This is particularly true if teachers are checking out materials that are being used by students in their class-rooms. In such cases, the teachers will need to be able to check out large numbers of materials.

Time Limitations

Policies related to time limitations for the circulation of materials de-pend on the needs of patrons. Usually students in an elementary school have a one-week check-out period for materials, with the date due being the day that the class comes to the media center if the school is on a fixed media center schedule. Sometimes the upper elementary grades are given a longer check-out period, perhaps two weeks. If you have a flexibly scheduled me-dia center and a large collection where there is not frequent demand for titles, it is advantageous to consider a longer circulation period. Some media specialists have experimented with having only one date each month when materials are due, regardless of when materials are checked out. It is most important to remember that you want to have circulation policies that will encourage the use of materials.

Secondary schools should have a longer check-out period, especially when books are being used for research purposes. If research assignments are stretched out over a long period in a high school, it makes sense to have at least a four-week circulation period for books. Having less time will result in very long overdue lists and will frustrate students, teachers, and media spe-cialists. Options for renewing materials should be made at all school levels. This, however, may be limited, particularly if titles are in high demand.

Teachers appreciate not having time limitations on materials they check out from a media center. However, it is advantageous to let faculty know what materials they have checked out since it is easy for teachers to put materials into a cabinet or closet and forget that they have not returned items to the media center. Most library automation systems allow individual patrons to view which items they have checked out, but many teachers neglect to use this feature.

Overdue, Lost, and Damaged Materials

For many years the collection of fines for overdue materials was con-troversial. Today most elementary schools do not collect such fines, partly because of the time and effort it takes to deal with the collection of small amounts of money and also because elementary media specialists should be encouraging reading and the use of the media center. In some cases, par-ents do not allow their children to check out books if they are consistently forgetting to return books and having to pay fines. Having some positive methods to encourage the return of materials is a better alternative for young children. This might be giving out stickers (or possibly candy) to all children who return books on time or maintaining a record of classes in which all children return books each week and then providing some type of treat (e.g. a pizza party or special field trip) to the class who has the best record at the end of each grading period. Some media specialists do not let children check out other books until the students return the materials that are due.

Secondary media centers sometimes collect fines from students. Some media specialists and also teachers think that older students need to learn responsibility for the return of materials on time. Other media specialists like to have the monies collected in fines to use for special purposes, such

Figure 11.1. Elementary school circulation policies

Lincoln Elementary School Media Center
Circulation Policies

Books, audiocassette kits, videos on the student shelves, and back issues of magazines may be checked out by students.

Students in kindergarten may check out one item at a time during the first semester and two during the second semester.

Students in 1st-5th grades may check out two items at a time.

Parents may check out three items at a time.

Media center materials are checked out to students and parents for a two-week period.

Students and parents may renew materials once, if no one else has requested the materials.

Reference books and current issues of magazines are for use only in the media center.

Teachers may check out as many items as needed. There is no time limit for materials checked out by teachers. At the end of each grading period, the media staff will send to each teacher a listing of materials checked out to him/her.

No overdue fines are charged.

Students will be charged the full replacement cost for any lost materials or items damaged beyond repair.

---

as purchasing holiday gifts for student volunteers or developing a special collection (graphic novels or CDs) that would not be possible within the general media center budget. It is the author's opinion that even at the secondary level it is preferable to use positive means, rather than punitive, to encourage the return of materials. The collection of fines at any grade level should be discussed with administrators and teachers before a policy is implemented or revised.

All students and sometimes teachers should be responsible for damaged or lost materials. Assessment for damaged or lost materials can be made either at replacement value (including processing charges), cost of original purchase, or percentage of replacement, depending on how long the item has been in the media center collection. Some policies do not charge teachers for damaged or lost items unless there is obvious irresponsibility and unreasonable loss. In such instances it is wise to involve the principal and inform the administrator of the monetary amount of such loss.

Figure 11.1 is a sample of circulation policies for an elementary school media center. Sample circulation policies for a high school media center can be found in Figure 11.2.

Circulation Procedures

The procedures for circulating materials should be included in your policy and procedures manual. If a media center is not automated, then

Figure 11.2. High school circulation policies

JEFFERSON HIGH SCHOOL MEDIA CENTER
CIRCULATION POLICIES

Students

Students must present their school identification card to check out library materials. The first time a student checks out an item, a patron barcode will be placed on the back of the library card.

Five items (books, videos, and CDs) can be checked out at one time. Items can be checked out for four weeks. Unless there are requests for the items, they can be renewed.

Reference books and magazines can not be checked out by students.

Fines for overdue items are $.10 a day, for a maximum of $5.00 per item.

Students are responsible for lost or damaged items. The cost will be based on the amount of damage or the price paid for the item plus a processing fee. A receipt will be issued; if the item is found a portion of the collected money will be returned (price paid minus the overdue charge).

Students withdrawing from the school need to present a withdrawal form for the librarian's signature. The librarian will note on the form any outstanding obligations.

Teachers

Teachers are responsible for all materials borrowed, whether the items are for class use or personal use. Their patron barcodes are kept in a file at the circulation desk.

There is no limit on the number of items that teachers can borrow from the media center.

All items must be returned to the media center at the end of each semester.

Teachers are responsible for the safe return of all equipment borrowed from the media center.

Interlibrary Loan Procedures

If materials are not available in the media center, a student or teacher may request an item through interlibrary loan. If the item is available in a media center within the school district, it will be delivered to the Jefferson High School Media Center, and the student or teacher will be notified by the librarian when it arrives. This process usually takes three to five days. If the item is not picked up within five days by the patron requesting the interlibrary loan, the item will be returned.

---

check-out cards and pockets to hold the cards will need to be ordered from a library supply company and attached to all library materials that circulate outside the media center.

Most media centers today, however, are automated, which makes circulation procedures much more efficient. Specific procedures vary according to the library automation system that is used. Generally each student and teacher has an identifying barcode, which is referred to as the patron barcode and serves as a library card. The barcodes that are placed on library items are material barcodes and are different from patron barcodes.

Although the same laser reader is used for all the barcodes, the automated library system will be able to identify whether the barcode that is being read by the laser is a patron or material barcode.

In some media centers a Rolodex file is kept at the circulation desk with identifying patron barcodes attached to the file cards; sometimes the barcodes are covered with a special, thin plastic made specifically for that purpose. When a patron wishes to check out an item, the media staff member finds the student's name in the file and passes the laser reader over the correct barcode.

Barcodes can also be placed on sheets of paper and retained in manila files, with the classroom teacher's name on the outside of each file. This works well for media centers that are on fixed schedules. In one school that the author visited, students decorated bookmarks on which their patron barcodes were placed. Each time the class came to the media center, the media specialist placed the bookmarks on a small table next to the circulation desk and all the children found their own bookmarks when ready to check out books. The media specialist collected all the bookmarks before the students left the media center so they would be available the next time the class came to the media center. Students who had been in the school for several years enjoyed seeing the bookmarks that they had made when they were in kindergarten.

Some schools require that students bring their own barcodes with them each time they check out items from the media center. This is often problematic in elementary schools in which students are not carrying wallets or book bags where they can safely keep their identifying barcodes.

Large secondary schools usually require students to have their barcodes with them when they check out materials. These barcodes can be placed on the back of a photo identification cards that are issued by the school administration or the media center staff can create cards using an automated library management system. Having the barcodes as part of a photo identification system is particularly helpful in large schools where it is difficult to know all the students. Unfortunately some secondary students tend to "borrow" other students library cards and items thus get checked out to the wrong students.

Usually the same patron barcode is used throughout the years that a student is in a school. If a media center is on a fixed schedule it is necessary for the media specialist to get a list of students in each class at the beginning of the school year in order to organize barcodes into classes. If a media center is on a flexible schedule it is still helpful to have class student lists so the media specialist knows where to send overdue notices. In secondary schools the expected graduation date of a student is often entered into the automation system, along with the identifying barcode number. This makes it possible to "retire" large groups of student barcodes all at once. It is important that each barcode number is unique; until students leave a school, barcode numbers should not be used again.

Material barcodes must also be unique. You can purchase barcodes from library supply companies, but you will need to keep track of the number range that you purchase to make certain you are not purchasing duplicate numbers. Some jobbers will also provide the barcodes and attach them to materials, but again you must provide the number range that is to be utilized.

In all schools, teachers and administrators will appreciate not having to carry their patron barcodes with them each time they come to the media center. Instead their barcodes can easily be kept on a Rolodex or in a separate file at the circulation desk. School media specialists can also locate teacher barcode numbers by typing names of teachers in the computer program that manages circulation.

If barcodes are not placed on all material formats and equipment, then separate circulation systems will need to be created for those items. This might consist of paper forms, check-out cards, or for equipment a check-out board, where the names of items and teachers can be written with erasable markers.

Procedures also need to be established for requests to reserve materials and equipment. Most library automation systems provide methods of reserving or "holding" items for patrons. Reserves for equipment that do not have barcodes attached can be handled by having a large laminated calendar on a wall, where teachers can write their names, the piece of equipment requested, and the times the equipment is needed. If equipment is checked out permanently to a room, it is best to either barcode the equipment or to keep a separate file for such items. The serial number of each piece of equipment should be indicated on the check-out record.

On many automation systems it is possible for patrons to renew barcoded items on their own, perhaps by accessing the card catalog from a classroom or from home. If you enable such a feature on an automated online catalog, then you will need to inform students and teachers that the feature is available to them.

Promoting the Collection

Media specialists spend much time and school monies developing collections to meet the needs of students and teachers. Yet in many cases the collections are not used to their fullest. Therefore media specialists should be aware of techniques that can help promote all or certain parts of the collection.

Media Center Web Page

One of the most effective ways of promoting a collection is through the use of a media center Web page. If the media center in which you are employed does not have a Web page, you should definitely create one. Today's students and many teachers spend large amounts of time accessing information online; if you create a helpful and interesting Web page, they will use it. Your Web page should be the default page on the computers in the media center so students and teachers are well aware of its existence. You can also advertise its use in newsletters or the school newspaper. The home page should be organized to serve many purposes, including collection development and promotion of the collection.

To promote your collection on a media center Web page, you can feature new materials as they arrive in the media center. Also, if you know that a grade level will soon be studying a particular unit, select some of the best resources that are in the media center on topics in the unit. Write short, useful annotations on the resources. You can include eye-catching pictures from online sites that provide royalty-free clip art. Spend time locating quality Web pages on the topics and provide links to those pages.

You can also offer to post teachers' assignments on the Web page under a "Teachers' Assignments" page. You can then direct students to the print and online resources that will assist them in completing the assignments.

You can promote titles by having online book discussion groups in which you list titles of books that can be used in discussions—perhaps selecting a book of the week. Summer reading lists should be posted during the last grading periods, and students can be encouraged to begin reading the titles on the list. Try to make it possible for students and teachers to check out materials during the summer months. During certain seasons of the year, books on holidays, current sports, or special events can be featured on the Web page.

If you continuously update the collection information on your Web page, it will keep the interest of your patrons. Of course, maintaining a library Web page can be time-consuming so try to recruit the assistance of students or parents. Parents who cannot ordinarily volunteer during the day because of work or family obligations might be very willing to spend some time in the evening or on a weekend working on Web page projects that will help promote the collection.

Reading

Sponsoring reading motivation programs is another excellent means of promoting a media center collection. The use of electronic reading programs, such as Renaissance Learning's *Accelerated Reader* or Scholastic's *Reading Counts* will certainly impact the circulation of books in a media center. However, if you have some philosophical problems with the use of these programs to motivate reading, you can easily create your own programs or projects to promote reading (and thus the media center collection). The following are a few such ideas:

- Organize book discussion groups that can meet at lunch, or before or after school.

- In collaboration with classroom teachers sponsor "fun" reading contests where everyone has the opportunity to win a prize or the principal agrees to some outrageous activity (dyeing his hair green or kissing a pig) if a certain number of books are collectively read by the students.

- Sponsor a poetry reading event, such as a poetry slam; set up a coffeehouse atmosphere and provide coffee, tea, and pastries.

- Hold programs on a variety of topics—collecting baseball cards, making films, or physical fitness; invite speakers and provide displays of materials on the featured topics.

- Have a mock Caldecott or Newbery Award election, featuring some of the notable current books.

- Show video clips of movies based on books; have copies of the books and videos, available for check-out.

- Encourage your school to have a DEAR (Drop Everything and Read) program for the entire school, including teachers and administrators.

- Sponsor an "Evening of Stars" and invite local celebrities (mayor, sports figures, TV weatherman, etc.) to come in and read aloud from their favorite books.

- Present exciting booktalks when you meet with students in the media center or in their classrooms; have multiple copies of the books available for check-out.

- Have students present booktalks on the morning news announcement program.

- Make large "Read" posters of teachers reading their favorite children's or young adult books and hang the posters in the media center and halls.

- Help organize a "Battle of the Books" contest.

- Hold a "Media Center Preview Party" for the faculty when new purchases arrive; provide refreshments and free bookmarks.

- Create attractive handouts or pamphlets of materials on specific topics or genres—mysteries, romances, graphic novels, books for the college-bound.

- Enlist the PTSA or a local bookstore to help sponsor an author visit to your school.

- Sponsor a "Rock and Read" corner in the media center, with comfortable rocking chairs and baskets of specially selected books and magazines next to the rocking chairs.

- Practice your informal reading advisory skills by spending time at the circulation desk and making positive comments about each book that is checked out ("This dinosaur book looks interesting; tell me about it when you return it" or "I know another great book about surviving in the wilderness. Would you like to check it out, too?").

- Sponsor a "Catch Them Reading" program in which you give out Hershey kisses to students and teachers when you see them reading books outside the media center.

- Create a "Wall of Readers" with photos of teachers and students in various poses reading their favorite books or magazines.

- Sponsor a weekly "Where is the Principal Reading?" contest in which a photo of the principal reading somewhere outside the school is posted, and the first person to identify the location is given a prize.

Additional ideas for promoting the use of particular collections, such as CDs, graphic novels, or natural history materials can be found in some of the articles listed under "Additional Readings" at the end of this chapter.

Displays and Bulletin Boards

One of the best ways to promote a media center collection is to display items that you would like to have circulated. This can be done in a variety of ways. The glass display cases in many schools, whether in the media center or in the hallways, are ideal places to create displays on specific themes or particular authors. If you are not fortunate to have access to such cases, you can make your own displays in the media center using the tops of book shelves, tables, file cabinets, or wide window ledges. Library supply companies also have furniture that can be used for displays. The revolving paperback stands are particularly effective for promoting materials in secondary school media centers.

The manner in which you display books on regular book shelves can promote specific items. This can be done by turning books to show their covers, instead of the book spines. Moving books from very low or very high shelves to eye-level shelves can be effective if certain materials are not circulating.

Students are sometimes asked to create pictures, dioramas, or models depicting scenes or characters from books. Displaying such student art work in the media center will create interest in the books.

Eye-catching bulletin boards have always been a great way to promote a media center collection. Creating attractive bulletin boards is definitely an art that features the promotion of books and other media center materials. However, if you do not have that special talent, you can easily find ideas for bulletin boards in books or online. Student aides and parent volunteers can also be of great assistance in preparing materials for bulletin boards.

One of the simplest and yet most successful promotion bulletin boards that the author of this book "created" in an elementary school with flexible scheduling was to talk with students when they returned a book to the media center and invite them to write the name of the book on a colorful "Post-It," along with their name, one brief sentence or phrase about the book, and a recommendation of which of their classmates they thought would enjoy the book. The students were then asked to stick the "Post-Its" on a bulletin board that was simply covered with white paper. As soon as word about the bulletin board spread, students came to the media center to check the board and see if anyone had recommended that they read specific books. Circulation of books greatly increased during the month of the "Post-Its" bulletin board.

Professional Collection

Many media centers have a special collection of professional materials for the teachers, support staff, and administrators in the school. This collection is sometimes referred to as the *professional library*. Often it is the collection that needs the most promotion.

It is important to have this collection in an area that is easily accessible for teachers and staff. If there is a teacher workroom located in a room adjacent to the main media center, that room is an ideal location. If you are fortunate to have an extra room in your media center (even a very small room), placing the professional collection in a room with one or two comfortable chairs, a pot of hot coffee and a plate of cookies, will do wonders for the promotion of the professional collection. If you have no extra rooms, then by using low shelving around two or three sides of a large table in the media center, you can create a work area for teachers. The materials can then be placed on the shelves for easy access, and materials that you want to promote can be put on display on the shelf tops or on the table.

Media specialists can also promote the professional collection by e-mailing teachers and inviting them to come to the media center to view new issues of professional journals or materials that might be helpful in their instructional areas. Presenting brief booktalks on professional library materials at monthly faculty meetings is another possibility. An even better idea is to recruit the principal or classroom teachers who have checked out professional books or journals to share how they used the information in their work.

Conclusions

To encourage the use of library materials, media specialists should develop workable circulation policies and procedures that are positive, rather than punitive. Circulation policies generally vary according to media center scheduling and the needs of the students in a particular school. Taking advantage of the many circulation features of automated library systems can save time for the media staff, as well as for patrons.

Media specialists should try various techniques to promote their collections and encourage the use of all types of materials. By working collaboratively with classroom teachers to sponsor school-wide reading contests, author visits, and other special events, media specialists can promote both reading and the media center collection. Making creative displays and bulletin boards that feature media center materials are other ways of promoting the collection. Strategically locating the professional collection and bringing teachers' attention to the items in the collection can encourage the use of professional materials.

Additional Readings

Belben, C. (2002). How library media specialists can promote physical fitness. *Book Report, 21*(3), 28–30.

Belben, C. (2003). Creating and promoting a natural history collection. *Knowledge Quest, 31*(3), 33–36.

Connolly, B. (2005). Promoting the library's CD collection via iTunes file sharing. *Computers in libraries, 25*(10), 6–8, 53–54, 56.

Fisher, J. D., & Hill, S. (2000). Showcase your library via a home page. *Book Report, 19*(3), 44–46.

Hammond, J. (2001). Community resources as part of the school library collection. *Library Philosophy and Practice, 4*(1). Retrieved June 26, 2006, from http://libr.unl.edu:2000/LPP/hammond.html

Miller, S. (2005). *Developing and promoting graphic novel collections*. New York: Neal-Schuman.

Stephens, C., & Franklin, P. (2005). To circulate or not to circulate: That is the question. *School Library Media Activities Monthly, 22*(1), 43–44.

Stinson, M. (2006). A library media center catch-22: Is there a workable solution? *Library Media Connection, 24*(7), 48–49.

Winkel, W. (2003). Time to join the club: Where are all the electronic book discussion groups? *School Library Journal, 49*(7), 37.

12

Evaluation of the Collection

The evaluation of any library collection, including a school library collection, should be based upon how well the collection serves the needs of its users. It should also take into account the goals and objectives of the library program. In your policy and procedures manual, you should include who evaluates the collection, what types of evaluation measures are used, and when evaluation of the collection takes place.

School media specialists should oversee evaluation of the collection. However, it is helpful to have input from faculty and students. Experts in subject areas can also assist with some evaluation methods.

Several different methods of evaluating library collections have been developed. Sometimes techniques are used independently, but more often several methods are collectively utilized. No one correct method of collection evaluation is available to use in all libraries; however, three general types of measures can help media specialists evaluate school library collections. Collection-centered measures include checking lists, catalogs, and bibliographies; examining the collection directly; age analysis; compiling comparative statistics; applying collection standards, and collection mapping. Use-centered measures include circulation studies, in-house studies, user opinion surveys, shelf-availability studies, and analysis of interlibrary loan statistics. Simulated-use studies include citation studies and document delivery tests.

As a new media specialist, you should set aside a time to develop a plan for evaluating the media center collection. The plan should include what methods of evaluation will be utilized, when data will be gathered, and what will be done with the results of the evaluation.

Why Evaluate?

Those who fund media programs need facts on which to base funding decisions, shifts in financial resources, expansion of programs, and cutbacks. As managers, media specialists need information on which to base decisions about collections and for communicating collection needs to administrators. The evaluation process can reveal answers to the following questions: Does the collection meet the users' needs? Is the collection integral to curricular and instructional needs? Does it provide access to materials from outside the school? Does it include formats that users prefer? Does it hinder or facilitate the media program? Is the collection responsive to changes in the school's program? These questions identify general areas of investigation that are broad and complex. One cannot examine all these questions simultaneously; to do so would be an overwhelming task. However, a media specialist can evaluate smaller issues—components of the larger questions.

Before beginning an evaluation project, one must identify what information to collect, how to record it, how to analyze it, how to use it, and with whom to share it and why. The Lincoln, Nebraska school district effectively used documentation to obtain increased funding. Willeke and Peterson (1993) described a project in which they developed a purposeful and thoughtful planning process that included a study of school media center collections in Lincoln. The study related the size, age, and assessment of the collections in response to curricular demands. They observed that although earlier principals, teachers, and media center staff had reported the outdated status of the collections, "It was the objective data, supporting subjective opinion, that resulted in the district's allocating additional monies for collection renewal" (p. 105).

A project to obtain library funding through analysis of school library collections was reported by Curtis (2000). The criteria used in this project were the currency of the collection, size of the collection, and the items per student of fifteen representative schools in the Baltimore Public Schools. The team working on the project requested and received $10.529 million over a three-year period of time to bring the secondary school library collections up to the state standards with resources that were current, age-appropriate, and supported the school curriculum. Curtis (2000) noted, "Budget requests are more likely to be funded when the rationale is based on statistical data that clearly demonstrates areas of need for collection development along with an understanding of how libraries contribute to student achievement" (p. 20).

Further evidence of the power of objective data to gain support is reported in *Managing and Analyzing Your Collection* (Doll & Barron, 2002). They also provide directions and useful work forms for analyzing collections in terms of (1) collection percentages; (2) copyright dates of the collection; (3) average age of the collection; (4) collection use; (5) comparison of the collection to standard bibliographies; (6) comparison of the collection to textbooks or periodical indexes; (7) teacher requests; (8) evaluation of a limited area; (9) estimating update costs and benefits; and (10) comparison of information in various formats.

Evaluation and Measurement

Evaluation is the process of deciding worth or value; measurement, a component of the evaluation process, is the process of identifying extent or quantity. We can count the number of items that circulate in any given period, but that information is not evaluative; counting provides quantitative data, an objective measure. The count gives us information about the number of items that circulated; there is no information about who used the materials (or whether anyone did) and under what set of circumstances, whether additional materials were used in other places, or even what materials were used within the media center. Merely counting the number of circulated science titles does not measure how adequately the collection supports the science curriculum. One must interpret additional quantitative data and perhaps consider some qualitative assessments before beginning to evaluate. The purpose of evaluating a collection determines whether one should use quantitative or qualitative techniques, or a combination of both. Although quantitative data lacks the element of judgment found in qualitative data, quantitative analysis does give us an objective basis for changing a collection policy.

Measurement can lead to meaningful evaluation. Professional judgment helps us decide what to measure, whether we can measure it, and how we interpret the results. The process can provide knowledge about alternatives, possible consequences, the effectiveness of operations, and insight into the managerial aspects of the collection program.

Evaluation produces information that can be judged by four criteria: validity, reliability, timeliness, and credibility. If the information is essential to a decision, it has validity. If we can reproduce the information when repeating the same techniques, the evaluation has reliability. If the information reaches the decision-makers when they need it, it has timeliness. If decision-makers trust the information, it has credibility. One should consider these criteria when planning how and when to evaluate.

Barriers to Evaluation

As with weeding, media specialists can fall into the trap of finding reasons for putting off or avoiding evaluation. Baker and Lancaster (1991) identify five barriers to evaluation. First, some people believe library services are intangible and library goals are impossible to measure objectively. However, media specialists who use a planning process recognize evaluation as a crucial component in the process. Assessment occurs in the context of each collection's philosophy, mission statement, constraints, users, and environment. Long-range goals guide the direction of the organization. The process also involves short-term, measurable objectives to guide day-to-day activities. Strategies help us to meet the objectives and identify measures for evaluating them.

A second barrier is concern about lack of staff time. Automation answers this argument. Automated circulation systems provide means to easily obtain circulation figures and to analyze use of a collection. This information helps one see patterns in a media center. Online public access catalogs can help media specialists to analyze other aspects of the collection, including the number of books in specific categories and the average copyright date of materials. These analyses can lead to evaluation, which in turn can lead to more efficient and effective operations, thus saving staff time.

Third, media specialists may lack experience with or knowledge about collecting and analyzing empirical data. Some ways exist to overcome this problem. For example, other members of the school's faculty can be asked to help with these operations. University courses and workshops on research methods provide opportunities to gain confidence in these activities.

Fourth, people who are unfamiliar with evaluation may fear the results. The results should be objective data that identify program strengths and weaknesses. The data can help one make collection decisions. An informed manager can use documented weaknesses to gain additional support of funds.

A fifth barrier is uncertainty about what to do with the results. Those responsible for the collection, including those who provide the funds for collections, must be ready to use the results to make necessary changes. The results of evaluation need to be shared and used, not filed away (Baker & Lancaster, 1991, pp. 4–7).

Techniques for Measuring Collections

You can use one of many ways to measure the value of a collection. The following sections describe the most commonly used techniques for measuring collection value. As you read about them, think about their appropriateness for your purposes. How will the results help you present the media center program to others? What type of data will you collect? What effort must you make to collect the data? How many people will you need to assist in evaluating the collection? What will the costs be? How much time will it take? Once you have obtained the information, how should you organize it? With whom can you share the information? How can you use the information to communicate with others? Analyzing measurement techniques with these questions in mind can help you select the most appropriate technique.

Collection-Centered Measures

To determine the size, scope, or depth of a collection, one can use collection-centered techniques. These are often used to compare a collection with an external standard. They include checking lists, catalogs, and bibliographies; examining the collection directly; age analysis; compiling comparative statistics; applying collection standards; and collection mapping.

Checking Lists, Catalogs, and Bibliographies

In this procedure, the titles in the OPAC are compared to a bibliography, list, or catalog of titles recommended for a certain purpose or type of collection. During the procedure, you should record the number of titles the media center owns and does not own. From this data you can obtain the percentage of recommended titles that the collection contains.

Lists that you can use for this technique include specialized bibliographies; basic subject lists; current lists; reference works; periodicals; lists designed to meet specific objectives; citations in textbooks or curriculum guides; or catalogs from jobbers, publishers, and producers. Examples of current lists include the Association for Library Service to Children's *Notable Children's Books, Notable Children's Videos, Notable Computer Software,* and *Notable Children's Recordings*; or the Young Adult Library Services Association's *Best Books for Young Adults, Selected DVDs and Videos for Young Adults, Outstanding Books for the College Bound, Great Graphic Novels for Teens, Popular Paperbacks for Young Adults,* and *Quick Picks for Reluctant Young Adult Readers*. Current lists of this nature identify highly recommended titles, but you must determine whether your collection needs those titles.

If your purpose is to measure the general coverage of titles appropriate for the audience served, standard catalogs, such as the H. W. Wilson series titles *Children's Catalog, Middle and Junior High School Library Catalog,* and *Senior High School Library Catalog* are useful. If comparison reveals that the collection has many of the recommended titles, then, presumably, the collection is successful. The more closely the purpose of the tool matches the purpose of the collection, the more beneficial the comparison will be. The collection development policy can provide a basis for judging the appropriateness of a specific list.

Advantages of this technique to help evaluate a collection are as follows:

- A wide range of lists is available.
- Many lists are selective and include informative annotations.
- Lists of this nature are frequently updated and revised.
- Lists can be compiled to meet the needs of a collection.
- Searching lists is a comparatively easy way to evaluate a collection.
- Most compilations have been prepared by competent professional media specialists or subject specialists.

Some disadvantages for utilizing this technique to evaluate a collection include the following:

- The lists that are readily available may be those used as purchasing guides.
- Some items may be out of print.
- The cost of the list may outweigh the benefit of its use.
- No single list can cover every subject or need.
- Bibliographies cover materials for all ages and may have limited usefulness for evaluating a collection established to serve a specific age-group.
- This approach does not give credit to titles in the collection that could be equal to or better than those the list recommends.

In schools where teachers use textbooks or curriculum guides that include bibliographies of recommended resources, media specialists can measure their collections against the recommended titles. Teachers appreciate having lists of titles that are available in the media center, along with the call numbers of the materials. Creating such lists for teachers can also alert you to gaps in the collection and simultaneously provide teachers with an opportunity to suggest alternate materials. A limitation of this approach is that titles listed in textbooks and curriculum guides may be out of print. However, newer materials may provide the same content.

Examining the Collection Directly

A physical examination of materials can reveal the size, scope, and depth of a collection. An assessment of the timeliness of materials and their physical condition can help identify which items need to be mended, repaired, bound, replaced, removed, or discarded. An examiner can be a member of the media center staff or an outsider. The latter is usually someone knowledgeable about materials on a specific subject.

A media center staff can examine the collection on two levels. The more cursory approach is to examine only the shelves while asking yourself questions. Are some shelves consistently empty? Is that a sign of popularity or improper distribution? Are teachers giving assignments that call for those materials? Does the collection development policy provide for adequate coverage in this area? Do some shelves have materials that are seldom used? Have students turned to electronic forms for this information? This cursory approach takes little time and can indicate a section of the collection that calls for more careful study.

A more in-depth approach is a systematic review of the collection. One examines the materials while considering the collection development policy. If users' needs have changed, a policy change is imperative. For subjects that have low priority in a collection, infrequently used materials are probably unnecessary. Knowledge of the collection policy and the extent to which materials are added, withdrawn, or replaced can help the media specialist to establish goals for the review program.

Selection criteria such as those presented in Chapter 7, "General Selection Criteria," can guide these decisions. Ideally, such a review is an ongoing process. It is easy to check the physical condition of books and periodicals when users return them. More time is required to check damage to software or audiovisual materials.

Advantages of directly examining a collection include the following:

- A cursory examination can be accomplished quickly.

- Media specialists considering resource sharing can readily identify a collection's weaknesses and strengths.

- Reviewing a collection on a systematic and ongoing basis ensures that both the collection policy and the collection are responsive to school goals and user needs.

- Establishing criteria for decisions about relegating, repairing, binding, replacing, and discarding materials facilitates and standardizes those processes.

Some disadvantages of this technique include the following:

- One must consider any materials that are being circulated during the examination study.

- The process, unless computerized or focused on one aspect of the collection, is time-consuming and requires trained personnel.

- If one does not consider the collection development policy and the rate of growth, individual items, rather than the collection as a whole, will be evaluated.

- Resources available through cooperative efforts are not considered. If a media center is participating in a resource-sharing program where another collection is responsible for collecting on a specific subject, those materials will not appear in the examination.

- People who are knowledgeable about the school program, as well as a subject area, may be difficult to locate and expensive to hire.

Age Analysis

One method of examining the collection is to estimate the age of the information in the materials. Doll (1997) explains that this can be done by selecting a random sample of materials and then computing the average copyright date.

The advantages of utilizing the age analysis technique are as follows:

- Others can easily understand the result.

- It is possible to match the result with anecdotal information, such as noting that the average age of the materials in the collection is twenty-five years and then recalling what was happening in the world at that time.

Disadvantages of this technique of evaluating a collection are as follows:

- It is difficult for one number to represent an entire set of materials. Sometimes it is better to use one number for fiction and another number for nonfiction.

- One must consider how old is too old for a children's collection. Presently no standard guidelines exist to determine the appropriate age for children's collections.

Compiling Comparative Statistics

Although the limitations of quantitative methods were discussed earlier in this chapter, there are reasons for collecting these types of data. For example, comparing data collected at various times of the year reveals patterns of use. State and federal agencies, professional associations, and accrediting agencies typically request circulation statistics.

Some writers have expressed concern about the lack of comparative national statistics that could document the contributions of media centers or the status of their collections. This information would be useful for policymakers. Garland (1993) found that a majority of state agencies collect three types of statistics from media centers: expenditures, holdings, and personnel. Comparing statistics among states is impossible because no single statistic is collected uniformly by all states, nor are terms or time periods standard.

Garland (1993) found that elementary and middle school media specialists collect circulation statistics for a variety of reasons, including reports to principals, superintendents, and boards of education. Viewing the importance of statistics as documentation of the contributions media programs make to education, she points out the need to share this information with policymakers at the state and national levels.

> Unfortunately, statistics describing the condition of library media centers and assessing their performance are rarely published. Library media specialists must make policymakers aware of the contributions of library media programs to the schools they support, and they must have supporting data. (p. 107)

Several types of statistics can be used with local, state, and national policymakers. Statistics can be collected about the following aspects of the collection: size, growth rate (volumes added within a given period of time), expenditures for materials, and collection overlap (how many individual titles are held in common among two or more collections).

Advantages of using comparison of statistics to evaluate a collection include the following:

- If records have been kept, statistics are easy to compile.
- If the application is clearly defined, it is easy to understand and compare the statistics.
- The method relates directly to the users in the case of requests filled or not filled.

Disadvantages of utilizing this technique for collection evaluation include the following:

- There is a lack of standard definitions of the content or quantity of a unit.
- It is difficult to count nonprint items and sets of materials.
- Significance may be difficult to interpret.
- Possible inaccuracy or inconsistency in data collection and recording exists.
- Statistics are usually non-applicable to a media center's goals and objectives.

The gathering of statistics is commonly used to compare one collection with another, to examine subject balance within a collection, and to decide whether to share resources or to allocate monies. When using data for comparative purposes, the participating agencies need to agree on the definition of each statistical component and use identical measurement methods. You will need to learn what your district or state considers a statistical component and which data-collecting methods are used.

If the collections in your district or state are being compared, data must be gathered in the same way. You should check for the district's or state's guidelines. Are you to use a volume or title count? If you are to count each volume of an encyclopedia set or each record in an album, the total size of the collection may be distorted. Some districts with centralized processing may count an item as it appears in its main entry. For example, because each school may have a separate main entry, a school that owns a kit containing two videos, five books, and a teacher's guide might record one kit; another school with only one of the videos and one of the books might record two items—a book and a video. An encyclopedia set cataloged as one item would count as one title. A multi-volume set in which each volume is separately cataloged would be recorded as the number of individual titles.

Automated catalog systems use barcodes, generally with each volume having an individual barcode. If an item in a kit can be checked out separately, each item would have a separate barcode. However, if the intent is for the kit to be checked out with all items included, one barcode is used for the kit. It is relatively easy to determine the number of volumes in a collection when the items are separately barcoded.

The use of online databases to access titles that are not physically in the media center can also complicate the counting of volumes and titles. Although the materials may not be physically in the media center, they are accessible, and the media center budget is being used to purchase their accessibility.

When information is to be used for allocating funds, there is an advantage to having uniform data about the quantity of materials accessible to each student. One could argue that several students can use an encyclopedia set; however, circulating materials, such as kits, are usually checked out to one person at a time. Data that include both a title and a volume count reveal more about the accessibility of materials than does a volume count alone. This dual procedure accounts for duplicate titles that can serve more people for a specific item but records the limit of the total resources available.

Statistics about unfilled requests can help determine what materials to add to a collection. It is a good idea to record requests by students and teachers for information or specific items not in the collection. You can then use these records when making selection decisions.

Applying Standards

In this procedure, the collection is compared to quantitative and qualitative recommendations that various standards, guidelines, or similar publications list. The issuing body may be professional associations, such as the American Association of School Librarians (AASL) and the Association for Educational Communications and Technology (AECT), who jointly published *Information Power: Guidelines for School Library Media Programs* (1988). These guidelines, which focus on qualitative standards and a planning approach based on the needs of individual media centers, note that "Quantitative descriptions are limited in value because the quantitative characteristics of programs vary in relation to needs and program activities. They are, by no means, the sole criteria by which individual programs should be evaluated" (p. 115). The guidelines provide qualitative and quantitative descriptions of state-of-the-art schools, which provide a basis for comparison of performance standards. Media specialists can compare their schools with others at the same level of service and with similar student populations.

Although the more recent school library media standards, such as *Information Power: Building Partnerships for Learning* (American Association of School Librarians & American Association of School Association for Educational Communications and Technology, 1998), do not include quantitative descriptions of school media collections, they do address the importance of the collections in their principles. Principle 5 under "Information Access and Delivery" emphasizes collaborative evaluation: "The collections of the library media program are developed and evaluated collaboratively to support the school's curriculum and to meet the diverse learning needs of students" (p. 90). The principles also relate to the document's information literacy standards, which note that "through collaborative collection development and evaluation, the program's collections promote active, authentic learning by providing a variety of formats and activities for linking information literacy with curricular objectives" (p. 90).

Accreditation agencies, such as the Southern Association of Colleges and Schools, are another source of standards. Typically such standards include basic criteria for evaluation of materials, level of financial support, size and condition of the collection, and access to materials. Accreditation agency standards are based on resources or inputs, such as the amount of money spent per student.

Advantages for evaluating your collection by applying standards include the following:

- The guidelines generally are relevant to the media center and the school's goals and objectives.
- Educators usually accept standards and guidelines and consider them authoritative.
- They can be used in persuasive ways to solicit support.

Disadvantages of applying standards to evaluate a collection include the following:

- The recommendations may be stated so generally that a high degree of professional knowledge and judgment may be needed to interpret the statements.
- Knowledgeable people may disagree about the application and interpretation of the statements.
- Minimum standards may be perceived as sufficient.

Use-Centered Measures

Use-centered measures can be used to determine whether, how often, and by whom materials are used. Circulation studies, in-house studies, user opinion surveys, shelf-availability studies, and analysis of interlibrary loan studies focus on the users and the use of materials.

Circulation Studies

Analysis of circulation data can help you examine the collection as a whole, or any part of it, in terms of publication data, subject, or user group. You can use this information to identify (1) low-usage materials, which may be ready to be removed from the collection; (2) high-usage materials, which may be titles to duplicate; (3) patterns of use in selected subject areas or by format; and (4) materials favored by specific user groups.

The advantages of utilizing circulation studies for evaluating a media center collection include the following:

- Data are easily arranged into categories for analysis.
- Flexibility in duration of study and sample size is possible.
- Units of information are easily compiled.
- Information is objective.
- Data can be readily available with automated circulation systems.
- Types of users can be correlated with the types of materials they use.

Disadvantages of using this technique to evaluate a collection include the following:

- In-house use is excluded, thus under-representing actual use.
- It reflects only materials found by users and does not record whether the user did not locate a desired item or whether the collection did not have that item.

- Bias may be present because of inaccessibility of heavily used materials.

- The method is not suitable for non-circulating collections, such as periodicals.

One can use the evidence from circulation statistics to show how well the collection supports the curriculum. Increased circulation of reading for pleasure may result from the introduction of whole-language or reading motivation programs. By documenting this increase, a media specialist could justify an increased budget allocation for fiction. New media specialists can use this technique to identify which courses and teachers make extensive use of which sections of the collection. By identifying weak areas of the collection, teachers and media specialists can work together to identify materials to fill those gaps.

In-House Use Studies

In-house studies can focus on either the use of non-circulating materials or on the users of materials within the media center. During these studies, users are asked not to shelve materials. This allows the media center staff to record use of the materials before returning the items to the shelves. You can also request that a database vendor provide you with statistics on how many times students from your school accessed a particular database. However, this service might add an additional charge to your database subscription.

Advantages of collecting data on in-house use of materials include the following:

- Types of users can be correlated with the types of material they use.

- A circulation study combined with the in-house use study about the same part of the collection provides more in-depth information about the use of that section.

- The method is appropriate for non-circulating materials.

- It can help one determine which journals to keep and for how long, which databases meet students' needs, areas in which students need help in developing search strategies, and gaps in the collection.

Disadvantages of this evaluation technique include the following:

- Users' cooperation is needed.

- If conducted during a high- or low-use period, results may be biased.

- Circulating items will not be included, and this may create bias.

- The method does not reflect a student's failure to locate and find desired information.

User-Opinion Surveys

A survey of users and user groups requires soliciting verbal or written responses through interviews, questionnaires, or a combination of methods. User opinions can be gathered informally, leading the media specialist to think that users' needs have been identified. Examples of informal surveys include asking students as they check out materials whether they found what they wanted and recording their answers.

A formal survey is more systematic and thorough. The formal approach involves a series of steps: identifying the objectives, selecting and designing the data collection technique, developing and testing the instrument, selecting the sample (the subgroup of the population), collecting and analyzing the data, and interpreting the results. Questions that could be addressed in a formal survey given to teachers include the following:

- Do your students have available resources to complete their projects and assignments?
- Do students have adequate resources for pleasure reading?
- Is there a variety of formats to support the learning styles of your students?
- Is there a balanced collection with a wide range of views on controversial topics?
- Is there sufficient access to electronic information and databases to meet your information needs and the needs of your students?
- Does the media center have adequate resources to support your curriculum?
- Does the media center have appropriate professional development materials?

Whether using a written questionnaire or conducting interviews, one can use carefully worded questions to identify the strengths and weaknesses of the collection as perceived by the users. The questions should be directed to specific goals, which may or may not be of significance to the user. Formulating questions that solicit the type of information you need can be time-consuming. Interviews, which take longer to administer, can provide more in-depth information. However, the length of time involved may mean that fewer individuals participate in the process. The results of either type of survey can provide the basis for making changes in the collection development policy.

Advantages of utilizing user-opinion surveys to evaluate a collection include the following:

- The survey can be developed to relate directly to the needs of users and to the goals and objectives of the collection.
- The information collected may reflect current interests.
- A survey can be used for most types of users.

Disadvantages of this technique of evaluation include the following:

- The method requires aggressive seeking of opinions.
- Those polled may be passive about participating or lack a point of comparison.
- Users' interests may be narrower than the collection development policy.

• Designing written questionnaires for young children may be difficult.

Shelf-Availability Studies

To determine whether users are finding specific works they seek, users can be interviewed or handed a brief questionnaire that asks them to identify titles they could not find. These data can help identify titles the media center does not own, titles for which the media center needs duplicate copies, items that have been improperly shelved, and insufficient directions for locating materials. One may also learn that the user had an incomplete or inaccurate citation, copied the call number incorrectly, or did not know where to locate the materials. This information about the collection and the user identifies areas that call for corrective action and changes.

Advantages of using shelf-availability information to evaluate a collection include the following:

• The method identifies failures that users face in trying to find materials.

• Data on possible changes in library policies and procedures are provided.

• The method can be used repeatedly to measure changes in library performance.

Disadvantages of using this technique include the following:

• User cooperation is required.

• Staff time in planning and collecting data is involved.

• The needs of non-users are not identified.

• Users may not remember titles.

Using a simple questionnaire, a media specialist can have students indicate what they are looking for and whether they find it. The results can indicate areas of the collection that need strengthening or areas where circulation is high and duplicate copies may be needed. Staff members may need to follow up on the survey by determining whether students had the wrong call number or whether materials were shelved incorrectly.

Analysis of Interlibrary Loan Statistics

Interlibrary loan requests represent materials people did not find in the collection and sought to obtain from other sources. Analyzing these requests can identify subject or format weaknesses in the collection, identify specific titles needed, and monitor resource-sharing agreements. You should compare analyses of subject areas with similar analyses of acquisition and circulation data to identify areas of heavy use or lack of materials. The results must be evaluated in terms of the collection development policy and existing resource-sharing agreements involving interlibrary loan.

Advantages of analyzing interlibrary loan requests to evaluate a collection include the following:

- The data are often readily available. For example, statistics on requests for periodical titles are usually kept to avoid copyright infringement.
- The items are needed by at least one person.
- Requests may indicate weaknesses in the collection.

Disadvantages of this evaluation technique include the following:

- The significance of the data may be difficult to interpret because it represents the request of only one person.
- Needs of users who personally go to other collections and skip making interlibrary loan requests are not identified.

Records of interlibrary loan requests can be analyzed to identify titles that patrons request. The results can be analyzed in terms of frequently sought subjects in which materials need to be added to a collection. Analysis of requests for articles can reveal heavily-used periodicals the collection may need.

Simulated-Use Studies

Information about the use of a collection can be gathered without directly involving users. These simulated situations include citation studies and document delivery tests.

Citation Studies

This method can be used if users of the collection utilize other libraries. If students write term papers or do independent projects, media specialists can check the bibliographies of student papers or projects to identify titles cited that are not holdings of the school collection.

Advantages of evaluating a collection by examining citations include the following:

- Lists are easily obtained from the students' project bibliographies.
- The method relates directly to users.
- The procedure is easy to apply.
- This method identifies works not in the collection.

Disadvantages of utilizing this method include the following:

- The value is limited if students use only the collection being evaluated.
- Citations are limited to the subject of the paper, a small portion of the total collection.
- The method is limited by the number of students who write papers.

Document Delivery Tests

This technique is similar to the shelf-availability study; however, members of the library staff, rather than users, perform the searching. It also carries the citation study a step further. It helps determine whether the collection includes a specific title, whether one can locate the item, and how long it takes to do so. The purpose of document delivery tests is to assess the capability of a library to provide users with the items they need at the time they need them. A typical approach is to compile a list of citations that reflects users' needs and determine the time it takes to locate each item.

Advantages of using tests of document delivery to evaluate the collection include the following:

- Objective measurements of the capability of the collection to satisfy user needs are provided.
- Data can be compared between libraries if identical citation lists are used.

Disadvantages of this evaluation method include the following:

- A representative list may be difficult to create.
- Because library staff members perform the searches, the test understates the problems users encounter.
- To be meaningful, tests need to be repeated or compared with studies conducted in other libraries.

Logs can be kept of interlibrary loan requests to record the requested item, the date of the request, the date the item was available to the requestor, and the response time (days between request and availability). The same type of information can be recorded about the response time for a teacher requesting a title for purchase. Further information can be obtained by asking whether the requestor still needs the item.

Collection Mapping

In recent years collection mapping has been one of the most popular evaluation techniques used by school library media specialists. It can involve some of the methods already described. Collection mapping is a visual display of the strengths and weaknesses of a library collection. Sometimes the entire collection is mapped, while in other instances specific areas of the collection are mapped. Often the areas selected correspond with particular areas of the curriculum; therefore it is important to have knowledge about the curriculum. When mapping only a specific area of the collection, these maps are sometimes called *emphasis maps* or *mini-maps*. Some media specialists try to select one area of the collection each year and create a mini-map project for that area.

Different ways are available to develop procedures for collection mapping and to graphically present a collection. Loertscher's (1996) book *Collection Mapping in the LMC: Building Library Center Collection in the Age of Technology* discusses several collection mapping techniques. *Building a School Library Media Collection: A Handbook with Internet Assist*

Figure 12.1. A sample collection map

Jane Doe Middle School Student Enrollment=950 January 2007		
Category	**Number of Books**	**Average Age of Books**
000 General	57	1992
100 Philosophy	42	1985
200 Religion	58	1989
300 Social Science	625	1996
400 Language	53	1990
500 Pure Science	895	1997
600 Applied Science	406	1999
700 The Arts	512	1987
800 Literature	304	1982
900 History/Geography	1087	1997
Biography	904	1992
Fiction	1603	1993
Short Stories	67	1990
Reference	489	2002

Total Number of Books = 7102
Books Per Student = 7.48
Average Age of Categories (Sections of the Media Center) = 1992

(Loertscher, Woolls, & Felker, 1999) provides collection mapping guidance for beginning school media specialists.

Figure 12.1 is a sample of a collection map for a middle school. This map provides a graphic representation of the number of books in the collection and the average age of the books. If analyzing the results of this collection map, it can be noted that the number of books per student (7.48) is low. Generally a school should have at least 10 books per student. Also, since the collection map was made in 2007 we can also conclude that the average age of the collection (1992) is old, but not as old as many school media collections. This is a collection that needs both weeding to update the average year of the collection, plus many additional new titles need to be added. Although the science categories are more up-to-date than some of the other categories, it is particularly important that books in these sections have recent, accurate information. Thus, this could be an area in which the media specialist might begin to weed and then purchase additional titles. The media specialist will need to find out from the science teachers what topics are studied in the classrooms and emphasize the purchase of materials to support those topics.

Other media formats (videos, DVDs, access to databases, etc.) can also be included in a collection map. Quality components, such as condition of the materials, diversity of formats, cultural representation, and diversity of reading levels can also be used in a collection mapping project. There are methods to determine what percentage should be recommended for each area of the collection and how well a particular collection is meeting those needs.

Advantages of creating a collection map include the following:

• A collection map can be read and understood fairly easily.

• A collection map can show the strengths and weaknesses of the collection.

- It can be used to indicate areas that need weeding.
- It can demonstrate areas of excellence and areas of need.
- A collection map can be used to develop collection goals.
- Collection mapping can be used to support the curriculum.
- A collection map can be used as a tool to request funding for specific needs.

Disadvantages of collection mapping include the following:

- The process of creating a collection mapping project can be time-consuming.
- Knowledge of the curriculum and research assignments must be obtained in order to ascertain curriculum needs.
- Assistance might be needed to analyze the results of a collection map.

Additional guidance for creating collection maps can be found at the Web sites listed under "Helpful Web Sites" at the end of this chapter.

Vendor Services

Several vendors provide online collection analysis services which make it easy to analyze a school library media collection. Follett Library Resources' *Titlewise* and Sagebrush's *BenchMARC* can quickly identify areas of the collection that are strong and areas that need weeding. In order to receive such a service the MARC records from a school library must be downloaded and submitted online to a vendor, who then compares the records with a standard based on award-winning library collections. Reporting on a school's collection areas is immediate. While there is no charge for entry-level reports, some vendors charge for more in-depth reports that evaluate certain aspects of the collection.

Conclusions

Several techniques can be used to evaluate media center collections. The methods are usually categorized under collection-centered or user-centered approaches. It is important to use both qualitative and quantitative measures when evaluating a school library media collection. Generally two or more methods are used together to obtain meaningful results. In recent years collection mapping, graphically representing a collection, has been used to demonstrate the strengths and weaknesses of a collection. Some vendors also provide online free collection analysis to school libraries.

The collection evaluation process provides an opportunity to work with students, teachers, and administrators to ensure that a collection meets their needs. Their involvement can lead to understanding why certain decisions are made.

References

American Association of School Librarians & Association for Educational Communications and Technology. (1988). *Information power: Guidelines for school library media programs*. Chicago, IL: American Library Association.

American Association of School Librarians & Association for Educational Communications and Technology. (1998). *Information power: Building partnerships for learning*. Chicago, IL: American Library Association.

Baker, S. L., & Lancaster, F. W. (1991). *The measurement and evaluation of library services* (2nd ed.). Arlington, VA: Information Resources Press.

Curtis, D. (2000). School library renaissance in Baltimore County. *Multimedia Schools, 7*(6), 18–24.

Doll, C. A. (1997). Quality and elementary school library collections. *School Library Media Quarterly, 25*(2), 95–102.

Doll, C. A., & Barron, P. P. (2002). *Managing and analyzing your collection: A practical guide for small libraries and school media centers*. Chicago, IL: American Library Association.

Garland, K. (1993). An analysis of school library media center statistics collected by state agencies and individual library media specialists. *School Library Media Quarterly, 21*(2): 106–110.

Loertscher, D. V. (1996). *Collection mapping in the LMC: Building access in a world of technology*. San Jose, CA: Hi Willow Research and Publishing.

Loertscher, D. V., Woolls, B., & Felker, J. (1999). *Building a school library collection plan: A beginning handbook with Internet assist*. San Jose, CA: Hi Willow Research and Publishing.

Willeke, M. J., & Peterson, D. L. (1993). Improving the library media program: A school district's successful experience with change. *School Library Media Quarterly, 21*(2): 101–105.

Additional Readings

Emanuel, M. (2002). A collection evaluation in 150 hours. *Collection management, 27*(3/4), 79–93.

Everhart, N. (1998). *Evaluating the school library media center: Analysis techniques and research practices*. Westport, CT: Libraries Unlimited.

Harbour, D. (2002). Collection mapping. *The Book Report, 20*(5), 6–10.

Hart, A. (2003). Collection analyses. *Library Media Connection, 21*(5), 36–39.

Hatcher, A. (2001). Fine-tuning your library media collection. *Book Report, 19*(5), 15–17.

Kachel, D. E. (1997). *Collection assessment and management for school libraries: Preparing for cooperative collection development*. Westport, CT: Greenwood Press.

Kachka, A. (2001). Evaluating your library media center collection. *Book Report, 19*(5), 19–20.

Marie, K. L. (2005). From theory to practice: A new teacher-librarian tackles library assessment. *Teacher Librarian, 33*(2), 20–25.

McGriff, N., Harvey, C. A., & Preddy, L. B. (2004). *Collecting the data, 20*(9), 27–29.

Nisonger, T. E. (2003). *Evaluation of library collections, access and electronic resources: A literature guide and annotated bibliography.* Westport, CT: Libraries Unlimited.

Willcoxon, W. O. (2001). Collection evaluation in a Georgia elementary school. *Knowledge Quest, 29*(5), 23–29.

Wolfe, G. (2001). How do you measure a library collection? *Multimedia Schools, 8*(3), 30–33.

Helpful Web Sites

Creadaro, A. (2001). *Collection evaluation in school libraries.* Retrieved July 12, 2006, from http://us.geocities.com/koalakid_1999/UNIVERSITY/TLshipCollEval.html?20067

Follett Library Resources. (2006). *Titlewise.* Retrieved July 12, 2006, from http://www.flr.follett.com/

Lamb, A., & Johnson, L. (2005). *Collection mapping.* Retrieved July 12, 2006, from http://eudscapes.com/sms/mapping.html

Lamb, A., & Johnson, L. (2005). *The school library media specialist: Evaluation.* Retrieved July 12, 2006, from http://eduscapes.com/sms/evaluation.html

Mesa, T. (2001). *Collection development evaluation plan.* Retrieved July 11, 2006, from http://www.accd.edu/pac/lrc/evaluatn/eval-cd.htm

National Library of Australia. (2004). *A guide to the collection assessment process.* Retrieved July 14, 2006, from http://www.nla.gov.au/libraries/help/guide.html

Sagebrush. (2006). *Quick, easy collection analysis and development.* Retrieved July 12, 2006, from http://www.sagebrushcorp.com/dataservices/benchmarc.cfm?CFID=715151&CFTOKEN=39545761

University of Wyoming Libraries Collection Development Office. (2002). *Collection Assessment.* Retrieved July 12, 2006, from http://www-lib.uwyo.edu/cdo/collass.htm

13
Ethical Issues and the Collection

Media specialists continually use decision-making skills when dealing with the various processes of collection development. Numerous collection development issues exist in school media centers today. Issues such as intellectual freedom and copyright have been present in media centers for many years, but others, like the use of acceptable Internet use policies or Internet filtering are more recent. In order to make both sound and ethical decisions regarding these issues, media center policies and procedures must be in place.

Ethical responsibilities are encountered not only with the selection of materials, but also with other processes of collection development—the acquisition of materials and equipment, students' access to materials, preserving and maintaining the collection, circulating materials, and evaluating the collection. This chapter discusses some issues and ethical responsibilities that involve decisions on the part of school library media specialists. For some of the issues, there are definite legal and ethical guidelines, but in other instances there may be more than one acceptable opinion about an issue. Therefore, a beginning media specialist should reflect on some of these issues and try to read some of the items listed in "Additional Readings" or "Helpful Web Sites" at the end of the chapter. At the end of this chapter are scenarios involving intellectual freedom, students' rights, access equality, and copyright. As you study them, bear in mind the very real possibility that you may one day face such situations.

Providing Access

Access to information involves both intellectual and physical access. Intellectual access addresses students' rights to hear, read, and view information; to receive ideas; to express ideas; and to develop skills to receive, examine, analyze, synthesize, evaluate, and use information. Physical access refers to an environment that permits the unimpeded location and retrieval of information. This involves provision of adequate media center staff, access to the media center during and after regular school hours; supplying a broad range of resources to meet students' needs in terms of learning styles and linguistic and cultural diversity; use of interlibrary loan; and access to computerized information networks or databases. The media specialist's commitment to intellectual freedom influences the extent of intellectual access provided. The media specialist's commitment to intellectual access and sensitivity to individual needs influence the extent of physical access provided. Commitment to intellectual and physical access affects the media specialist's response to collection issues.

Intellectual freedom is a principle upon which almost all library collections are based. However, when collections are to be utilized by children or young people, the concept of intellectual freedom becomes much more controversial. Two questions that need to be considered are:

- How does the concept of intellectual freedom apply to children and young people?
- Should there be limits on students' rights to read, view, and listen? If so, who has the right to impose those limits?

Children's Rights and Intellectual Freedom

The information you make available to students reflects the value you place on intellectual freedom and students' rights. In the United States, the First Amendment serves as the basis of intellectual rights. Intellectual freedom is the basis of the First Amendment's three major sections: freedom of religion, freedom of expression, and freedom of association. These three rights have been topics of controversy and court cases. A child's intellectual rights can be viewed as legal rights, as well as ethical rights. The application of the First Amendment to children generally arises in matters dealing with public education, particularly in court cases concerning censorship.

How does the First Amendment apply to children and to intellectual freedom? Moshman (1986) edited a book on the intellectual rights of children in which he addresses this subject. He lists the following legal intellectual rights as they apply to children:

- *Free expression*—Government may not control a child's right to form or to express ideas.
- *Freedom of Nonexpression*—Government may not require a child to adopt or express belief in a particular idea.
- *Freedom of Access*—Government may not restrict children's access to ideas and sources of information.
- *Free Exercise of Religion*—Government may not restrict children from acting according to their religious beliefs.
- *Distinction of Child from Adult*—Limiting First Amendment rights must be based on compelling reasons by showing that harm would occur because the children in question are less competent than the typical adult. (p. 27)

Moshman (1986) also addresses the moral rights of children, noting that they are consistent with the philosophy of the First Amendment:

- *Free Expression II*—A child has the right to form, express, and communicate ideas.

- *Freedom of Nonexpression II*—A child has the right to choose not to adopt or express belief in particular ideas.

- *Freedom of Access II*—Individuals responsible for children's development have an obligation to provide access to diverse sources of information and to diverse opinions and perspectives.

- *Free Exercise of Religion II*—Children have a right to act according to their religious beliefs unless such actions would be harmful or illegal.

- *Distinction of Child from Adult II*—Restrictions on children's intellectual rights should be based on the individual child's circumstances and intellectual limitations.

- *Right to Education*—Children have the right to the type of environment that will facilitate their intellectual development to the extent of their intellectual limitations. (p. 27)

Moshman (1986) goes so far as to say that First Amendment rights are more important to children than to adults. When one denies an adult access to diverse ideas, one is restricting available input; when one denies such access to a child, however, one is also restricting development of the ability to consider differing views. When one denies an adult free expression, one is denying the opportunity to communicate; when one denies free expression to a child, however, one is also restricting development of the ability to form one's own ideas. In short, in denying First Amendment rights to a child, one is restricting not merely the present exercise of those rights, but also the further development of precisely those intellectual competencies that make the First Amendment meaningful. Contrary to the suggestion that children have little at stake, it appears that as future adults they may have more to lose than present adults from governmental restriction of their intellectual freedom.

How do First Amendment rights apply to children? As one example, Moshman (1986) examines these rights in the context of censorship cases involving school libraries. He notes

> that schools must make choices; they cannot use every text or stock every book in the library. Selections should, however, be made in accord with educationally relevant, written criteria aimed at providing as wide a variety of views and ideas as students can handle. Removals should follow carefully designed procedures in which these criteria are carefully applied and claims of harm based on alleged lack of cognitive competence are seriously scrutinized. (p. 35)

How have the courts interpreted children's rights? The representative court case for children's First Amendment rights is *Tinker v. Des Moines* (1969). This is the first time the Supreme Court declared a government action unconstitutional because it violated minors' rights to freedom of expression. The Supreme Court said:

> School officials do not possess absolute authority over their students. Students in school as well as out of school are "persons" under our Constitution. They are possessed of fundamental rights which the State must respect, just as they themselves must respect their obligations to the State. (*Tinker v. Des Moines*, 1969)

Librarians tend to take one of two positions in response to the question "What intellectual rights do children have?" One position, the protector, assumes that adults know what is best for children, what will harm them, what information they need, and how their needs should be met. The other position, the advocate, assumes an open stance, perceiving children as capable of defining both their information needs and their resource needs. The first position strives to protect students from themselves, from others, and from ideas. The second strives to help students identify, evaluate, retrieve, and use information.

Barriers to Access

Common barriers to access include inequality of access; fiscal limitations; physical limitations of materials, equipment, and individuals; design of resources, such as interactive retrieval systems; attitudes and practices regarding reference and interlibrary loan services; and censorship.

Inequality of Access

We are increasingly aware of inequality in accessing computer-based information. These inequalities result from factors such as the following:

- More girls than boys are computer-aliterate.
- Software is designed to appeal to boys, not girls.
- Wealthy school districts continue to own more computers than less wealthy ones.
- The technology gap between rich and poor schools and wealthy and poor homes is widening.
- Minority students may have less computer experience.
- Schools without media specialists may have computers, but lack trained personnel who are able to assist students in effective computer use.

Neuman (1990) recommends actions to meet the challenge, including the following:

- Look for software that appeals to girls.
- Provide adaptive input and output devices (for example, guarded keyboards for students with physical impairment and large print monitors for students with visual impairment) designed for students with disabilities.
- Ensure equitable scheduling.
- Explore ways to use new technologies to promote equity.

Fiscal Limitations

Budgetary constraints limit available resources, including personnel. Lack of a materials and equipment replacement plan encourages media specialists to hold onto out-of-date materials and equipment. Media specialists who automate circulation and cataloging systems or expand software and online services without outside funding have fewer funds for books and audiovisual materials.

Physical Limitations

Physical barriers to access limit the use of resources and restrict the number of people who can use them. The physical environment of the media center can create limitations: lack of seating and work space, shelving beyond people's reach, lack of electrical outlets for equipment, or an insufficient number of terminals. Provisions for people with disabilities are discussed in Chapter 15, "Special Groups of Students." Barriers created by administrative decisions include rigid schedules, limited hours for use, restrictive circulation and interlibrary loan practices, and limited student pass systems. Inappropriate or missing catalog subject headings can also inhibit access to resources.

Inadequate Design of Resources

Another aspect of access is the effectiveness of interactive information retrieval systems for children. Jacobson (1991) calls for an evaluation of exactly how children use these systems; such research reveals whether software is properly designed. She describes the challenge:

> There are clearly many issues to be explored in evaluating information retrieval systems in youth services. Until recently, designers seem to have assumed that products initially developed for adults also would meet the needs of children and young adults. But unlike paper-based systems, electronic systems are fluid in nature. They can be adapted and modified; they also can be developed specifically for targeted user groups. Researchers and practitioners have a unique opportunity to influence this process by communicating their concerns to product developers. Certainly, the potential for truly responsive systems is worth the effort. (Jacobson, 1991, p. 112)

Publishers, producers, and vendors can benefit from media specialists' alerting them to areas that need materials or improvements. Regional library and education associations can collect comments and suggestions or sponsor a workshop on this topic at a conference.

Internet

Before the 1990s, the majority of censorship challenges dealt with materials that were housed in the school media center. However, with increased access to the Internet in school libraries, one of the main targets of censorship has been the use of the Internet.

The Internet is very different from other resources in the school library in that it is composed of a huge number of resources, many of which provide rich research materials for students. However, the Internet also provides access to numerous sites that a school media specialist would not consider useful or appropriate for students' use in the school library. Initially, the choice was an all-or-nothing proposition for school libraries: Either provide access to the Internet or don't provide it. Because of the possibility of accessing inappropriate sites (particularly those that were sexually graphic), many parents, organized groups, and legislators challenged access to the Internet in media centers (or anywhere in the school).

The Communications Decency Act (CDA), hotly debated in 1998, was an unsuccessful federal legislative attempt to legislate "safe" Internet use. Its original intent was to protect children from inappropriate sites, but its broad wording potentially deprived adults of nonsexual information in areas such as science, health, and art. The U.S. Congress, however, was successful in passing the Internet Protection Act (CIPA) and the Neighborhood Children Internet Children's Protection Act (NCIPA) to address concerns about access to offensive Internet materials in schools and libraries. These acts went into effect on April 20, 2001. They place certain requirements on schools or libraries that receive support from federal grants or the "E-rate" program, a program that makes technology more affordable for eligible schools and libraries. Schools are required to certify that they have an Internet safety policy in place and that they have Internet filters to block materials that might be harmful to minors. Schools must also adopt and enforce a policy to monitor the activities of minors. Even before these laws were passed most schools with Internet access had an Internet safety or acceptable use policy. In some schools this policy is sent home for parents to sign, while in other schools parents are notified about the policy and if they do not want their children to have Internet access at school, then it is the parents' responsibility to contact the school.

Many commercial companies have produced filters for the Internet, which, according to the companies, eliminate objectionable materials. A problem with some of the filters is that they do not always work as intended, for they sometimes block potentially educational sites while permitting access to other "inappropriate" sites. Software programmers, however, have continually improved the filters and have made them much more sophisticated. The filters can now allow administrators to determine categories of materials to block and to allow various levels of access determined by user passwords.

Many states and school districts have passed legislation dealing with the use of filters on individual computers in schools. Other districts and some states have moved to proxy servers (on external computers) that filter all files before they arrive at individual computers. Some Internet service providers (ISPs) also offer a filtering service for a small fee in addition to their regular Internet service fee.

Regardless of whether a filter on each computer or a proxy server controls Internet access or whether there is open access to the Internet, it is important that a school have a written Internet policy or an acceptable use policy (AUP) that includes parental consent on the use of the Internet. It is essential that school media specialists be well acquainted with any policies (state, district, or school) that relate to Internet access in their school libraries. There are several items that should be addressed in an Internet or acceptable use policy. These include:

- A statement addressing the educational uses and advantages of Internet access in the school

- The responsibilities of teachers, administrators, and library media specialists

- The responsibilities of students

- The role of parent(s) or guardian(s)

Figure 13.1. A sample Internet student use agreement form

JOHN DOE MIDDLE SCHOOL COMPUTER AND INTERNET

STUDENT USE AGREEMENT

I understand that:

That the use of computers and Internet at school is a privilege that can be revoked.

The use of school computers is only for school work.

I am not permitted to use school computers to access or create material that is offensive, dangerous, inappropriate, or illegal.

If I use e-mail at school it is only for school work and that I do not give anyone on the Internet personal information about myself or anyone else.

If I accidentally come across material that would not be allowed in school that I immediately remove it from the screen and contact a teacher or the media specialist.

I do not interfere with any other files on the network and I use only authorized software.

I take care of all technology equipment.

I print out only the information that is important to my school work.

I respect copyright guidelines for all material on the Internet, and I cite appropriately all sources from the Internet that I use for school assignments.

I do not give out passwords provided to me, nor do I use other students' passwords.

I have read this agreement and know the importance of school rules for the use of computers and the Internet. I understand that if I break these rules, I could lose the privilege of using a school computer and that the school personnel can take disciplinary action against me.

Student Name:

Student Signature: Date:

- A code of conduct describing how the Internet should be used in the school
- A description of acceptable and unacceptable uses of Internet
- A description of network etiquette
- A description of the consequences for violating the policy, including first offenses and loss of the privilege of using the Internet.
- A statement regarding the need to maintain personal safety and privacy while accessing the Internet

- A statement regarding the need to comply with copyright fair use guidelines
- A statement explaining that the use of the Internet is a privilege and not a right.
- A signature form that will be signed by the Internet user (and usually by a parent or guardian).
- Assurance that the policy will be enforced
- A disclaimer absolving the school or school district from responsibility
- A statement that the policy is in compliance with state and federal telecommunication rules and regulations

You can find some actual Internet policies of school districts by searching online. Some of these are listed at the end of the chapter under "Helpful Web Sites." Ideally you should have your Internet policy examined by a lawyer. Many school districts have consulting lawyers for such tasks.

The agreement form that users are asked to sign before using the Internet in a school should be clearly written and easy to understand. Figure 13.1 is a sample student use form that could be utilized in a school.

Copyright

As respecters of creative contributions, media specialists have a responsibility to ensure that copyright laws are honored. These professional responsibilities include educating teachers and students about fair use guidelines and the copyright laws, placing copyright notices near copy machines and computers, identifying copyrighted materials, and monitoring the use of copyrighted materials. Chapter 8, "Criteria by Format," describes copyright regulations for various formats. The fair use guidelines can be found on Web sites listed under "Helpful Web Sites" at the end of this chapter. Copyright guidelines for resource sharing are discussed later in this chapter under "Acquisition of Materials and Equipment."

Selecting Materials

Some of the most important ethical decisions made by media specialists are in the selection of materials. All selection policies should uphold the principle of intellectual freedom for all the users of the media center collection. The *Code of Ethics of the American Library Association* addresses this topic: "We uphold the principles of intellectual freedom and resist all efforts to censor library resources" (American Library Association Council, 1995).

Selection and Censorship

What is the difference between selection and censorship? Selection is by nature exclusive. In choosing materials to include in the collection, the media specialist excludes the materials not chosen. Selection and censorship can be differentiated. Selection is a process of choosing among materials. The choices are relative as one item is compared with others. In choosing materials, the media specialist strives to give each item fair consideration and makes a concerted effort to suppress personal biases. In censorship, an individual or a group attempts to impose certain values on others by limiting the availability of one or more items. By examining definitions of selection and censorship, one can see how censorship creates barriers to intellectual freedom and how selection can promote intellectual freedom.

Reichman (1993) describes the differences between selection and censorship:

> In general, selection is carried out by trained professionals, familiar with the wide variety of available choices and guided by a clear graph of the educational purposes to be fulfilled.... By contrast, the censor's judgment is that of the individual, and it is most frequently based on criteria that are inherently personal and often intolerant.... Where the censor seeks reasons to exclude materials, those engaged in the process of selection look for ways to include the widest possible variety of... library materials.... Censorship responds to diversity with suppression; the selection process seeks instead to familiarize students with the breadth of available images and information, while simultaneously erecting essential guideposts for the development of truly independent thought. (p. 46)

Censorship can be described in terms of who is doing the questioning, which materials they are questioning and what is being questioned, and how the questions are handled. Policies and procedures to guide these situations are described in Chapter 6, "Selection."

Common objections to materials include sexuality (including sexual orientation), profanity, obscenity, immorality, witchcraft, nudity, occultism, and violence. Less frequently cited reasons include incest, mental illness, and slavery. Censors state family values and the immaturity of students as reasons for their challenges.

Who are censors? The list of those who initiate challenges is long. Individuals include parents and other members of students' families, teachers, students, principals, and other school administrators, school support staff, community members, library media supervisors, library support staff, and even librarians. Groups include school boards, local government officials, and organized groups who share political or religious beliefs. Reichman (1993) reminds us that:

> The word "Censor" often evokes the mental picture of an irrational, belligerent individual. In most instances, however, it is a sincerely concerned parent or citizen interested in the future of education who complains about curricular or library materials. Complainants may not have a broad knowledge of literature or of the principles of intellectual freedom, but their motives in questioning the use of educational materials are seldom unusual. Complainants may honestly believe that certain materials will corrupt children and adolescents, offend the sensitive or unwary reader, or undermine basic values and beliefs. (pp. 14–15)

Media Specialists and Personal Biases

Unfortunately some media specialists' choices are colored by their personal values, rather than commitment to intellectual freedom. Not taking into consideration one's biases or special interests when making selections for a media center collection is not easy for some media specialists. However, it is necessary that this be done if media specialists are to follow ALA's *Code of Ethics*, which states that "We do not advance private interests at the expense of library users, colleagues, or our employing institutions" and that "We distinguish between our personal convictions and professional duties and do not allow our personal beliefs to interfere with fair representation" (American Library Association, 1995).

Knowing one's self is a prerequisite for selection. Media specialists should be aware of their own biases and preferences so that personal prejudices do not inadvertently affect selection decisions. A media specialist with a strong belief in higher education may be tempted to purchase more college-oriented materials than items for vocational courses. A media specialist who advocates online searching as a major teaching tool may be overzealous in budgeting for online services. A media specialist whose hobby is cinema may buy numerous materials about movies and equipment for video production. College-preparatory materials, online databases, books on cinema, and video production equipment are all worthy resources; however, the media specialist's personal interests should not unduly influence selection decisions.

When you next visit a media center, examine the collection. Can you detect any bias on the selector's part? Does this indicate the need to involve others in the selection process? One purpose of the collection is to fulfill the needs of everyone in the school. If you sense that your personal views may be outweighing your professional judgment, seek other people's opinions.

Providing Balance in a Collection

Some people define a balanced collection as one that contains materials that represent all sides of various issues. Advocates of this position express the belief that young people should learn to gather and evaluate information; they believe these skills are necessary to preserve democracy. Opponents argue that students need to be directed or guided to materials selected by adults to reflect the adults' beliefs and values.

Another debate centers on whether it is possible to objectively present any controversial subject. Would oversimplification and generalization result? Attempting to be objective may put constraints on the writer who is well informed about an issue and cares about the outcome. Authors who attempt to present both sides may become bogged down in phrases such as "some experts believe." Fortunately, many writers achieve objectivity while stimulating curiosity.

A more realistic goal of collection development is to maintain objectivity by including works that present differing views. Some students may not be aware of the wide range of viewpoints that exist about a particular subject. Media specialists should encourage students to seek many sources of information and not stop at the first source encountered.

When examining materials about controversial subjects, you should consider not only content, but also presentation. Excluding relevant facts is only one way to slant information. Word choice and connotations, use of visuals, vocal inflection, or filming techniques may be used to elicit emotional responses.

One benefit of a balanced collection containing many diverse viewpoints is that there will be materials on hand to counter criticism of controversial works. For example, one can anticipate questions about contemporary works on creation science, sexuality, birth control, and homosexuality. One response to critics is to refer them to works that present a different perspective on adolescents' problems. To address this situation, some media specialists select some works that reflect traditional, conservative, or various religious views.

Popularity Versus Literary Merit

To achieve balance within a collection, media specialists must grapple with the conflict between popular appeal and literary value. At one end of this spectrum is a collection that includes only popular items lacking literary merit. At the other end is a collection that contains classic works of little or no interest or relevance to many young people. Proponents on both sides argue vehemently, generating lively debate in conversations and in print. Some say that appeal is more important than quality; others promote the role of libraries in preserving and providing quality materials.

The issue of demand selection versus literary selection cuts across the boundaries of content, format, reading level, and intellectual freedom. You may want to ask yourself some questions. Should the media specialist purchase popular material that contains racial, ethnic, or sexual stereotypes? Should one buy mostly visual materials and software because "no one reads anymore"?

Some people argue that if children do not find items they want in the media center, they leave with a negative attitude about libraries that endures for life. Others argue that a media specialist's professional responsibility is to motivate young people by exposing them to materials that will aid the development of their literary and aesthetic tastes. Many people feel that responding to readers' requests encourages reading. Their position is that children will reach a saturation point with a series and will then turn to media specialists for recommendations. Others argue that limited budgets demand that media specialists encourage readers to explore worthy works that are less advertised.

An ongoing debate centers on the inclusion of series titles from "fiction factories," where hired writers complete a prepared character and plot outline ("formula writing"). The debate, active since the 1920s, when the series in question were Nancy Drew and The Hardy Boys, is a prime example of the demand-versus-quality issue. Similar debates center on the widely advertised Junie B. Jones or Dora the Explorer series for younger readers, Baby-Sitters Club series books, and the paperback young adult romance series Sweet Valley High, which are just a few of the numerous series on display in mall bookstores. As a media specialist you will need to decide whether to include series books in your collection and how to determine which series titles to include.

The issues concerning series apply to other materials as well. Comics, materials from the popular culture, and materials based on popular television programs are a few examples. Should comics be in the collection? Are there differences in value among *Peanuts*, *Mad Magazine*, and comic books based on classics? Are these materials more or less valuable than graphic novels or nonfiction presented in comic book form?

Those who say comics have a place in the collection call for clear guidelines for selection. These criteria address the visual art, social values, potential use for language development, and quality of the story.

Acquisition of Materials and Equipment

From whom to purchase materials and equipment can also involve ethical decisions. In many cases there may be more than one jobber or vendor who can provide the material or the equipment that the media specialist has selected to purchase. Since vendors are in the business to make money, it is possible that they can entice media specialists to purchase items from them. Such enticements might involve personal gifts or free dinners. Although these enticements might occur through the mail, more often they occur at conferences. At conferences frequently vendors offer special luncheons or dinners to customers or potential customers. They may also provide gifts, such as tote bags or candies, at their exhibits. The author of this book has attended such special events and accepted the small items at exhibit booths. However, one must be careful not to let the acceptance of meals or gifts influence the "best" selection of vendors to furnish the needs of a media center. This is why having a policy for acquisitions and following that policy is so important. Purchases should be made for appropriate reasons—good quality of items, savings for the media center, and excellent service record—not because the media specialist is able to personally gain from doing business with particular vendors.

School media specialists also have ethical responsibilities to the businesses with whom they deal. These include paying bills on time, not over-encumbering funds, and not asking for special favors or non-library funding from the vendors. It is always wise to have written agreements made between the vendor and the school so both parties are well aware of their ethical obligations.

If a school media center is involved in resource sharing and obtains some materials through interlibrary loan, then there are some ethical decisions and obligations that must be considered. Most of these issues deal with the amount of copying and number of interlibrary loans that can be made. The National Commission on New Technological Uses of Copyrighted Works (CONTU) provides guidelines for interlibrary loans. The guidelines describe the procedures that need to be followed to comply with copyright laws. You should become familiar with copyright laws; pleading ignorance cannot be used as a legal defense. School media specialists have an ethical responsibility to stay informed on copyright laws and guidelines and to keep a file of information that can be utilized by the teachers in your school.

If your school is purchasing access to online databases, there are license agreements that need to be signed and should be followed. If your school shares funding for the databases with other schools in the district, then making a single copy of an article for another school is considered an intralibrary loan and is allowable. However, making copies for school media centers that do not share in the funding of the online databases is neither legal nor ethical.

Maintaining and Preserving the Collection

Ethically, media specialists have many responsibilities in the area of maintaining and preserving collections. With tight educational budgets it is imperative that we take good care of the materials and equipment in the media center. Media specialists should train children and teachers on the proper care of materials and equipment. Copy machines should be available to cut down on possible destruction of materials when students are in need of information that is in non-circulating materials, and if economically feasible a security system can be installed to alleviate the loss of materials. Making certain that proper lighting and humidity control is maintained is also a maintenance responsibility as is weeding or de-selecting materials to maintain an atmosphere of care and order. Additionally, properly disposing of weeded materials is an ethical obligation. Giving de-selected materials that contain inaccurate information to classrooms or community organizations is not ethical.

Circulating the Collection

Besides treating all users fairly when enforcing circulation rules, the major ethical concern in the area of circulation is confidentiality. ALA's *Code of Ethics* addresses this important principle of librarianship by noting that "We protect each library user's right to privacy and confidentiality with respect to information sought or received and resources consulted, borrowed, acquired or transmitted" (American Library Association, 1995). Almost all states have confidentiality laws that apply to libraries. Some of the state laws include school libraries, while others do not. Whether or not you live in a state that has passed legislation on the confidentiality of school library circulation records, it is important to try to protect the privacy of students and teachers. Displaying overdue lists of materials by linking them to student names is not ethical. Supplying information about a student or teacher's reading habits is also not appropriate. If a person asks who has a particular book checked out, it is not ethical to provide that information, but you may tell the person requesting that information that you will try to *recall* the material. Such a recall will let the person who has the material checked out know that someone else is requesting the use of that particular item.

Sometimes there may be legitimate reasons to share information about the materials that a child has checked out of the media center. In the lower grades teachers or parents may need to help students locate the books they have checked out. However, the privacy rights of older students, particularly teenagers, should be protected, and any circulation issues should be discussed directly with these students. If you fear that a student may be checking out information that might be used to injure themselves or someone else, then obtaining some guidance from the school administrator or guidance counselor is warranted.

The U.S. Patriot Act passed by the U.S. Congress in 2001 and renewed in 2006 can impact the confidentiality of school library records. The law makes it possible for government agents to access library records without possible cause and without notifying patrons. Under the law, the government can have access to user circulation information for all types of materials, as well as Internet history logs (Web sites visited), e-mail messages, and student projects. You, as the school library media specialist, are not allowed to tell anyone of the agents' actions.

Placing materials on "restricted shelves" and only allowing certain students to check out the items or requiring a parental signature to let a student see restricted materials also infringes on the intellectual freedom of patrons by restricting access to information. Additionally, if a student is checking out a book that a media specialist thinks may be too difficult or may contain advanced information, it may be appropriate to provide some reading guidance, but the final decision on whether to check out a book should rest with the student.

Evaluating the Collection

Ethical decision-making also needs to be made in the evaluation of the collection. It is the responsibility of the media specialist to make certain that the collection is meeting the needs of the users. This can be done by one or more of the various methods discussed in Chapter 12, "Evaluation of the Collection." Evaluation should be done in light of the policies in place and the goals of the media center. Evaluation should not be done to weed out controversial materials. On the other hand, materials should be added to the collection when evaluation provides evidence of a need. When the curriculum in a school changes, then a media specialist should re-evaluate the collection and purchase appropriate materials to support the curriculum. Failing to do so is not meeting the needs of users.

Professional Responsibilities

As professionals, media specialists' responsibilities for intellectual freedom and access extend to collection activities other than selection. As selectors, media specialists need to be aware of their own biases. As managers of the collection, they need to ensure adequate funds to support the collection. As respecters of the creative contributions of authors, illustrators, and producers, media specialists need to ensure the enforcement of copyright practices. Commitment to intellectual freedom and balance in the collection come into play in all of these areas.

A media specialist's professional responsibilities include obtaining funding that will support and strengthen a collection. This may mean presenting facts about the collection, noting its condition, anticipating replacement costs, informing those who make the budget decisions of the average costs of materials, deciding how much of the budget should go toward the purchase of online databases, or seeking outside funding through grants.

Scenarios

Think about how you would handle the following situations and discuss them with your colleagues:

1. A school board member removes books from a high school media center because a citizen said the books contain offensive language. Neither the citizen nor the board member has read the books in question.

2. A minority student who rides a bus to school tells you that he does not have Internet access at home and he has no study hall period in which to complete a research assignment that his social studies teacher has made.

3. The principal checks out some books that have gay and lesbian characters in them. He fails to return them, but offers to pay for them.

4. Your media clerk tells a high school parent that the parent's son is checking out books on religious cults.

5. One of your teachers is checking out many videos and returning them the following morning. You suspect that she is making copies of the videos at home.

6. The music teacher is using a copy machine in the media center to make copies of a piece of choral music that is going to be sung at an upcoming school choral concert.

7. Two teachers are coming into the media center after school hours and are downloading pictures from pornographic Web sites.

8. A parent comes into your media center and asks that you restrict her son, who is in middle school, from checking out any graphic novels.

9. The site-based council informs you that they want the materials budget to be spent on online databases this year, with no new purchases of print materials.

10. The assistant principal, whose hobby is antiques, has requested fifteen books on various types of antiques and antique collecting.

11. A parent comes to the media center to inform you that her family is moving and she needs a list of all the books checked out by her daughter, who is in middle school, so she can make certain all books that have been checked out are returned before the family moves.

12. Two high school students come to the media center and ask you to help them obtain some interlibrary loan materials that will describe how to build a bomb.

Conclusions

Ethical situations and potential dilemmas of collection development are inescapable. School media specialists need to be prepared to face these dilemmas, whether they involve challenges to materials in the media center, equality of access to needed information, or protecting the intellectual freedom rights of young people. Every school media specialist should be familiar with the *Code of Ethics of the American Library Association* and be ready to support the principles on which librarianship is based. It is important to have written policies and procedures for any potential collection development issue that might be encountered. Considering possible scenarios that involve ethical issues and discussing professional responsibilities with other professionals will help prepare school media specialists for the real situations that occur in their schools.

References

American Library Association Council. (1995). *Code of ethics of the American Library Association*. Retrieved August 10, 2006, from http://www.ala.org/ala/oif/statementspols/codeof ethics/codeofethics.htm

Jacobson, F. F. (1991). Information retrieval systems and youth: A review of recent literature. *Journal of Youth Services in Libraries, 5* (1) 109–113.

Moshman, D. (1986). Children's intellectual rights: A First Amendment analysis. In D. Moshman (Ed.), *Children's Intellectual Rights* (pp. 25–38). San Francisco: Jossey-Bass.

Neuman, D. (1990). Beyond the chip: A model for fostering equity. *School Library Media Quarterly, 18*(3), 158–164.

Reichman, H. (1993). *Censorship and selection: Issues and answers for schools.* Chicago: American Library Association; Arlington, VA: American Association of School Administrators.

Tinker v. Des Moines Independent Community School District, 393 U.S. 503 (1969).

Additional Readings

Abram, S. (2005). The top priorities for school libraries and their districts. *Multimedia & Internet@Schools, 12*(1), 19–22.

Anderson, J. (2002). When parents' rights are wrong: Should parents be able to prohibit their kids from reading school library books? *School Library Journal, 48*(11), 43.

Butler, R. B. (2003). Television, teaching, and copyright. *Knowledge Quest, 32*(2), 52–53.

Campbell, S. (1998). Guidelines for writing children's Internet policies. *American Libraries, 29*(1), 91–92.

Carefoot, L. (2003). Student access to the school library. *Teacher Librarian, 30*(4), 69–71.

Cornette, L. (1998a). A censor: Do you know one when you see one? *Ohio Media Spectrum, 49*(4), 13–14.

Cornette, L. (1998b). Intellectual freedom is a concern for all media specialists. *Ohio Media Spectrum, 50*(3), 13–14.

Farmer, L. (2002) Issues in electronic resource services in K-12 school library settings. *Education Libraries, 25*(2).

Feret, A. J. (2006). Book series and character development: An unlikely but powerful duo in book choice for read-alouds. *Teacher Librarian, 33*(3), 24–27.

Fisher, C. (2004). Internet issues in elementary school library centers. *PNLA Quarterly, 68*(4), 39–43.

Johnson, D. (2004). Lessons school librarians teach others. *American Libraries, 35*(11), 46–48.

Jones, P. (2001). Nonfiction: The real stuff. *School Library Journal, 47*(4), 44–45.

Jones, P. (2003). To the teen core: A librarian advocates building collections that serve YA readers. *School Library Journal, 49*(3), 48–49.

Kastner, A., & Allen, R. (2002). Feasting on forbidden fruit, *30*(2), 18–20.

Kravitz, N. (2002). Censorship and the school library media center. Westport, CT: Libraries Unlimited.

Lamb, A., & Johnson, L. (2004). *Rights of library users*. Retrieved August 30, 2006, from http://eduscapes,com/sms/patriot.html

Libraries and the law. (2002). *The School Librarian's Workshop, 22*(9), 5–6.

Miller, J. (2004). Intellectual freedom and the Internet: Developing acceptable use policies. *School Libraries in Canada*, 23(3). Retrieved August 25, 2006, from WilsonWeb database.

Minkel, W. (2001). Company touts device as alternative to filters. *School Library Journal*, *47*(7), 16.

Russell, C. (2001). Stolen words. *School Library Journal*, *47*(2), 40–43.

Russell, C. (2003). A tough act to follow. *School Library Journal*, *49*(11), 52–54.

Russell, C. (2005). Singing a different tune. *School Library Journal*, *51*(3), 35.

Shirley, L. J. (2001). Intellectual freedom in school libraries. *Louisiana Libraries, 64* (2). 17–19.

Simpson, C. (2003). *Ethics in school librarianship: A reader*. Worthington, OH: Linworth.

Simpson, C. (2003). Rights tracking in school libraries. *Tech Trends*, *4*(1), 11–12, 32.

Simpson, C. (2004). Should I or shouldn't I? An ethical conundrum. *Library Media Connection*, *23*(2), 18–21.

Simpson, C. (2005). *Copyright for schools: A practical guide*. Worthington, OH: Linworth.

Sipley, M. (2003). Operation-Patriots Act: The role of school libraries in promoting a free and informed society. *Progressive Librarian* (22), 52–61.

Sullivan, E. (2000). More is not always better. *School Library Journal*, *46*(4), 42–43.

Thomson, V. (2004). Children's rights in the library. *School Libraries in Canada*, 24(4). Retrieved August 25, 2006 from WilsonWeb database.

Torrans, L. E. (2003). *Law for K-12 libraries and librarians*. Westport, CT: Libraries Unlimited.

Ujiie, J., & Krashen, S. (2006). Are prize-winning books popular among children? An analysis of public library circulation. *Knowledge Quest*, *34*(3), 33–35.

Wolinsky, A. CIPA: Understanding and complying. *School Executive*, *39*(1), 23.

Helpful Web Sites

American Library Association. (2000). *The censor: Motives and tactics*. Retrieved August 28, 2006, from http://www.ala.org/alaorg/oif/censormotives.html

American Library Association. (2005). *Intellectual freedom issues*. Retrieved August 28, 2006, from http://www.ala.org/ala/oif/ifissues/Default883.htm

American Library Association. (2006). *Code of ethics of the American Library Association*. Retrieved August 28, 2006, from http://www.ala.org/ala/oif/ statementspols/codeofethics/codeethics.htm

American Library Association. (2006). *Copyright: Fair use legislation.* Retrieved August 28, 2006, from http://www.ala.org/ala/washoff/WOissues/copyrightb/fairuseleg/fairuselegislation.htm

Arizona Department of Library Archives and Public Records. (n.d.) *Intellectual freedom.* Retrieved August 28, 2006, from http://www.lib.az.us/cdt/intell.htm

Chicago Public Schools. (2003). *Acceptable use policy.* Retrieved August 28, 2006, from http://www.cps.k12.il.us/AboutCPS/Acceptable_Use_Policies/acceptable_use_policies.html

Cleveland Municipal School District. (2004). *Internet acceptable use policy.* Retrieved August 28, 2006, from http://www.cmsdnet.net/AUP/internetAUP.htm

Davis School District. (2002). *Internet use policies.* Retrieved August 28, 2006, from http://www.davis.k12.ut.us/DIST/AUA.htm

Des Moines Public Schools. (2000). *Student acceptable use policy statement.* Retrieved August 28, 2006, from http://www.dmps.k12.ia.us/schooldir/stpolicy.htm

East Meadow Public School. (n.d.). *Acceptable use policy.* Retrieved August 28, 2006, from http://eastmeadow.k12.ny.us/parents/computer_policy.htm

Federal Communications Commission. Consumer & Governmental Affairs Bureau. (1999). *Children's Internet protection act.* Retrieved August 28, 2006, from http://www.fcc.gov/cgb/consumerfacts/cipa.html

Indiana Department of Education. Office of Learning Resources. (2005). *Acceptable use policy.* Retrieved August 28, 2006, from http://ideanet.doe.state.in.us/olr/aup/welcome.html

Los Angeles Unified School District. (n.d.). *Acceptable use policy.* Retrieved August 28, 2006, from http://notebook.lausd.net/portal/page?_pageid=33,136640&_dad=ptl&_schema=PTL_EP

Ramsey, I. L. (n.d.). *Intellectual freedom.* Retrieved August 28, 2006, from http://falcon.jmu.edu/~ramseyil/free.htm

Randolph Public Schools. (2002). *Randolph Public Schools: Internet acceptable use policy.* Retrieved August 28, 2006, from http://www.randolph.mec.edu/district_pages/aup.html

Student guidelines for multimedia and web page production. (n.d.). Retrieved August 28, 2006, from http://mciunix.mciu.k12.pa.us/~spjvweb/guidelines.html

U.S. Copyright Office. (2006). *Copyright.* Retrieved August 28, 2006, from http://www.copyright.gov/

Virginia Department of Education. (n.d.). *Acceptable use policies: A handbook.* Retrieved August 10, 2006, from http://www.pen.k12.va.us/VDOE/Technology/AUP/home.shtml

14
The Curriculum

A major purpose of the collection is to support the school curriculum. The American Association of School Librarians and the Association for Educational Communications and Technology (1998) state this as one of the principles of information access and delivery. Their statement reads as follows: "The collections of the library media program are developed and evaluated collaboratively to support the school's curriculum and to meet the diverse learning needs of students" (p. 83).

The wide range of instructional programs and practices in a school creates many demands upon its media collection. To be well versed about instructional programs, a media specialist must understand the school's approaches to education, be knowledgeable about the curriculum, and be aware of any educational trends that might affect the curriculum.

The School's Purpose

A look at a high school mission statement can illustrate the complexity of demands for educational support. Some high schools serve a single, overriding purpose. Sometimes this purpose is expressed in the name of the institution, with adjectives such as "vocational," "technical," "preparatory," or "alternative." For some schools the purpose is narrowly defined, and thus the role of the media program can be relatively narrow in scope.

More often a high school serves more than one purpose. A multi-purpose or comprehensive high school exerts varied demands on the media center collection and presents added challenges to the media specialist. In some comprehensive high schools, the purposes may not be clearly defined, which may lead to problems for budget allocations.

Middle schools and elementary schools also have mission statements. Like high schools, some of these schools have specific purposes that can affect a school media center's program and collection. For instance, a school for gifted students in grades 2–12 has as its mission statement: "to provide a qualitatively different learning environment that nurtures a passion for intellectual curiosity, encourages risk taking, independence and innovation, and is committed to a tradition of academic excellence and social responsibility." (Pine View School, 2006). The school also participates in special programs, including Academic Olympics, Artists in Residency, TAPS (a character education program), and Math Counts. At this school the mission statement, purpose of the school, and the special programs affect resources and services provided by the media center.

In order to determine the type or purpose of a school one should ask the following questions. Is the school a comprehensive high school with both academic and practical courses and departments? Is it a vocational school emphasizing specific job-related courses? Is the school a performing arts or technical school offering special programs for talented students? Is there a non-traditional or an alternative program? A media specialist should consult with administrators, teachers, curriculum coordinators, and students to learn about the school's purposes and programs. The school board's annual report to the community can also offer additional insight into the purposes of the school and its place in the district's overall education plan.

A school's purpose has implications for the collection. Each of the schools just described requires different sources in its collection. Some general materials, such as ready-reference works, may be in the collections of all the schools. In the case of a relatively expensive multi-volume work, such as *The New Grove Dictionary of Music and Musicians* (Oxford University Press, 2001) all schools may not need to own a copy; however, a school that emphasizes performing arts may want its own copy.

Educational Program

A school achieves its purpose through its educational program—the curriculum. The curriculum may be in response to mandated standards that the school district, the state, professional organizations, or even the federal government issues. The standards may call for specific content, establish sequencing of experiences, prescribe the teaching methods, and define the learner. If a school is teaching to specific standards that have been established by the state or school district, it is essential that you obtain copies of those standards for each of the subject areas taught in your school. You need to make certain that you have the print and nonprint resources available to support the teaching of all of the standards in your state or school district.

Most schools develop curriculum plans to meet the school's purpose or particular standards. A typical curriculum plan includes a statement of goals and objectives, the content teachers must cover, the organization (or sequencing) of that content, teaching strategies designed to meet the objectives or organizational requirements, and a program for evaluation. Curriculum plans may emphasize one or more of these elements. Each element of the curriculum plan has implications for the media program and its collection.

You should examine the curriculum plans for your school. This may be a time-consuming task since curriculum plans vary in scope, and there may be plans for all subject areas. Some plans are comprehensive, covering all educational programs; others cover specific subjects or specific learning situations. Curriculum plans may be general or give very specific directives to teachers. The general approach outlines the broad tasks of the school and identifies the teachers' responsibilities. More specific curriculum plans prescribe when, how, to whom, with what, and under what conditions teachers are to function. Specific plans may also offer more direct practical information for the media specialist than the general curriculum. However, both types of plans will be helpful guides for deciding material purchases for the media center collection.

An analysis of a curriculum plan can indicate what content or subject matter is required or recommended, when and to what depth it will be covered, and how it will be presented. If several classes will be studying the same unit simultaneously, you most likely will need to have duplicate copies of some materials. In other cases, the media specialist can work with teachers to decide whether certain units can be taught at different times of the year. The curriculum plan might indicate why a unit is recommended for a specific time and whether altering its sequence would be detrimental to the learning process.

Many schools go through an involved process of curriculum planning and present their curriculum in a graphic representation called a *curriculum map*. Generally all members of the teaching staff, including the media specialist, participate in the planning. Curriculum maps present data about implemented curriculum, using data collected from individual teachers. These may then be integrated into grade levels or subject areas. The maps offer a scope of what is taught, the sequence of the content taught, the processes involved, and the assessments that are utilized to evaluate student learning. By reviewing curriculum maps educators can determine if there are redundancies or gaps in the curriculum, as well as documenting the relationship of components of the curriculum with intended student learning outcomes. The maps also can help identify interdisciplinary opportunities. Curriculum maps are reviewed and updated on a regular basis. For further information about curriculum mapping, including Web site links to actual curriculum maps, refer to listings under "Helpful Web Sites" at the end of this chapter.

Range of Course Offerings

To explore a school's unique demands on its collection, you should examine the range of courses the school offers. A high school may offer basic courses in art, computer education, dance, drama, foreign languages, health, humanities, language arts, library media, mathematics, music, physical education, safety and driver education, family and consumer services, science, and social studies. The social studies department may offer anthropology, economics, global studies, and history. History courses may include African, Asian, U.S., and world history. The school may offer courses in agribusiness, natural resources, business, health occupations, industrial occupations, marketing, public-service occupations, and technology. Additional courses may be designed to meet the needs of exceptional students, including gifted students and students with disabilities.

The state department of education in each state most likely has lists of approved courses. This information may be available through the department's Web site or obtained from the principal or curriculum coordinator.

If a collection is to support a wide variety of courses, it must provide some level of coverage for all subjects. Again, you will need to ask some questions. Is the subject covered at an introductory, advanced, or remedial level? Are there honors courses? Do honor students have access to a nearby college collection? Has a shift in the local population created a need for materials that present concepts in simple English or bilingual formats? How are the subjects organized or approached? For example, is art history taught as a separate course, or is it integrated into a study of humanities?

Extracurricular groups and programs create demands for specific subject materials. A debate society needs timely information and opinions on controversial issues. A drama club needs plays, information about costumes, and ideas for set designs. After school programs require information about crafts and sports.

New programs or changes in organization create new demands. An example is the case of an actual school district in which it was decided to open a centrally located high school media center to serve students from all schools in the district during after-school hours and on Saturdays. Media specialists from various schools took turns overseeing the media center. They found that the reference collection needed to expand in order to meet the needs of students from diverse programs. In another community, students in adult education programs began meeting in a high school during evening hours. They had access to the high school media center. Although the students used some of the materials that daytime students used, they also needed materials to support additional subjects taught in the adult education programs; thus other resources were added to the collection.

Special Programs and Events

Often schools initiate special programs that will influence the media center collection and activities. Usually these occur after much discussion and planning at the district level. It is important for media specialists to be involved in these discussions. Sometimes the programs are long-term, lasting several years; in other cases a program may be in place for only a year or two. Examples of such programs are literature-based reading programs and electronic reading programs.

In a literature-based reading program, trade books (the types of books found in libraries and bookstores in contrast to instructional textbooks) are used to teach reading to students. In these programs large amounts of print materials must be made available to teachers and students. If the literature-based reading program is used across disciplines, as is usually the case, then these materials must include both fiction and nonfiction materials. Often these programs are set up around thematic units developed by individual teachers or more frequently by grade-level faculty. It is essential that a media specialist be aware of these themes and the teachers' plans to use media center materials in thematic units. Figure 14.1 is a sample of a form that could be used to maintain records of units taught each year. The media center collection may not be adequate to support the themes the teachers select; thus, the media specialist may need to order special materials. Sitting in on grade-level curriculum-planning sessions will enable you to know in advance what types and quantities of materials might be needed (frequently sets of particular titles are used in literature-based reading programs). Such a program will greatly affect the monetary demands on the media center budget. It is advisable that you address this topic as early as possible. A meeting with school administrators and faculty may make it possible to shift textbook funds to the media center budget to meet the needs of the literature-based reading program.

Another program that has had great impact on media center collections and programs is the use of electronic reading programs, such as *The Accelerated Reader"* (produced by Renaissance Learning) and *Scholastic Reading Counts* (produced by Scholastic). In these programs students read specific books with designated reading levels and take computer tests on those books. Thus, there is much pressure on the media specialist to have specific titles in the media center and to have them labeled with reading levels. This

Figure 14.1. Unit resource form

UNIT RESOURCE FORM

Unit Theme:

Grade: Teacher:

Special Student Needs:

Objectives:

Information Skills Required:

Resources Required   Call # or Source   Evaluative Comments

---

may not make it possible for the media specialist to purchase other materials that are needed by the curriculum or that would be of particular interest to students. Also, a media specialist may have a philosophical problem with labeling books that teachers say are to be read by only certain students. There is much controversy about these programs, including their effects on student reading and their impact on collections in school media centers. It is important for you to be aware of these programs and the controversy. If there is discussion about initiating such a program in your school, you should participate in the discussions. Share your views on the programs and the ways that they might impinge on both students and the media center collection.

These are just a few of the special programs that have been introduced into schools that have had significant effects on media center collections. Whenever there is discussion at your school about initiating a new program, be prepared to share your views by participating in discussions and serving on committees.

Schools often hold special events that need to be supported by the media center resources. Examples of such events are author visits, science fairs, and participation in Battle of the Books. Often for such events you will need to collaborate with classroom teachers to plan the event and provide the necessary media center resources.

Educational Reforms and Trends

An educational reform that often affects school media centers is the initiation of block scheduling in high schools or middle schools. Numerous models are used for block scheduling. Block scheduling typically involves having classes meet on only certain days of the week, but for longer periods of time than in the traditional class-period scheduling. This type of scheduling can also have an impact on the school media center. Teachers whose students have not been doing research requiring the media center collection may find that by using block scheduling they are able to have large blocks of time that can be used beneficially in the school media center. Thus, the media specialist may need to order materials to fit those research needs.

The increase in the number of students who are being home schooled is another educational trend that can affect school media centers. In recent years some school districts have partnered with parents of home-schooled students so that the students can take part in various school activities and use some of the public school facilities and resources. Thus, there can be increased demand for the resources in a media center. In some cases the home-schooled students follow a different curriculum so additional materials may need to be added to the collection.

Some other educational trends or reforms that can affect the media center program and collection include site-based management, school choice, distance education, inclusion, school-to-work programs, and cooperative learning. You should become knowledgeable about educational trends and issues and consider how they can impact school media centers.

Assessment of Student Learning

With the introduction of national and state standards in the 1980s and 1990s, several states began to develop their own state-wide student tests. National assessment programs were also implemented, with the National Assessment of Educational Progress (NAEP) sometimes referred to as the nation's report card. High academic standards and accountability have become the emphasis in education, and much pressure from the new standardized tests has been put on both teachers and students. These tests and the standards upon which they are based have greatly affected curriculum.

Some educators disagree with the emphasis on standardized testing; they have advocated alternative assessments of student learning, such as performance-based learning experiences that involve higher order of thinking skills. The use of student projects and portfolios of students' works are two alternative assessments that are sometimes utilized in schools.

No matter what type of assessment of student learning is utilized in a school, media specialists need to work collaboratively with classroom teachers to ensure that the resources needed to prepare the students for assessment are available. Many of the standardized tests emphasize information skills; thus, media specialists should work with classroom teachers to make certain students obtain the information literacy skills included in *Information Power: Building Partnerships for Learning* (American Association of School Librarians & Association for Educational Communications and Technology, 1998). These skills include being able to effectively access information, critically evaluate information, and to use information accurately. The literacy skills relating to becoming an independent learner include being able to pursue information related to personal interests, appreciating literature and other creative expressions of information, and striving for excellence in information seeking. Other literacy skills emphasize social responsibility: contributing positively to society and recognizing the importance of information in a democratic society; practicing ethical behavior in regard to information, including information technology; and effectively participating in groups to pursue and generate information.

Media centers and media specialists have also been affected by the recent trend of standardized testing, student learning, and accountability. Many school districts have cut budgets for any programs that cannot demonstrate that they are directly affecting student test scores. The school library media profession has become much more proactive and has been demonstrating their impact on student learning through research studies and positive public relations. You should be aware of the findings of such studies and share them with teachers, administrators, and parents. Citations for some of the studies are listed under "References" in Chapter 4, "The Media Center Program."

Distribution of Learning Materials

Another factor influencing subject- and program-oriented materials is the location of the materials themselves. When departmental libraries or resource centers are established to support particular subject areas, their relationships to the collection housed in the media center must be determined. Are the centers' materials purely instructional? Are the materials considered part of the media center collection, but housed conveniently near the classrooms?

Another pattern of housing occurs when materials are stored in the classroom or teaching areas where they are used most frequently. For instance, cookbooks might be housed in a home economics classroom, and materials on woodworking in a woodworking shop. A tour of the school helps you identify the distribution pattern. If materials are not housed in the media center, you need to determine who is responsible for them. You may need to ask some additional questions. What are the circulation procedures? Who is responsible for inventory, maintenance, and control? Have the materials been entered on the OPAC? Are separate funds used to buy these materials, or are they purchased with media center funds?

Professional Collection

You will also need to provide professional resources for staff members in your school. Staff members include people with teaching responsibilities, as well as those who work with children in other ways: administrators, guidance counselors, social workers, nurses, speech therapists, aides, secretaries, and technical staff. The portion of the collection designated to fulfill these people's needs is usually called the *professional collection*. Frequently a professional collection is housed in a specified area in the media center; other times the collection is in a separate room, such as a teacher workroom. The professional collection should be placed in a location that is convenient for teachers and where it can get adequate exposure.

As is true with the rest of the collection, a variety of formats and resources should be available. If the collection does not contain the materials the school staff needs for their professional duties, then the media specialist should know where one can obtain those materials.

Some of the resources that compose a professional collection should relate to the student standards for the various subjects. If a school is participating in special programs, such as block scheduling or literature-based reading, materials dealing with those programs should be in the professional collection.

Resources for Particular Grade Levels

Other resources are also available that will assist teachers at the various grade levels. People who are responsible for preschoolers will find Barbara Taylor's *A Child Goes Forth: A Curriculum Guide for Preschool Children*, 10th edition (Prentice Hall Career & Technology Division, 2004) to be a helpful guide for selecting materials and activities for young children. *A to Zoo: Subject Access to Children's Picture Books*, 7th edition (Libraries Unlimited, 2005) by Carolyn W. and John A. Lima can assist preschool and primary-level teachers in locating picture books about particular topics.

Teachers in elementary or middle schools that utilize thematic units for instruction will especially appreciate a subscription to *Book Links: Connecting Books, Libraries, and Classrooms* (American Library Association), which reviews old and new materials for individual units and provides suggestions for using the materials with children. *Weaving the Literacy Web: Creating Curriculum Based on Books Children Love* (Redleaf Press, 2005) by Hope Vestergard provides information relating to book-based webbing with young children. Cora M. Wright's *More Hot Links: Linking Literature with the Middle School Curriculum* (Libraries Unlimited, 2002), which is arranged by categories and curriculum areas, is another useful source for teachers using thematic units or literature across the curriculum.

Literature and Genre Materials

Survey books about children's and young adult literature can be helpful to teachers and media specialists as they work with students in classrooms and in the media center. *Huck's Children's Literature in the Elementary School*, 9th edition (McGraw-Hill Humanities/Social Sciences/Languages, 2006) by Barbara Kiefer, Janet Hickman, and Susan Hepler is a classic survey of children's literature. A smaller book focusing on literary aspects is Rebecca J. Lukens's *A Critical Handbook of Children's Literature*, 8th edition (Allyn & Bacon, 2007). The second part of each chapter in Donna Norton's *Through the Eyes of a Child*, 7th edition (Prentice Hall, 2007) includes activities on how to use each genre of children's literature in the classroom, while the first part deals with the books themselves. Carol Lynch-Brown and Carl M. Tomlinson's *Essentials of Children's Literature*, 5th edition (Allyn and Bacon, 2005) interweaves the history of each genre with the selection and evaluation of such materials. Their chapter on multicultural and international literature is the most extensive coverage found in any of the titles mentioned. Catherine Barr and John T. Gillespie's *Best Books for Children: Preschool Through Grade 6*, 8th edition (Libraries Unlimited, 2005), Gillespie and Barr's *Best Books for Middle School and Junior High Readers* (Libraries Unlimited, 2004), and Gillespie and Barr's *Best Books for High School Readers* (Libraries Unlimited, 2004) are all useful tools that include lively annotations for numerous titles.

Elementary classroom teachers dealing with the genre of picture books will find over 200 books organized into categories in Patricia J. Cianciola's *Informational Picture Books for Children* (American Library Association, 2000). *Popular Series Fiction for K-6 Readers: A Reading and Selection Guide* by Rebecca L. Thomas and Catherine Barr, covers selected series books, which are annotated and arranged alphabetically by the series name.

You will want to include award-winning books in your collections for teachers to use. *Newbery and Caldecott Awards: A Guide to the Medal and Honor Books* (American Library Association, 2006) provides annotations for all the winning and honor titles since the inception of the awards. Other books on award-winning titles can be found in Chapter 15, "Special Groups of Students."

Teachers interested in working with particular genres will find *Genreflecting: A Guide to Popular Reading Interests*, 6th edition (Libraries Unlimited, 2005) by Diana Tixier Herald and Wayne A. Wiegand valuable as it contains over 5000 titles. Herald's *Teen Genreflecting*, 2nd edition (Libraries Unlimited, 2003) is a well-organized resource that can be used as a reading advisory tool for middle school and high school students. Ruth Nadelman Lynn's comprehensive guide *Fantasy Literature for Children and Young Adults*, 5th edition (Libraries Unlimited, 2005) can be especially helpful in recommending titles for young readers.

Specific Subject Areas

Few books are designed to connect literature and specific subject areas. These books are especially helpful to teachers who want to have their students utilize the media center resources. Lynda G. Adamson has written several books that connect literature to history. Her most recent book *Thematic Guide to Popular Nonfiction* (Greenwood, 2006) groups nonfiction books into themes, such as "American Dream" and "Race Relations." A similar work in the area of science is Carol M. and John W. Butzow's *Science Through Children's Literature: An Integrated Approach*, 2nd edition (Libraries Unlimited, 2000).

Teachers and media specialists who work in schools that specialize in the fine arts have other needs. Titles such as *Halliwell's Film Video and DVD Guide*, 21st edition (HarperCollins, 2006) edited by John Walker and *1-2-3-4 for the Show: A Guide to Small-Cast One Act Plays* (Scarecrow, 1999) by Lewis Heniford might be useful resources for such teachers and media specialists. *Television Production*, 2nd edition (Libraries Unlimited, 2004) by Keith Kyker and Christopher Curchy is an excellent choice for teachers or media specialists who teach television production in secondary schools.

Journals produced by professional organizations provide worthwhile information. Many carry reviews and produce bibliographies. Titles you might consider for a professional collection are *Language Arts, School Talk*, and *English Journal* (National Council of Teachers of English), *American Music Teacher* (Music Teachers National Association), *Educational Leadership* (Association for Supervision and Curriculum Development), *History Teacher* (Society for History Education), *Journal of Geography* (National Council for Geographic Education), *Journal of Family & Consumer Services* (American Association of Family & Consumer Sciences), *Journal of Physical Education, Recreation & Dance* (American Alliance for Health, Physical Education, Recreation, and Dance), *Teaching Children Mathematics, Mathematics Teaching in the Middle School*, and *Mathematics Teacher* (National Council of Teachers of Mathematics), *Reading Teacher* and *Journal of Adolescent & Adult Literacy* (International Reading Association), *Science* and *S B & F Science Books and Films* (American Association for the Advancement of Science), *Science & Children, Science Scope*, and *The Science Teacher* (National Science Teachers Association), and *Social Studies and the Young Learner* and *Social Education* (National Council for the Social Studies). Several of the associations have journals specific to either elementary, middle, or high schools so you should select the journals that are most appropriate for the level of your school.

Conclusions

A media specialist is responsible for ensuring that a collection meets a school's curricular and instructional needs. To carry out this responsibility, one must be knowledgeable about the purpose of the school and the curriculum. A media specialist should be aware of conditions for use of materials, including who will use the resources and for what purposes. As curricula and teaching methods change, media specialists must re-evaluate items in the collection in terms of how effectively the resources contribute to the teaching and learning process. Standardized testing, educational reforms, extracurricular activities, special events, and programs adopted by a school can also affect a media center collection.

Media specialists should provide a professional collection for the school staff so classroom teachers are able to obtain materials that support their instruction. They should have a budget that can be used to purchase some of the resources described in this chapter. Through cooperative efforts, teachers and media specialists can make selection decisions that will meet the school's curricular needs.

As you get caught up in the day-to-day administrative activities and are busy coping with technological advances, do not forget that the common goal we share as educators is to create an effective environment for the educational experience.

References

American Association of School Librarians & Association for Educational Communications and Technology. (1998). *Information power: Building partnerships for learning*. Chicago, IL: American Library Association.

Pine View School. (2006). *Pine View mission statement*. Retrieved September 15, from http://www.sarasota.k12.fl.us/pvs/PV_mission.html

Additional Readings

Abilock, D. (2003). Collaborating with science teachers. *Knowledge Quest, 31*(3), 8–9.

Bishop, K. (2003). *Connecting libraries with classrooms: The curricular roles of the media specialist*. Worthington, OH: Linworth.

Bishop, K., & Larimer, N. (1999). Literacy through collaboration. *Teacher Librarian, 27*(1), 15–20.

Buddy, J. W. (2005). A library media specialist's introduction to international baccalaureate programmes. *School Library Media Activities Monthly, 22*(4), 56–58.

Carter, B. (2000). Formula failure. *School Library Journal, 46*(7), 34–37.

Chenoweth, K. (2001). Keeping score. *School Library Journal, 47*(9), 48–51.

Copeland, B. S. (2005). *Collaborative library lessons for the primary grades: Linking research skills to curriculum standards*. Westport, CT: Libraries Unlimited.

Corey, L. (2002). The role of the library media specialist in standards-based learning. *Knowledge Quest, 31*(2), 21–23.

Everhart, N. (2002). Long-term tracking of student participants' reading achievement in reading motivation programs. *Knowledge Quest, 30*(5), 43–46.

Greer, J. (2003). A positive experience with Accelerated Reader. *Teacher Librarian, 30*(4), 32.

Hancock, M. R. (2003). Children's books in the classroom: Milestones and memories of the literature-based revolution. In L.M. Pavonetti, (Eds.). *Children's literature remembered* (pp. 225–244). Westport, CT: Libraries Unlimited.

Hartzell, G. (2001). The implications of selected school reform approaches for school library media services. *School Library Media Research, 4.* Retrieved September 5, 2006, from http://www.ala.org/ala/aasl/aaslpubsandjournals/slmrb/slmrcontents/volume42001/hartzell.htm

Harvey, C. A. (2006). Leveling for leverage. *Library Media Connection, 24*(4), 42–43.

Howard, S. N. (2001). A school librarian's dilemma: Computerized reading incentive programs. *The Book Report, 20*(3), 52–53.

Jordan, J. H. (2001). The teachers' professional collection materials: Stimulating use. *Knowledge Quest, 29*(2), 18–21.

Kindig, J. (2006). Here, there, and everywhere: Reading First in the library. *Library Media Connection, 24*(7), 28–29.

Krashen, S. (2002). Accelerated Reader: Does it work? If so, why? *School Libraries in Canada, 22*(2), 24–26, 44.

Krashen, S. (2005). Accelerated Reader: Evidence still lacking. *Knowledge Quest, 33*(3), 48–49.

Mardis, M. A. (2006). It's not just whodunit, but how: Science learning, and the school library. *Knowledge Quest, 35* (1), 12–17.

Moyer, M. (2006). Accelerated Reader sparks high school reading excitement. *Knowledge Quest, 35*(1), 34–39.

Nilsen, A. P. (2005). The future of reading: An educator explains why she's worried and wonders what next. *School Library Journal, 51*(1), 38–39.

Obama, B. (2005). Bound to the word. *American Libraries, 36*(7), 49–52.

Pappas, M. (2004) School libraries organized by AR or lexile scores? *Knowledge Quest, 33*(2), 69–70.

Persinger, J. M. (2001). What are the characteristics of a successful implementation of Accelerated Reader? *Knowledge Quest, 29*(5), 30–35.

Scott, E. (2003). Making the standards a "hit" with teachers. *Tech Trends, 47*(1), 27–28.

Scott, T. J. (2005). Analyzing student search strategies: Making a case for integrating information literacy skills into the curriculum. *Teacher Librarian, 33*(1), 21–25.

Seaver, K., & Hare, P. (2002). The effects of block scheduling on high school library media information centers, or the conversion of two library media specialists to blockheads. *Ohio Media Spectrum, 54*(1), 10–17.

Small, R. V. (2005). Block scheduling. *School Library Media Research, 8.* Retrieved September 5, 2006, from http://www.ala.org/ala/aasl/aaslpubsandjournals/slmrb/editorschoiceb/bestoferic/besteric.htm

Smith, M. (2004). California DREAMin': A model for school-public library cooperation to improve student achievement. *Public Libraries, 43*(1), 47–51.

Stefl-Mabry, J. (2005). Computer-aided reading promotion: Accelerated reading—silent sustained reading camouflaged in a computer program. *School Library Media Research, 8.* Retrieved September 5, 21006, from http://www.ala.org/ala/aasl/aaslpubsandjournals/slmrb/editorschoiceb/bestoferic/besteric.htm

Stripling, B. K., & Hughes-Hassell, S. (Eds.). (2003). *Curriculum connections through the library.* Westport, CT: Libraries Unlimited.

Walker, C. (2004). Are you the gatekeeper or the keymaster?: The role of the library media specialist in reading. *Knowledge Quest, 33*(5), 46–47.

Whelan, D. L. (2004). SLJ's book buying survey. *School Library Journal, 50*(9), 42–46.

Helpful Web Sites

Baltimore County Public Schools. The Library Office. (2001). *Roles of library media specialist.* Retrieved September 5, 2006, from http://www.bcps.org/offices/lis/office/teacher.html

CitizenLink. (2005). *Focus on social issues: Home schooling.* Retrieved September 15, 2006, from http://www.family.org/cforum/fosi/education/hs

Core Knowledge Foundation. (2006). *Developing a curriculum plan for implementation.* Retrieved September 5, 2006, from http://coreknowledge.org/CK/schools/curriculum_plan.htm

Education World. (2006). *Curriculum mapping.* Retrieved September 15, 2006, from http://www.education-world.com/a_curr/virtualwkshp/virtualwkshp004.shtml

Education World. (2006). *National standards.* Retrieved September 11, 2006, from http://www.education-world.com/standards

Glencoe/McGraw-Hill. (2005). *Roadmap to success: A curriculum mapping primer.* Retrieved September 12, 2006, from http://www.glencoe.com/sec/teachingtoday/educationupclose.phtml/35

Lamme, L. L., & Beckett, C. (1992). *Whole language in an elementary school library media center.* ERIC Digest. Retrieved September 5, 2006, from http://www.ericdigests.org/1992-3/library.htm

National Home Education Research Institute. (2006). *Welcome to the National Home Education Research Institute.* Retrieved September 15, 2006, from http://www.nheri.org

Powers, M. A. (1999). *Block scheduling: Lessons from experience—a case study.* Retrieved September 5, 2005, from http://www.ala.org/ala/aasl/aaslpubsandjournals/kqweb/kqarchives/volume28/282Tegera.htm

Shemeley, L. (2006). *Save the school librarian.* Retrieved September 5, 2006, from http://www.libraryvideo.com/articles/article17.asp

Starr, L. (2005). *Strong libraries improve student achievement.* Retrieved September 5, 2006, from http://www.educationworld.com/a_admin/admin/admin178.shtml

Whelan D. L. (2004). *Why 'No Child Left Behind' is your chance to become indispensable.* Retrieved September 5, 2006, from http://www.schoollibraryjournal.com/article/CA372997.html

15
Special Groups of Students

One of the primary purposes of school media centers is to meet the needs of all students in a school. Thus, it is important to understand and address the needs of special groups of students. Trends in our society and in public education in the past few decades have resulted in many more "special" students in today's schools. Some of these trends include the mainstreaming of students with disabilities; acknowledgment that gifted and talented students have specific needs; an increase in ethnic and cultural diversity in the population, including the addition of large numbers of families whose first language is not English; a decrease in student reading test scores; recognition of gay and lesbians in society; and the inclusion of pre-school programs in some public schools.

Although each person is unique, he or she may be part of a group sharing characteristics that require special consideration in the collection. Meeting the needs of special groups of students affects selection of resources, as well as accessibility of materials. Consideration of the needs of these students can also impact circulation policies.

Students with Disabilities

People with special needs based on disabilities may not only be students, but also teachers and staff members. Not until the author of this book had a paraplegic teacher join the faculty at the high school where she was a media specialist did she realize the physical access problems in the school's media center. School media centers should have as one of their goals to ensure that students, teachers, and staff members with disabilities have access to both print and electronic resources. The following discussion provides basic information about different types of disabilities and identifies resources that can be helpful to media specialists, teachers, other staff members, parents, and caregivers.

Two pieces of national legislation of particular relevance for this discussion are the Education for All Handicapped Children Act of 1975 (Public Law 94-142), now called the Individuals with Disabilities Education Act (IDEA), and the Americans with Disabilities Act (ADA; Public Law 101-336). The IDEA addresses the needs of the child and calls for an individualized educational program (IEP) based on each child's needs. Media specialist should cooperate with teachers to learn about the methods they are using for IEPs in order to offer support. An older, but frequently cited work, that helps media specialists, parents, and teachers understand the process of ensuring the child's rights under IDEA is *Negotiating the Special Education Maze*, 3rd edition (Woodbine House, 1997) by Winifred Anderson, Stephen Chitwood, and Deidre Hayden. Other more recent books dealing with special education and IEPs include *The Special Educator's Survival Guide* (Jossey-Bass, 2004) by Roger Pierangelo and *Special Education and the Law: A Guide for Practitioners*, 2nd edition (Corwin Press, 2006).

Information about the characteristics of disabilities and the materials recommended to meet the needs of people with disabilities can guide collection activities. The characteristics of a specific disability, however, might not apply to everyone with that disability. Also, many children have needs identified with more than one type of disability.

In working with these students, you have a responsibility to learn about the different characteristics and the implications for resources. School staff members can help. Teachers can describe students' behavior-management programs, abilities, and learning styles. The media specialist can learn which disabilities call for modifications or adaptations and how to implement them. Specialists at the district or state level can also provide information and advice.

The ALSC (Association for Library Services to Children) Library Service to Special Population Children and Their Caregivers Committee recommends several books that deal with children with disabilities. The resources, which include working with autistic children, providing disability etiquette tips, including families with special needs, and mainstreaming services in school and public libraries, are particularly useful for teachers and media specialists. The Web site that lists and annotates the resources is listed at the end of the chapter under "Helpful Web Sites."

Other sources of information are national organizations and clearinghouses. The Council for Exceptional Children (CEC) provides information about education for both children with disabilities and gifted children. CEC provides suggested resources and professional development opportunities, advocates for appropriate governmental policies, and sets professional standards. The Canadian Council for Exceptional Children (CCEC) assists educators, support personnel, and parents who work with special students. They also provide professional development and a newsletter, as well as helping develop responsible legislation. The National Information Center for Children and Youth with Disabilities (NICHCY) is a central source of information on disabilities in children and youth, IDEA, and how No Child Left Behind (NCLB) relates to children with disabilities. They also provide research-based information on effective educational practices. The home pages for these organizations are listed under "Helpful Web Sites" at the end of this chapter. Journals of interest to adults working with special education children include *Exceptional Children* and *Teaching Exceptional Children* (Council for Exceptional Children), and *The Exceptional Parent* (Exceptional Parent).

Not only do media specialists need to know the materials in the collection that are appropriate for children with disabilities, but they also have a responsibility to be aware of the resources available in the community. These may include rehabilitation agencies, information agencies, and other educational or recreational programs. For example, some communities have recreation areas designed to accommodate wheelchairs or to provide information that children can learn through a variety of senses. In one recreational area, trails provide easy access to picnic areas, a fishing pier, and nature paths.

Along the trails, information stations use models, large charts, printed information, and recorded messages to point out items of interest. Messages written in Braille encourage people to feel an object or to smell it. Sheltered eating areas provide spaces for wheelchairs interspersed at the picnic tables. The media specialist should make information about such facilities available and suggest them as possible destinations for field trips.

Formats and Assistive Technologies

Students with special needs use the same range of formats that other students use, but in some cases alternatives or adaptations are necessary. For instance, paperbacks are ideal for students with upper extremity weakness. Students with cognitive disabilities may find audio, video, toys, and multimedia formats useful. Large print books and magazines are helpful to students with visual disabilities.

In recent years many technologies have been adapted to assist persons with special needs. Frequently these technologies are referred to as *assistive technologies*, which are defined by the Technology-Related Assistance for Individuals with Disabilities Act, 1988, U. S. Public Law 100-407 as "any item, piece of equipment or product system, whether acquired commercially, off the shelf, modified, or customized, that is used to increase or improve functional capabilities of individuals with disabilities" (University of Iowa. Iowa Center for Assistive Technology Education and Research, 2006). In *Adaptive Technologies for Learning & Work Environments*, 2nd edition (American Library Association, 2001) Joseph Lazzaro provides a comprehensive coverage of these technologies. A CD-ROM to support users with disabilities is available separately. *Assistive Technology* (AT Network) is published monthly and provides helpful articles and resources. Figure 15.1 lists some of the technologies and their uses.

Visual Impairment

Persons who have vision problems may require special types of materials. Some people with partial sight can use regular print materials, whereas others need large-print materials. One cannot make the assumption that large-print materials are appropriate for all students with partial sight. Low-vision aids, hand-held magnifiers, or closed-circuit televisions can magnify standard print materials. Trained students can use Braille books, games, and outline maps. A blind person can read printed materials by using optical machines that allow users to feel sensation on their fingertips. For others, taped materials may be most useful.

Students with visual disabilities can participate in all media center activities. Useful pieces of equipment include rear projection screens, which permit students to get close to the screen without blocking images; tape recorders; speech compressors, which eliminate pauses between words and thus reduce the time needed to access recorded materials; talking calculators; and computers with voice-recognition software.

People with visual and other physical disabilities can use talking books, which are tapes or records of books, textbooks, and magazines (available in English and other languages, including Spanish). Talking books are a free service of the National Library Service for the Blind and Physically Handicapped, part of the Library of Congress. Arrangements can be made through the local public library. Titles can be found in plaintext catalogs and bibliographies obtained from the National Library Service for the Blind

Figure 15.1. Adaptive technologies
Source: Base on Joseph J. Lazarro's *Adaptive Technologies for Learning & Work Enviroment* (American Library Association, 2001)

ADAPTIVE TECHNOLOGIES

For Persons with Vision Impairments
Speech synthesis hardware and software: Translates text into human sounding speech through the use of speech engines
Computer sound cards: Supports software engines and makes it possible to hear speech, music, and sound effects
Computer screen readers: Provides voice output for word processing, databases, browsers, and spreadsheets
Computer magnification systems: Enlarges computer text and graphics through optical aids
Braille systems: Make it possible for printers to provide Braille output
Braille software: Converts standard text into Braille
Braille note takers: Provide Braille keyboards for input and speech synthesizers and Braille displays for output
Optical character recognition (OCR): Transmits printed materials into a personal computer so they can be read using speech, Braille, or magnified output
Closed circuit television: Allows persons to read books and other materials independently

For Persons with Hearing Impairments
Text telephones (TDDS): Send typed messages over telephone lines
Braille text telephones: Make it possible for output to be in Braille
Cordless and cellular phones (some brands): Allow persons to send and receive text messages
Alphanumeric pagers: Allow for visual communication over long distances; permits persons to send and receive phone messages and e-mail messages
Computer-assisted access: Creates an accessible environment in which persons who are deaf or hard of hearing can use networks, electronic mail, bulletin boards, Web sites, and instant messaging
Instant messaging: Makes it possible for persons to send messages over the Internet using a wide variety of platforms
Online chat: Permits persons to type messages back and forth over the Internet
Signaling systems: Transform sound communication to visible, tactile, or vibrating signals; examples are doorbells or telephones which have receiver lamps that flash or alarm clocks that vibrate
Captioning systems: Provide text messages of dialog at the bottom of television or video screens
Electronic amplification systems: Boost sound energy to make it possible to hear the spoken word and music more easily; hearing aids and assistive listening devices are examples

For Persons with Motor and Speech Impairments
Adapted keyboards: Allow persons with motor disabilities greater access to personal computers
Alternative input systems: Use assistive software in their operation; devices include adapted switches, scanning keyboards, Morse code systems, and word-prediction software
Speech-recognition systems: Provide the hardware and software to listen to spoken words and send commands to the computer as if the words were typed on the keyboard
Environmental control systems: Permit persons with motor disabilities to control appliances and other devices by using a computer or a stand-alone control unit

---

and Physically Handicapped, or they can be downloaded online. Information on the books can be found in the print and online versions of *Braille Book Review* (1932–) and *Talking Books Topics* (1935–) from the National Service for the Blind and Physically Handicapped (NLS). These titles are available free to the blind or people with other disabilities. In 1998 plans were made for evolving the audiobooks program from analog to digital technology.

In 1999 the Library of Congress introduced the Web-Braille service, which offers in electronic format many Braille books, some music scores, and all Braille magazines produced by NLS. Because of copyright laws, access to Web-Braille is limited to NLS patrons and eligible institutions that provide services to the blind. Links to Web-Braille books are included in the NLS online catalog.

The Complete Directory of Large Print Books and Serials (Bowker, 2006) lists adult, juvenile, and textbook titles and indicates the type size and the physical size of each book, as well as full-contact information on publishers, wholesalers, and distributors. The American Foundation for the Blind develops, publishes, and sells useful books, pamphlets, periodicals, videos, and electronic materials for students and professionals. They also publish the *Journal of Visual Impairment and Blindness*.

The American Printing House for the Blind (APHB) publishes Braille books, magazines, and large print texts, as well as materials in recorded and computer disk formats. They also produce an online monthly newsletter, which includes brief reviews of new recreational books in Braille.

Deafness or Hearing Impairment

Children with hearing impairments have difficulty hearing spoken language, and as a result they often have difficulty understanding written and spoken language and abstract concepts. Visual formats are useful for these children. The visuals should be large and present a single, distinct concept or idea. Illustrations and print should be immediately recognizable. Language patterns and sentence structures need to be simple. Repetition and reinforcement are helpful.

Captioned videotapes, CD-ROMs, and DVDs are useful for children with hearing impairments. These materials can be obtained free through a loan program of over 4000 open-captioned materials provided by the Captioned Media Program, whose services are available through the U.S. Department of Education. The materials can be found on the Captioned Media Program Web site, which lists captioned media that can be borrowed by deaf and hard-of-hearing people. Check with your local educational television station for information about captioned programming and the equipment necessary to receive it.

You can provide materials to students who have learned sign language. Books, videotapes, and other materials in sign language are available from the Alexander Graham Bell Association for the Deaf and Hard of Hearing and Gallaudet College Bookstore. Weston Woods produces audiovisual adaptations of several children's books with sign language narration. These materials are intended for young children who cannot yet read captioned media. The American Speech-Language-Hearing Association publishes the newsletter *The ASHA Leader*, which includes articles for persons working with the deaf and hard of hearing. It can be accessed online at <http://www.asha.org/about/publications/leader-online/>. Media specialists who take a course in sign language can greatly increase rapport with students who are deaf or have hearing impairments.

Other Disabilities

Other students who are officially identified through an assessment process include learning disabled (LD), emotionally disturbed (ED), behavior disordered (BD), or mentally retarded (MR). Learning disabled children may have difficulty acquiring and storing information, but their visual and auditory senses are fully functional. Students with behavior disorders may have several behavior problems, including depression, unusual behavior in normal circumstances, and chronic misbehavior such as aggressiveness. Students with intelligence quotients (IQs) below 70 are considered mentally retarded and may have low adaptive behaviors. Students with autism, brain injuries, and other health impairments may also have physical disabilities that require special attention. It is important that all these students have media center privileges although in some cases it may require special education teachers or teacher assistants to accompany the students to the media center.

School media specialists should include in their collection materials appropriate for all students, including those with disabilities. The students should be guided to the materials that will fit their special needs and interests. For instance, children who are mentally retarded will need materials that are simple and sequential. School media specialists may need to modify assignments and materials when teaching library skills to students with disabilities.

One of the most important ways of serving students with disabilities is to provide books and other materials that deal with disabilities. Media center collections should include not only nonfiction resources about disabilities, but also fiction titles in which persons with disabilities occur as main or minor characters. All students with disabilities need to see themselves represented in books and other media center materials. Additionally, other students need to be exposed to materials which have in them persons with disabilities so they can better understand their peers with handicaps. Mason Crest Publishers has produced an entire series of books (15 volume set) on youth with special needs. The books, which are geared for middle school and high school readers, combine factual information with fictional stories and address the challenges and triumphs of youth with special needs, including physical, mental, and emotional disabilities.

Gifted and Talented Students

As any parent of a gifted or talented child knows, gifted students also have special needs. Often these needs are not addressed in public schools as some school systems spend most of their "special" monies on programs that help students who are physically or learning disabled. Yet many gifted students have problems adjusting to school, perhaps because of boredom, feeling uncomfortable about their abilities, or being seen by other students as misfits. Gifted students can also have learning disabilities, and some of them perform far below their abilities. Gifted and talented students will be many of our future leaders in society so it is important to address their educational needs.

At one time gifted students were identified only though IQ tests. But educators in recent years have moved to an expanded definition of giftedness in which intelligence is seen as multifaceted. The current definition of gifted and talented means "children and youth who give evidence of high performance capability in areas such as intellectual, creative, artistic or leadership capacity, or in specific academic fields..." (U.S. Congress, 1988).

Some school programs that deal with gifted and talented students involve enrichment activities that are not included in the regular curriculum and others concentrate on higher-level thinking skills, such as problem solving and critical thinking. With either type of program media resources are frequently needed, and often teachers of gifted and talented students work closely with school media specialists to assist the students in conducting independent research projects.

Many professional organizations deal with gifted and talented students. The National Association for Gifted Children (NAGC) deals specifically with the needs of gifted students and publishes *Gifted Child Quarterly*. Prufrock Press is the largest producer of materials in gifted education. They also publish three periodicals—*Gifted Child Today Magazine, Journal for the Education of the Gifted,* and *Journal of Secondary Gifted Education.*

Gifted and talented students frequently use media center resources to pursue their special interests and talents. It is especially important that they learn to access, evaluate, and use information so they can work independently. Media specialists can help assist these students obtain the literacy skills that they need to be successful in their research.

It is also essential that media specialists develop collections that meet the needs of the gifted and talented students. Good reading advisory can be especially helpful to gifted students and can lead them to quality literature. These students should also be introduced to the classics. Knowing the interests of gifted and talented students is important to matching the students to appropriate materials. Research has shown that gifted students have particular preferences for certain genres—fantasy, science fiction, humor, and series books, such as *The Chronicles of Narnia* (Carter, 1982; Chrisman & Bishop, 1985; Jackson, 1999). Thus, it is important to include in a collection challenging materials in these genres.

Just as is true for other special needs youth, gifted and talented students need to see themselves in books and to gain self-understanding and social understanding. *Gifted Books, Gifted Readers: Literature Activities to Excite Young Minds* (Libraries Unlimited, 2000) by Nancy J. Polette is a valuable resource for selecting books and activities for these students. Judith Wynn Halsted's *Some of My Best Friends Are Books: Guiding Gifted Readers from Preschool to High School*, 2nd edition (Great Potential Press, 2002) contains summaries of approximately 300 books, as well as research on the reading needs of gifted students. *Hoagies' Gifted Education Page* (http://www.hoagiesgifted.org/reading_lists.htm) has numerous links to bibliographies of books recommended for gifted and talented students.

Diversity and Students

Multicultural materials support individual needs as well as the curriculum. These materials help students learn about people whose backgrounds are different from their own. Seeing their culture represented in materials helps raise the self-esteem of members of minority groups. It is important for the school media specialist to be aware of the diversity of a school's students and to make certain that materials are available to meet those students' needs. If there are large numbers of non-English-speaking students in the school population, the media center needs to have materials available in languages other than English.

The topic of multicultural materials can raise heated debate. Questions center on a few issues:

- *Definition of multicultural materials:* Does it include books from or about other nations? How does it define a cultural group? Should Vietnamese, Cambodian, Chinese, and Japanese materials all be labeled

"Asian American" when the differences between these cultures are significant?

- *Background of authors:* Who is qualified to write about ethnic and cultural experiences? Should only those who are actually members of a culture write about that group? Can an author successfully write about a culture if he or she has gained insight into it through extensive research or experience in the culture?

Because you will want to select high-quality multicultural materials to include in your collection, a third issue—the quality of the literature—deserves your special attention as a school media specialist. It is important to remember that the standards for any good literature also apply to multicultural and international literature. However, additional criteria should be considered:

- The materials should be culturally accurate. This includes the illustrations in a book as well as text.

- Ethnic materials should contain authentic dialogue and depict realistic relationships.

- The materials should avoid racial and cultural stereotyping. Characters should be regarded as distinct individuals.

- The materials should not contain racial comments or clichés.

- Details in a story should help the reader gain a sense of the culture.

Some resources address multicultural materials. Sherry York's *Ethnic Book Awards: A Directory of Multicultural Literature for Young Readers* (Linworth, 2005) is a comprehensive listing of the award-winning titles of several multicultural awards. Sylvia and Ken Marantz's *Multicultural Picturebooks*, 2nd edition (Scarecrow, 2004), reviews and evaluates picture books with a multicultural theme for grades K-4. *Venture into Cultures: A Resource Book of Multicultural Materials and Programs*, 2nd edition (American Library Association, 2001) by Olga R. Kuharets is especially helpful for creating multicultural programs for children. *Multicultural Projects Index: Things to Make and Do to Celebrate Holidays Around the World* (Libraries Unlimited, 1998) is an index of multicultural projects in more than 1,700 books. *Multicultural Resources on the Internet: The United States and Canada* (Libraries Unlimited, 1999) annotates URL sites for Native American, African American, Hispanic American, Asian American, Chinese American, Japanese American, Asian Indian American, Jewish American, Americans of Middle Eastern descent, French Canadian, Cajun and Creole, and Hawaiian American cultures. *Culturally Diverse Videos, Audios, and CD-ROMs for Children* (Neal-Schuman, 1999) recommends more than 1,000 multicultural titles. In order to locate quality multicultural books, you should become familiar with Lee & Low, a publishing company that specializes in multicultural literature for children.

The following sources can help you select African American titles for your collection. *The Coretta Scott King Awards Book: 1970–2004* (American Library Association, 2004) edited by Henrietta M. Smith features annotations of winning and honor titles, as well as biographies of their authors and illustrators. Pamela Toussaint's *Great Books for African-American Children* (Plume, 1999) lists 250 books that celebrate the African-American culture. *Black Books Galore: Guide to More Great African American Children's Books* by Donna Rand and Toni Trent Parker includes over 400 titles, as well as profiles of selected authors and illustrators.

The Pura Belpré Awards: Celebrating Latino Authors and Illustrators (American Library Association, 2006) edited by Rose Z. Trevino covers the first ten years of the Pura Belpré Awards. It annotates the award-winning titles and provides biographies of the authors and illustrators. Other helpful resources for selecting Latino titles for your collection are Sherry York's *Picture Books by Latino Writers: A Guide for Librarians, Teachers, Parents, and Students* (Linworth, 2002) and York's *Children's and Young Adult Literature by Latino Writers: A Guide for Librarians, Teachers, Parents, and Students* (Linworth, 2002). Isabel Schon's *The Best of Latino Heritage, 1996–2002: A Guide to the Best Juvenile Books about Latino People* (Scarecrow, 2003) also is a valuable collection development tool. Schon's *Recommended Books in Spanish for Children and Young Adults: 2000–2004* (Scarecrow, 2004) is an essential selection aid for purchasing materials in Spanish. *Programming with Latino Children's Materials: A How-to-Do-It Manual for Librarians* (Neal-Schuman, 1999) provides background on the Latino culture and reviews books, folktales, and recordings that can be used in programming.

Recent selection tools for Native American Indian materials are more difficult to locate. Sherry York's *Children's and Young Adult Literature by Native Americans: A Concept Guide for Librarians, Teachers, Parents, and Students* (Linworth, 2003) covers titles in print for fiction, folklore, drama, poetry, and nonfiction. An older source *Through Indian Eyes: The Native Experience in Books for Children* (American Indian Studies Center, 1998) includes critical evaluations of books by and about Native Americans.

Reviews of new print and nonprint resources, as well as articles about multiculturalism can be found in *MultiCultural Review: Dedicated to a Better Understanding of Ethnic, Racial and Religious Diversity*. This quarterly journal published by the Goldman Group is designed for educators and librarians at all levels.

Sources that are particularly helpful for international materials include Carl M. Tomlinson's *Children's Books from Other Countries* (Scarecrow, 1998), Susan Stan's *The World Through Children's Books* (Scarecrow, 2002), *Crossing Boundaries with Children's Books* (Scarecrow, 2006) edited by Doris Gebel, and Beth B. Zarian's *Around the World with Historical Fiction and Folklore* (Scarecrow, 2004). *Bookbird: A Journal of International Children's Literature* is a refereed journal published quarterly by the International Board on Books for Children. It features articles of interest on international literature for children, and it also reviews selection tools.

Bibliographies of multicultural materials for the groups discussed, as well as for Asian Americans, can be found on several Internet sites. Some of the sites are listed under "Helpful Web Sites" at the end of this chapter. Additionally the Web sites for some awards that are given for books that deal with minorities are also listed. These lists can be helpful selection aid resources since the winning titles are some of the best books published about the represented minorities. It is important for media specialists to purchase these books and give these award-winning titles the recognition that they deserve.

Poor and Reluctant Readers

Poor or reluctant readers have always been a challenge to teachers and media specialists who teach literature appreciation and encourage reading. The poor reader reads below capacity. This is not a reflection of that person's potential to read. A reluctant or resistive reader is one who has the skills needed to read, but prefers not to read. Sometimes these students are referred to as aliterate. Books with high appeal and appropriate reading levels can help these students. The phrases "high interest/low vocabulary" (hi-low) or "high interest/low reading level" (HILRL) are often used to describe these works. Some helpful criteria for evaluating such books include:

- Cover—should be "catchy" and attractive
- Good blurb
- Appropriate format—appealing balance of text and white space
- Clear writing without long, complex sentences or sophisticated vocabulary
- Direct and simple narrative
- A few well-defined characters
- Use of dialogue and action
- Well-organized and direct information
- Repetition of main points
- Illustrations to explain the text
- Humor when appropriate
- Presented in chronological order

The topic of reluctant readers has been addressed in library literature during the past few years. *Connecting with Reluctant Teen Readers* (Neal-Schuman, 2006) by Patrick Jones, Maureen L. Hartman, and Patricia Taylor provides ideas on the types of books that will entice teens to read. Lists of over 600 books, series, and magazines are included. Edward T. Sullivan's *Reaching Reluctant Young Adult Readers: A Handbook for Librarians and Teachers* (Scarecrow, 2002) is also a useful resource to confront the problem of teen aliteracy. Michael Sullivan has researched the problem of aliteracy among boys. His book, *Connecting Boys with Books: What Libraries Can Do* (American Library Association, 2003) contains practical ideas on how to connect boys with books. *More Rip-Roaring Reads for Reluctant Teen Readers* (Libraries Unlimited, 1999) by Betty D. Ammon and Gale W. Sherman describes both fiction and nonfiction titles for reluctant readers in middle and high school grades. Each year the Young Adult Library Services Association (YALSA) selects "Quick Picks for Reluctant Young Adult Readers." The Web site for these lists, as well as other lists for reluctant readers can be found under "Helpful Web Sites" at the end of this chapter. Other books that appeal to reluctant and resistive readers include graphic novels, series books, and picture books for older readers.

Unfortunately some educators equate reading only with books. Some even think of reading as only the reading of fiction. In reality, today's youth are doing much reading in formats other than books. Magazines, newspapers, and comics are appealing not only to reluctant or resistive readers, but to teenagers in general. It is important to remember that the time that students spend on computers and playing video games also involves reading. If we want to motivate students to read, we must first find out their interests, including what they are reading. We can then be more successful in matching their interests to reading materials.

Criteria for selecting books for ESL (English as a Second Language) students include some of the same considerations. According to McCaffery (1998, xiv), these books should have the following:

- An appealing format
- Appropriate reading and content levels
- Appropriate illustrations
- Accurate text and illustrations
- Access to information through an index
- A glossary of terms
- Bibliographies for further exploration

ESL books need to be representative of the culture they describe and effectively explain that culture. *Book Bridges for ESL Students: Using Young Adult and Children's Literature to Teach ESL* (Scarecrow, 2002) by Suzanne Elizabeth Reid is a valuable resource for both librarians and teachers.

Gay/Lesbian Students

For the most part school library services for gay and lesbian students have been grossly inadequate. Internet filtering on school library computers has seriously affected these students' capabilities to access information about their sexual orientation, and many school media specialists are hesitant to include gay literature in their collections because they fear controversy and book challenges. Yet without vital books and resources, gay students can often end up in high-risk situations. Having information available on gays and lesbians can not only provide the information needs of LGBT (lesbian, gay, bisexual, and transgender) students, but it also can discourage the teasing and harassing of LGBT students that exist at many schools. Reading gay-themed books can help LGBT students realize there are other young people like them. Students, including young children, living in families with gay or lesbian parents need to see their families represented and accepted in literature.

A growing number of quality gay-themed titles are available so it should not be difficult to find materials to purchase. *Lesbian and Gay Voices* (Greenwood, 2000) by Frances Ann Day is a much-needed resource that contains more than 275 titles of books that are appropriate for young readers and that feature lesbian and gay characters.

Other Special Groups of Students

Other special groups of students can benefit from materials geared to their needs and interests. Some of these groups include students with attention deficient disorders (ADH) and students with serious or chronic illnesses, such as cerebral palsy or HIV/AIDS. Nonfiction materials on all of these conditions should be available in a media center collection. Additionally, all of these students need to see themselves represented in fiction materials.

Transient students include children and teenagers who live in campgrounds, on migrant farms, in homeless shelters, or with foster parents.

Mobility often is accompanied by poverty, hunger, and exposure to violence. Often there is a lack of stability in the lives of transient students, as well as a lack of consistency in their education. It is especially important to make these students welcome in the media center. Materials and media center programs to help these students become aware of their value to society can be beneficial in lowering their anxieties and building their self-esteem. There also may be instances when circulation policies may need to be adapted for these students.

In recent years there has been a growing population of pre-school children in our schools. This means that we, as media specialists, need to educate ourselves about how children learn in the early years. These children should be welcomed into the media center with storytelling programming and learning experiences relating to the care of books. If pre-school children are present in your school, your collection should include appropriate age-level books, with sturdy library binding.

Attention to student dropout populations is another recent issue, both for educators and for society in general. These students are referred to as *at-risk youth*. Some characteristic that contribute to students dropping out of school include low family income, weak family cohesiveness, parental apathy, frequent family mobility, low self-esteem, conflict with other students, poor academic achievement, and behavior problems in school. One of the major deficits of students who are not doing well in school is the lack of reading skills. Media specialists can help with the dropout problem by providing materials that support students' various learning styles, reading levels, and interests. Keeping a media center open after school so at-risk students can obtain tutoring or homework help is another way to help with dropout prevention. Most important is making the media center a safe and welcoming environment for all students, and being particularly supportive of students who are struggling to fit in with their peers.

Sheila B. Anderson's *Extreme Teens: Library Services for Nontraditional Young Adults* (Libraries Unlimited, 2005) provides tips on building a collection and providing library services to connect with non-traditional young people, including juvenile delinquents, pregnant teens, the homeless, and many others. Articles relating to some of these non-traditional young people are listed in "Additional Readings" at the end of this chapter.

Conclusions

One of the responsibilities of school media specialists is to provide materials and services to meet the needs of students, including students who have special needs. Several changes in our society and in education have resulted in many special groups of students in our schools who have needs that impact the school media collection. Such groups include students with physical disabilities, such as sight or hearing impairments; young people with learning disabilities or health problems; gifted and talented students; students from ethnic minority groups; youth whose first language is not English; gay and lesbian students; transient young people; and at-risk students. School media specialists should purchase materials that address the needs of all these groups, including books that have these young people as major characters. Additionally, school media specialists should provide safe, welcoming environments in their media centers for all of these students who often face challenging situations with their peers.

References

Carter, B. (1982). Leisure reading habits of gifted students in a suburban junior high school. *Top of the News*, *38*(4), 312.

Chrisman, L. G., & Bishop, K. (1985). Reading preferences of academically talented students at a "parent-controlled" private school: A look at a study and its implications for library media specialists. *School Library Media Quarterly*, *13*(3/4), 200–207.

Jackson, T. D. (1999). Reading attitudes, interests, and habits, and their relation to giftedness and gender (Master's Thesis, University of Alberta, 1999).

McCaffery, L. H. (1998). *Building an ESL collection for young adults*. Westport, CT: Greenwood.

University of Iowa. Iowa Center for Assistive Technology Education and Research. (2006). *Assistive technology glossary*. Retrieved September 12, 2006, from http://www.education.uiowa.edu/icater/AT_glossary.htm

U.S. Congress Public Law 100-297, Title IV, Sec. 4103 (1988).

Additional Readings

Agosto, D. E. The cultured word: Cultural background, bilingualism, and the school library. *School Libraries Worldwide*, *7*(1), 46–57.

Akin, L., & MacKinney, D. (2004). Autism, literacy, and libraries. *Children and Libraries*, *2*(2), 35–43.

Alexander, L. B. (2005). ADA resources for the library and information professions. *Journal of Education for Library and Information Science*, *46*(3), 248–257.

Asselin, M. (2003). Bridging the gap between learning to be male and learning to read. *Teacher Librarian*, *30*(3), 53–54.

Beaman, A. (2006). YA Lit 2.0: How technology is enhancing the pleasure reading experience for teens. *Knowledge Quest*, *35*(1), 30–33.

Braxton, B. (2003). Bait the boys and hook them into reading. *Teacher Librarian*, *30*(3), 43–44.

Braxton, B. (2004). Encouraging students to read for pleasure. *Teacher Librarian*, *31*(3), 39–40.

Chu, C. (2000). See, hear, and speak no evil: A content approach to evaluating multicultural multimedia materials. *Reference and User Services Quarterly*, *39*(3), 255–264.

Clyde, L. A., & Loban, M. (2001). A door half open: Young people's access to fiction related to homosexuality. *School Libraries Worldwide*, *7*(2), 17–30.

Crawford, P. (2004). A novel approach: Using graphic novels to attract reluctant readers. *Library Media Connection*, *22*(5), 26–28.

Crawford, P. C. (2006). A juvenile miscellany: Americana popular culture and the comics. *Knowledge Quest*, *35*(1), 50–53.

Delisle, J., & Galbraith, J. (2002). *When gifted kids don't have all the answers: How to meet their social and emotional needs*. Minneapolis, MN: Free Spirit.

Dunnewind, S. (2006). Do's and don'ts for getting kids to read. *Teacher Librarian*, *34*(1), 28–29.

Hopkins, J. (2003). Assistive technology for the school library. *Library Media Connection, 21*(6), 46–48.

Hopkins, J. (2004). New support for visual and reading disabilities. *Library Media Connection, 22*(4), 48–50.

Hopkins, J. (2004). School library accessibility: The role of assistive technology. *Teacher Librarian, 31*(3), 15–18.

Hopkins, J. (2005). Extending inclusive learning: Library and special education collaboration. *Library Media Connection, 23*(6), 17–19.

Hopkins, J. (2006). Assistive technology: 10 things to know. *Library Media Connection, 25*(1) 12–14.

Horton, R. (2005). Boys are people too: Boys and reading, truth and misconceptions. *Teacher Librarian, 33*(2), 30–32.

Jones, J. (2006). The numbers are astounding: The role of the media specialist in dropout prevention. *Library Media Connection, 25*(2), 10–13.

Juozaitis, V. (2004). Serving the needs of our students with LD in the school library. *School libraries in Canada* (0nline), 23(1).

Kennedy, A. (2003). Eat, drink, and be literate. *School Library Journal, 49*(9), 45.

Kozol, J. (2000). An unequal education. *School Library Journal, 46*(5), 46–49.

Lane, D. (2002). The emergence of gay literature for young people. *Young Adult Library Services, 1*(1), 18–21.

Martin, R. (2003). Connecting with boys at lunch: A success story. *Teacher Librarian, 30*(3), 27–28.

McElmeel, S. L. (2004). Good intentions are not enough: Creating a book climate of diversity. *Library Media Connection, 23*(3), 28–29.

Meloni, C. (2006). Teen chick lit. *Library Media Connection, 25*(2), 16–19.

Mestre, L. S. (2000). Improving computer-use success for students of diverse backgrounds. *Knowledge Quest, 28*(5), 20–28.

Schrader, A. M., & Wells, K. (2004). *Queer perspectives on social responsibility in Canadian schools and libraries: Analysis and resources.* Retrieved October 10, 2006, from http://www.schoollibraries.ca/articles/151.aspx

Selverstone, H. (2001). Equity of access for all: Serving our underserved populations. *Knowledge Quest, 29*(4), 5–6.

Selverstone, H. (2003). Tech for kids with disabilities. *School Library Journal, 49*(6), 36–37.

Snowball, C. (2005). Teenage reluctant readers and graphic novels. *Young Adult Library Services, 3*(4), 43–45.

Souder, P. (2004). *A different way of seeing: Youth with visual impairments and blindness.* Broomal, Pa: Mason Crest.

Watson, J., & Stencel, J. (2005). Reaching reluctant readers with nonfiction. *Young Adult Library Services, 4*(1), 8–11.

Weldon, C. (2005). Addressing the gender gap in boys' reading. *Teacher Librarian, 32*(4), 44–45.

Whelan, D. L. (2006). Out and ignored: Why are so many school libraries reluctant to embrace gay teens? *School Library Journal, 52*(1), 46–50.

Wilson, R. (2006). Multicultural graphic novels. *Library Media Connection, 24*(6), 32–33.

Winkel, W. (2004). New ways to learn: A cooperative program in Milwaukee helps learning-disabled kids with technology. *School Library Journal, 50*(1), 24–26.

Woody, D. (2000). African American biographies: A collection development challenge. *Journal of Youth Services in Libraries, 13*(2), 5–9.

Zirkel, P. A. (2002). Decisions that have shaped U.S. education. (2001/2002). *Educational Leadership, 59*(4), 6–12.

Helpful Web Sites

About: Children's Books. (2006). *Resources for reluctant readers.* Retrieved October 10, 2006, from http://childrensbooks.about.com/od/reluctantreaders/

American Library Association. (2005). *Coretta Scott King Award.* Retrieved October 9, 2006, from http://www.ala.org/ala/emiert/corettascottkingbookawards/abouttheawarda/cskabout.htm

Association for Library Service to Children. (n.d.). *Children with disabilities and library programs.* Retrieved September 14, 2006, from http://www.ala.org/ala/alsc/alscresources/forlibrarians/Chldrnnwithdisabilities.htm

Association for Library Service to Children. (n.d.). *The Mildred L. Batchelder Award.* Retrieved October 9, 2006, from http://www.ala.org/ala/alsc/awardsscholarships/literaryawds/batchelderaward/batchelderaward.htm

Association for Library Service to Children. (n.d.). *The Pura Belpré Award.* Retrieved October 9, 2006, from http://www.ala.org/ala/alsc/awardsscholarships/literaryawds/belpremedal/belprmedal.htm

Association of Jewish Libraries. (2005). *Sydney Taylor Book Award.* Retrieved October from http://www.jewishlibraries.org/ajlweb/awards/st_books.htm

Books for reluctant readers. (n.d.). Retrieved October 10, 2006, from http://the2rs.com/Books_For_Reluctant_Readers

Brodsky, A. (n.d.). *Children's books about disability: A bibliography-teacher's guide.* Retrieved September 23, 2006, from www.state.nj.us/humanservices/dds/publications/Master%20Biblio-childrens%20disabilitybooks.pdf

Canadian Council for Exceptional Children. (2004). *Welcome.* Retrieved September 14, 2006, from http://canadian.cec.sped.org

Council for Exceptional Children. (2006). *About us.* Retrieved September 14, 2006, from http://www.cec.sped.org/AM/Template.cfm?Section=About_CEC

Eccleston. S (2005). *Gay / lesbian materials for young children.* Retrieved October 10, 2006, from www.teachers.ab.ca/ . . . /9B31CA70-1B36-4839-B5C1-8F944642FE7A/0/GayLesbianMaterialsforYoungChildren.ppt

ICDL. (n.d.). *International Children's Digital Library.* Retrieved October 7, 2006, from http://www.icdlbooks.org

Internet Public Library. (2006). *Native American authors.* Retrieved October 7, 2006, from http://www.ipl.org/div/natam

Internet School Library Media Center (n.d.). *Asian American, Asian & Pacific Islands Children's literature.* Retrieved October 7, 2006, from http://falcon.jmu.edu/%7Eramseyil/mulasia.htm

KidSource Online. (2003). *A guide to children's literature and disability: 1989–1994.* Retrieved September 23, 2006, from http://www.kidsource.com/NICHCY/literature.html

Lanehart, W., & Ramsey, I. (n.d.). *African-American bibliography for children*. Retrieved October 7, 2006, from http://falcon.jmu.edu/~ramseyil/mulafro.htm

Library of Congress. (2006). *That all may read ... National Library Service for the Blind and Physically Handicapped (NLS)*. Retrieved September 18, 2006, from http://www.loc.gov/nls

Mele, Joe. (n.d.). *Multicultural book reviews*. Retrieved October 7, 2006, from http://www.isomedia.com/homes/jmele/joe.html

National Center for Culturally Responsive Educational Systems, (2003). *Childrens literature*. Retrieved October 7, 2006, from http://nccrest.edreform.net/subject/childrensliterature

National Council for the Social Studies. (2006). *Carter G. Book Awards*. Retrieved October 18, 2006, from http://www.socialstudies.org/awards/woodson/

National Dissemination Center for Children with Disabilities. (2001). *Children's literature & disability*. Retrieved September 23, 2006, from http://www.nichcy.org/pubs/bibliog/bib5txt.htm

National Education Association. (n.d.). *Asian American booklist*. Retrieved October 7, 2006, from http://www.nea.org/readacross/resources/aabooks.html

National Information Center for Children and Youth with Disabilities. (n.d.). *National Dissemination Center for Children*. Retrieved September 14, 2006, from http://www.nichcy.org/index.html

National Library Service for the Blind and Physically Handicapped. (2002). *NLS reference bibliographies*. Retrieved September 23, 2006, from http://www.loc.gov/nls/reference/bibliographies/library.html

Pacific Rim Voices. (2006). *Papertiger.org: Asian Pacific Award for Literature*. Retrieved October 9, 2006, from http://papertigers.org/resources/USA?AsianPacificAmerican.html

Smith, R. F. (n.d.). *Celebrating cultural diversity through children's literature*. Retrieved October 7, 2006, from http://www.multicultrualchildrenslit.com

SNOW—Special needs opportunity windows. (n.d.). Retrieved September 14, 2006, from http://snow.utoronto.ca/index.html

Steelman, P. (2006). *Select bibliography of children's books about the disability experience*. Retrieved October 9, 2006, from http://www.ala.org/ala/awardsbucket/schneideraward/bibliography.htm

Texas State University—San Marcos. College of Education. (2005). *Tomás Rivera Mexican American Children's Book Award*. Retrieved October 18, 2006, from http://www.education.txstate.edu/subpages/tomasrivera/index.html

University of Wisconsin—Milwaukee. Center for Latin American and Caribbean Studies. *Américas Book Award for Children's and Young Adult Literature*. Retrieved October 9, 2006, from http://www.uwm.edu/Dept/CLACS/outreach/Americas.html

Walling, L. L. (2006). *Linda Lucas Walling collection: Materials for and/or about children with disabilities*. Retrieved October 3, 2006, from http://www.libsci.edu/facst/walling/bestfolder.htm

Young Adult Library Services Association. (n.d.). *Quick picks for reluctant young adult readers*. Retrieved October 10, 2006, from www.ala.org/yalsa/booklists/quickpicks

16

Fiscal Issues Relating to the Collection

Media specialists face the reality that a single collection cannot be composed of all available resources, nor can it meet all of its users' demands. In meeting this challenge media specialists must address some issues. Among these is the question of ownership versus access. Should a media specialist use funds to purchase an item or should the media specialist obtain a license so patrons can use that item? Other questions deal with technologies. Should one add new formats such as e-books to the collection? How often is it necessary to upgrade the current technology?

Unfortunately in many school media centers there are not enough funds to purchase even basic print materials. Thus, media specialists are faced with the challenge of how to raise additional monies, perhaps through fundraising projects or by applying for grants.

The Budget

Given these situations, how do media specialists plan a budget and allocate funds for acquiring or accessing resources? Very few persons become school media specialists because they have a special interest in developing budgets; however, budgeting is an important part of the program administration role of the media specialist. Dickinson (2004) notes that the budgeting cycle is a three-step process, involving knowledge (having sound understanding of the budget process), planning, and implementation.

Knowledge of the Budget Process

In most schools the principal has a major role in deciding how funds will be dispersed. Some states require that a certain amount of money based on student enrollment be allocated for media center resources, but this is generally a minimum amount. In some instances, particularly in schools utilizing site-based management, a school committee also has input into how monies are allocated in the school. In many cases you will be competing with other units in the school for the same funds. Therefore, it is essential that you understand the funding process and are able to clearly communicate in writing the needs of the media center, with well-documented costs of the resources that you think need to be purchased for the media center.

Planning and Implementing

In order to decide which resources or services to purchase, you should decide on some collection management goals and establish yearly budget priorities. The collection must be assessed to determine how closely the current resources respond to curriculum needs. A collection development plan should then be created to fill any gaps in the current resources. This plan should be reviewed annually. When requesting funds for resources, it is important to include the dollar amount needed to replace old and worn items, in addition to filling any identified gaps.

Budget requests can be presented in various formats, but all budgets should include itemized dollar amounts and justification for the purchase of each item or service. In today's educational setting it is wise to relate justification to student learning and achievement.

Allocation of funds can be based on curriculum areas, subjects, curriculum mapping, formats, and users. Other approaches include historical (how allocations were handled in the past), anticipated loss/replacement, and age of the collection. Allocation of funds also reflects a media center's stance on the amount of electronic access versus ownership (the more traditional position).

Escalating costs are another factor media specialists face. The average cost of books continues to increase. However, at the same time the costs of videocassettes, CDs, and DVDs are decreasing. One can consult the April issue of *Publishers Weekly* or the latest edition of the *Bowker Annual Library and Book Trade Almanac* (R. R. Bowker, 1955–) for an annual update on this type of information.

It may be possible that the amount of money requested to fully fund the needed resources is not well received; however, it is our responsibility as media specialists to submit a well-justified budget each year. Even if the initial request for funding is not completely fulfilled, that is not a reason to quit asking for funding or to lower the amounts requested. As long as you are basing requests on evidence-based facts, you should continue in your pursuit of requesting funds. It may be necessary for you to become proactive and gather support from others (parents, teachers, students) who can benefit from the resources that you think should be in the media center. Good public relations—attending PTSA meetings, sponsoring extracurricular activities, presenting staff development workshops—will also aid in increasing the chances that the media center program will be funded (Dickinson, 2004, p. 17).

Licensing

In the future, licensing or access fees for electronic resources may make up the major portion of the media center's non-personnel budget. With the advent of being able to access digital information, rather than obtain outright ownership, media specialists are learning to negotiate licensing agreements. These agreements define appropriate use and specify a given time period. Both the media center as buyer (licensee) and the vendor (licensor) are bound by the negotiated terms. Common issues in licensing electronic resources are the following:

- Resolving the issue of ownership and access
- Defining how the content may or may not be used (fair use)
- Determining whether the content is to be accessed within the library or remotely
- Defining who is authorized to use the resource

When examining access licenses, other practical advice includes the following:

- Select the clauses in license agreements with which you agree.
- Create a licensing template of those terms.
- Develop a checklist of terms and conditions that are appropriate for your situation.
- Be sure the license follows the copyright laws.
- Avoid licenses that hold the media center liable for each and every infringement by authorized users.
- Avoid non-cancellation clauses.
- Avoid non-disclosure clauses.
- Make sure time limitations are clearly defined.
- Avoid licenses that permit subcontracting to an agent.

For further suggestions see the "Additional Readings" and "Helpful Web Sites" at the end of this chapter.

Resource Sharing

The basic concept of sharing bibliographic information and collections is not new. However, the advent of telecommunications and other technologies has increased the opportunities to share resources. Although location of information is an important aspect, delivery of the desired items is of greater concern. Changes in technological delivery systems make it possible to address the needs of individual learners more effectively regardless of geographic location. These multi-type library organizations (that is, academic, public, school, and special libraries) establish formal cooperative organizations of independent and autonomous libraries or groups of libraries to work together for mutual benefit. Networks or consortiums are not limited to regions—they can be found within a school system or at the community, county, state, national, and international levels.

The traditional library network was a cooperative in which participating members shared resources on formal and informal bases. These early consortia shared union lists of serials, provided loans through their interlibrary lending (ILL) network, or jointly owned a film collection. The current use of the term *networking* acknowledges the development of online infrastructures through which members are linked to resources through some type of telecommunications connection. The participants include multi-state and multi-type libraries.

Successful networks are characterized by a financial and organizational commitment from the members, who agree to perform specific tasks and adhere to specific guidelines. In return, the member library has immediate access through computer and communications technology to databases that originate in the public or private sector. Commonly held beliefs about networks are the following:

- Opportunity to access information is the right of each individual.
- Networks do not replace individual collections; rather, they enhance existing ones and expand their range of services.
- Participating libraries are responsible for meeting the daily needs of their users and for contributing to the network.
- Networking is not free. Costs include equipment, materials, computer time, postage, telephone, copying expenses, and staff time.
- Effective communication among participants is essential.
- Commitment to participation is made at the school-district level.
- Local, district, and regional levels of service must be clearly defined.
- School-level personnel need to be notified early in the process and kept informed about plans.
- Decisions must be made as to which services—for example, bibliographic retrieval, cataloging, or interlibrary loan—the network will provide.
- Delivery systems for bibliographic data and information retrieval must be spelled out.
- Remuneration to or from systems must be mutually agreed upon.
- Legislative issues and governance must be agreed upon.

Several states have developed network projects that can be used by school library media specialists. Wisconsin's BadgerLink is a project begun in 1998 by the Wisconsin Department of Education whose services are available in the state's public, school, academic, and special libraries. They contract with five vendors (EBSCO, ProQuest, Thomson Gale, Newspaper Archive, and TeachingBooks) to provide users access to articles from newspapers and periodicals, image files, specialized reference materials, and Web sites. INFOhio, a virtual K-12 library, is funded by the state of Ohio. Its resources are available to all of Ohio's K-12 students and teachers. As of August 1, 2006, Florida's SUNLINK project had over 1.7 million titles from 2,695 schools in 67 districts in Florida. Also included were over 25,000 Web sites, over 396,000 book jacket cover images, 500 images from Florida memory, and almost 2,000 files of streaming video. These resources are available to K-12 schools in Florida. Additionally, many of the resources can be accessed by other individuals. These types of projects provide extremely valuable services to their users, including access to electronic materials, interlibrary loan transactions, and cataloging information.

Alternative Funding

It is a sad time in education when schools are not able to provide the funds to purchase the necessary materials and equipment to support the curriculum of a school and to provide resources for the personal interests of young people. Nonetheless, this is the reality in many communities. Besides fulfilling the four major roles of media specialists—teacher, information specialist, instructional partner, and program administrator—in recent years, media specialists have also needed to develop skills in both fundraising and grant writing.

Fundraising

With rising costs of materials and tightening of budgets, many media specialists have taken up projects for fundraising. While it is possible to sell school supplies out of the media center office or hold garage sales to obtain alternative funding, this author does not recommend such endeavors. Rather, it seems more appropriate to undertake projects that can contribute to the goals of a media center and at the same time raise monies. Sponsoring a book fair is a good example of such a project. Book fairs, however, can be very time-consuming so you should solicit the help of parent volunteers or the PTSA organization. While the profits can sometimes be very large for schools with large enrollments or where the economic status of the students is high, in other instances the profit share can be low compared to the amount of time and effort necessary to conduct a book fair. Scholastic and Troll are two publishers who provide book fair materials to many school media centers. Bookstores in a community are sometimes willing to provide materials for a school book fair. If you are a school media specialist in a parochial school, you can ask a local religious store if they are interested in collaborating with you on a book fair. Most companies or bookstores that help sponsor book fairs provide either a smaller monetary cash profit (typically 20–30 percent of the sales) or a larger amount if you purchase materials from them with a share of the profits.

Another creative idea for fundraising is to conduct a "read-a-thon" in which students get pledges from family and friends for the number of books that the students read. Students often earn prizes for their fundraising efforts. Local merchants can be asked to provide prizes. Such a project can raise monies for the media center while also encouraging reading.

If your school plans an author visit, you should contact a local bookstore to see if they would like to collaborate with you by having multiple copies of the author's books available for sale—providing you with a share of the profits, of course. Most authors are happy to autograph their books, making them even more special to students. Remember to provide adequate time in an author visit for the sale and autographing of the books.

Most of the fundraising projects that you may want to sponsor will take much extra time and effort. Organizing a Friends of the Library group or meeting with the PTSA to share your ideas about fundraising can result in finding able helpers for your projects.

Grant Writing

Media specialists can obtain outside funding through grant proposals, with monies coming from local, regional, or national sources. Many of the grant opportunities can be found by searching on the Internet. Some school districts also hire professional grant writers to be in charge of researching possible grants and assisting in the writing of grant proposals. You should be proactive and ask your administrator and classroom teachers to provide you with information on possible grants that could enhance your collection. Don't simply wait for announcements or calls for grant proposals.

Most grants are very specific, and the funds can be used only for specific purposes. Some of the possible funding opportunities include adding new technologies, upgrading technology, purchasing computer software and audiovisual materials, financial support for resource sharing, subscribing to online databases, and improving facilities. Since student reading test scores have been emphasized in recent years, several grants provide funding for materials and projects that can improve literacy.

Each grant has its own specifications that must be carefully followed in order for a media center to be considered as a possible recipient of funds. Typical elements in a proposal are the following:

- *Cover sheet*: Brief identification of project, goals, and beneficiaries of the project
- *Abstract*: Brief summary of project
- *Table of contents*
- *Introduction:* Description of applicant, purpose, programs, constituents, credibility of organization and its accomplishments, and credibility of proposed program
- *Needs statement*: Need, support data, and experiences
- *Goals and objectives*: Intent and anticipated outcomes of the proposed project
- *Project design*: Plan of action, activities, and methods planned to achieve the project objectives
- *Budget*: Costs and expenditures for personnel (includes wages, salaries, and fringe benefits) and non-personnel (includes equipment and supplies)
- *Evaluation design*: Plans for determining whether goals are met, assessing process and product, and identifying who will monitor and evaluate
- *Dissemination*: Identification of what will be reported to whom and how that information will be distributed
- *Plans for the future*: Outline of how the project will be supported after outside funding runs out
- *Appendix (you should refer to these items in the narrative)*: Examples of items to include are the mission statement, bibliography, vitae of personnel, and letters of commitment and endorsement

The Foundation Center (http://foundationcenter.org), established in 1956, is a national non-profit organization whose mission is to strengthen the non-profit sector by advancing knowledge about U.S. philanthropy. The center maintains a comprehensive database on U.S. grant makers and their grants. *Fundsnet Services Online* (http://www.fundnetservices.com) is another useful Web site that provides grant seekers with opportunities to obtain information on financial resources. The "Additional Readings" and "Helpful Web Sites" listings at the end of this chapter identify additional sources.

Conclusions

Media specialists must face fiscal issues when dealing with their collections. They must have knowledge relating to budgeting processes and how to request the funds needed to administer effective media center programs. Since it is not possible to purchase all available resources that are desired or needed, alternative methods of obtaining materials should be considered. One means of obtaining use of materials is to subscribe to online electronic resources. With such subscriptions, licenses must be negotiated. Many issues need to be considered when agreeing to licenses. Some issues include who is authorized to access materials, whether remote access outside of a school is needed, and deciding how content of the materials can be used.

In order to make more materials available to their users, some media centers participate in resource sharing, which are generally set up through electronic networks with libraries in their own school district or state, or perhaps with other types of libraries. In this way, they are able to provide their users with materials through interlibrary loan. Other means of obtaining the funds needed for a school media collection include fundraising (sponsoring book fairs or read-a-thons) and writing grants.

Reference

Dickinson, G. (2004). Budgeting as easy as 1-2-3: How to ask for—and get—the money you need. *Library Media Connection, 22*(6), 14–17.

Additional Readings

Anderson, C. (2001). *Write grants get money.* Worthington, OH: Linworth.

Anderson, C. (2002). Write a grant? Me? *Book Report, 21*(1), 15.

Braxton, B. (2006). Bring the books to students with a book fair. *Teacher Librarian, 33*(4), 52–53.

Davis, S. K. (2004). Harnessing the power of parent volunteers: Starting a Friends of the Library group at your school. *Knowledge Quest, 33*(1), 30–31.

Dembowski, S. (2005). Read-a-thons: A new fundraising opportunity. *Library Media Connection, 24*(3), 33.

Hall-Ellis, S. D. & Jerabek, A. (2003). *Grants for school libraries.* Westport, CT: Libraries Unlimited.

Mardis, M. A. (2005). The improving literacy through school libraries program of No Child Left Behind: Tips for writing a winning grant proposal. *Teacher Librarian, 32*(4), 38–40.

Maxwell, D. J. (2005). Money, money, money: Taking the pain out of grant writing. *Teacher Librarian, 32*(3), 16–21.

Nutt, P. (2003). Anatomy of a grant proposal. *Tech Trends, 47*(1), 33–35.

Nutt, P. (2005). Free cash giveaway: A can't-miss guide to writing winning grants. *School Library Journal, 51*(2), 42–44.

Politzer, L. (1999). You've got a friend. *School Library Journal, 45*(4), 30–31.

Running a personalized book fair. *School Librarian's Workshop*, *25*(3), 16.

Tahouri, P. (2005). Winning grants. *Library Media Connection*, *24*(2), 46–47.

Helpful Web Sites

Fernandez, D. (2006). *Welcome to school grants.* Retrieved October 25, 2006, from http://www.schoolgrants.org/welcome.htm

Foundation Center. (2006). *Times have changed.* Retrieved October 25, 2006, from http://foundationcenter.org

Fundsnet Services Online. (2006). Retrieved October 25, 2006, from http://www.fundsnetservices.com

The Laura Bush Foundation for America's Libraries. (n.d.). Retrieved October 25, 2006, from http://www.laurabushfoundation.org

Massachusetts Department of Education. (2004). *Grants for schools: Getting them and using them, a procedural manual.* Retrieved October 25, 2006, from http://finance1.doe.mass.edu/grants/procedure/default.html

SUNLINK (2006). Retrieved October 25, 2006, from http://www.sunlink.ucf.edu

U.S. Department of Education. (n.d.). *Grants & contracts.* Retrieved October 25, 2006, from http://www.ed.gov/fund/landing.jhtml?src=rt

What is INFOhio? (2006). Retrieved October 25, 2006, from http://www.infohio.org/Parent/OutreachKit/Video2005.html

Wisconsin Department of Public Instruction. (n.d.). *What is BadgerLink?* Retrieved October 25, 2006, from http://www.badgerlink.net/about.html

17

Opening, Moving, or Closing the Collection

When student populations shift or there is a change in grade levels served by a school, media specialists respond by creating initial collections, combining collections, or closing a collection. The media center might also be moved to a different location within the same school campus. Each situation presents different demands upon media specialists' knowledge and skills. A media specialist's human-relations skills may be tested in the tensions of these experiences. Emotions can run high when a school is closed or a favorite group or grade level is lost.

Creating Initial Collections

The opening of a new school calls for the creation of an initial collection. When a new building is being planned, various patterns of preparation for the initial collection can occur. The optimal time to begin planning is when the building contract is awarded. In an ideal situation, a media specialist and faculty are hired to plan during the year preceding the opening of the building. This procedure has definite advantages. The media specialist can benefit from participating with faculty members as they identify philosophies and goals, create a curriculum, and develop plans. The media specialist's major responsibility during the year is to ensure that the desired types of learning environments will be ready on opening day. The media specialist must place orders early enough to allow for delivery, processing, and time to make any necessary substitutions. Admittedly, school districts rarely have the financial resources or educational foresight to provide a whole year of planning.

Even if an entire faculty is not engaged in planning during the year prior to opening a school, the collection needs to be ready on opening day. If the school's staff has not been appointed, the responsibility often rests with district-level staff. Those planning the new facility need to be aware of the long-range goals and objectives of the district's educational program and the equipment and materials needed for an initial collection. Planners should design flexibility into plans to accommodate changes that may occur in teaching styles, subjects taught, and the needs of unknown users. An example of such flexibility would be to save a portion of the collection budget so it could be spent by the school media specialist in the first few weeks of the school year when more information about the users of the collection is available.

Districts follow various patterns for handling orders for a new building. Some districts use one-third of the initial collection budget to buy materials to have on opening day. One-third is reserved for recommendations by the principal and professional staff. The remaining third is reserved for orders generated by the media specialist, who works with teachers and students to make selections. Other districts spend the entire first year's budget prior to the opening of the school. When making a budget, a school district must also consider the cost of licensing electronic resources for the collection.

School districts with recent student population growth patterns may have lists of recommendations for the initial collection or have electronic holdings records of such collections. In some cases, these districts are willing to share or sell their lists. This type of list is designed to cover the broad scope needed by teachers and students in widely varying school communities and may be revised annually. You should contact district school media supervisors to determine if such lists exist in their school districts.

Major book jobbers also offer pre-packaged opening-day collections. Even though such a package, or any list developed by other school districts, may not address your school's unique needs, there are some advantages to these packages. Current costs are known, out-of-print titles are excluded, time and effort is saved by not having to consider unavailable items, the media specialist can add additional materials, and the printout of online orders saves time. Such a list, however, has disadvantages. Direct-order and standing-order items will not be covered, items requiring licensing will not be included, and the unique needs of the school may not be met.

General guidelines about the number of items that should be in an initial collection may also be available from the state's school library media consultant or state school library association. These guidelines may outline the formats, as well as stages of development, from the initial collection to one considered to be excellent.

By using selection aids, one can identify specific titles for a collection. Useful sources include *Children's Catalog* (H. W. Wilson), *Middle and Junior High School Library Collection* (H. W. Wilson), and *Senior High School Library Collection* (H. W. Wilson). Additional helpful resources can be found in the Appendix, "Resources." The broad scope and coverage of these tools help media specialists identify titles to match the wide range of information needs that will be experienced during the opening days of a collection.

Shifting or Moving Collections

Sometimes it becomes necessary to shift or move entire collections. This might occur because of redesigning, remodeling, simply outgrowing space for the present collection, or relocating the entire media center. Moving or shifting a collection is no easy task. Planning is essential in order to avoid many frustrations that can result from such a move. The following suggestions can help you successfully move a collection with a minimum number of problems:

1. Weed the collection before making a move or shift. You have no reason to move books that are not being used.

2. Read the shelves to ensure that all the books are in order.

3. Measure the floor, wall, and shelf space that will be available for the collection.

4. Make a paper model (to scale) of the media center to which you are moving. Be sure to draw in windows, furniture, and cabinets. Also indicate the electrical outlets.

5. Measure and log the amount of space needed for each section of books (as they presently line the shelves). Write in the sections on your paper model, making certain you leave adequate space for each section.

6. Choose sturdy boxes that are not too large for packing the books. Books are heavy, and you may need to move some of them yourself.

7. Pack boxes in reverse order beginning with the last book on each shelf. When you unpack, the books will be in shelf order.

8. In large letters, label the boxes on the side, identifying which books are in each box. For instance, the easy picture books might be labeled "E AAR-ADA." Consider color-coding boxes, using different color marking pens—blue for books that go in the easy section, yellow for fiction, green for nonfiction, and red for computer equipment.

9. Number the boxes and create a database that includes what is inside each box.

10. Put all unpacking supplies (scissors, utility knives, tape, pens, cleaning rags, and your Rolodex of phone numbers) in one box. Label it, "Supplies—Open Me First."

11. Have the movers place all the boxes (in numerical order) near the bookcases where they will be shelved to avoid overlooking a box. If the labels are color-coded it will help the movers quickly locate the part of the library where the boxes should be placed.

12. Choose your "un-packers" carefully and watch closely over their work.

13. Do not fill all the shelves. Leave at least one-quarter of each shelf to allow for expansion.

14. If space allows, do not use the bottom shelves. It is difficult to read the labels on the spines on the bottom shelves. Also, this will again leave room for expansion in individual sections.

15. Do not forget to plan for your online collection as well. Plan the location of computers so they are accessible to electrical outlets and away from the heavy traffic areas. Be sure adequate work surfaces are available next to each computer.

16. Have technicians install and test the equipment, including the computers that house the circulation system.

If these steps are followed when moving a collection, it should avoid many possible problems, but you should also remember to "expect the unexpected" and not get frustrated with situations that are out of your control.

Closing Collections

When schools are closed, consolidated, or have attendance districts re-organized, the full impact might not be felt until the formal announcement is made. Someone should be responsible for determining the procedures for removing materials. Media specialists must be involved in the planning to avoid confusion and inefficiency.

Consolidation and reorganization of attendance districts can be "hot" issues calling for special handling by the media specialist. Knowledge about the situation, diplomacy, and tact will help. Perhaps the loss can be turned into a gain for other schools in the district. Planning is the key factor in retaining items that a collection needs, while also preparing for the transfer of other items. Send information about available items, with plans for their transfer, to the receiving school. Assess each of the newly formed collections in terms of their weaknesses and strengths in meeting the new demands.

When schools close, answers to the following questions can guide the planning process. What will the disposition of the materials, equipment, and furniture be? What legal guidelines are there for the disposition of materials and equipment? Are there local constraints? What are the closing deadlines? Will extra help be available?

Once the target date is known, you should create a timeline with specific goals. This information can be posted to alert users and staff so they will be aware of when the media center plans to curtail services. Teachers who are moving to other schools can help you by indicating the titles they want available in the other schools. These items should be allocated first so they can be processed into the collections.

You should refer to your policies to see if there are criteria that might relate to the closing of a collection. For instance, does the policy on gift materials provide for transferring the materials to another school? You also need to check to determine if there are additional materials that other regulations or agreements cover. This should be done before deciding on how to dispose of items.

You can provide a list of remaining materials in your media center and distribute the list to other schools in the district so media specialists can request specific titles. Any items that are not requested will need to be stored, distributed, or discarded. Distribution possibilities include storing materials at an exchange center where they can be examined, or donating the materials to other agencies serving children, such as youth centers. Policies within the district will govern how you can disperse materials; the district may grant approval for sale to other library collections or to individuals.

Conclusions

In some instances a collection may need to be opened, moved, or closed. In each case, a media specialist will need to follow specific guidelines, as well as be aware of the emotions that may accompany the shifting of a grade level to another school or closing down a school. Early preparations for creating a new collection can make it possible for the media center to be open on the first day that a new school begins operation. Useful selection aids can assist in the selection of an initial media center collection. If a grade level leaves a school or a new grade is added to a school, the collection will need to be assessed and adjusted to meet student and curriculum needs. Following specific guidelines and tips for moving an entire collection can save time and prevent much frustration. When closing an entire collection, it is essential that media specialists follow any existing policies or regulations for the disposition and disposal of resources.

Additional Readings

Habich, E. C. (1998). *Moving library collections: A management handbook*. Westport, CT: Greenwood.

Mitchell, L. (2002). Transformation of a school library media center. *Knowledge Quest*, *31*(1), 9–10.

Taylor, K. (2000). Reflections on opening a new library media center. *Florida Media Quarterly*, *25*(4), 8–9.

Wilson, L. (2004). Bringing vision to practice: Planning and provisioning the new library resource center. *Teacher Librarian*, *32*(1), 23–27.

Appendix: Resources

This list identifies books, journals, and electronic sources useful in dealing with collection matters. In January 2007 books began to be assigned ISBN numbers containing thirteen digits, instead of ten. When available, both the ten-digit numbers and the thirteen-digit numbers are included in this listing. The newer, longer number is preceded with a "13." It should be used when possible for ordering purposes or you may want to include both numbers. For additional resources, see the listings at the end of chapters.

1-2-3-4 for the Show: A Guide to Small-Cast One-Act Plays. Lewis W. Heniford. Lanham, MD: Scarecrow, 1999. ISBN 0-81083-600-9 (vol. 2).

    A guide to both published and unpublished plays, indexed by author, cast size/gender, and title. Provides bibliographic information and genre. Describes how to obtain scripts through publishers or library collections.

A to Zoo: Subject Access to Children's Picture Books. 7th ed. Carolyn W. Lima and John A. Lima. Westport, CT: Libraries Unlimited, 2005. ISBN 1-59158-232-6, ISBN 13 978-1-59158-232-8.

    Identifies more than 22,000 titles (fiction and nonfiction) for preschoolers through second graders. Five sections: subject headings, subject guide, bibliographic guide, title index, and illustrator index.

Abridged Readers' Guide to Periodical Literature. See *Readers' Guide to Periodical Literature.*

Accelerated Reader. Advantage Learning Systems, Inc. Wisconsin Rapids, WI: Renaissance Learning, 2005. ISBN 1-59455-200-2, ISBN 13 978-1-59455-200-7.

    Reading comprehension software, reading ability testing software for elementary to high school level. Two CD-ROMs. Includes: one software manual, installation guide, and four reading practice lists.

Accessible Libraries on Campus: A Practical Guide for the Creation of Disability-Friendly Libraries. Tom McNulty, ed. Chicago, IL: Association of College and Research Libraries, 1999. ISBN 0-8389-8035-X, ISBN 13 978-0-8389-8035-4.

    Focuses on academic libraries but is equally appropriate for other institutions. Covers creating a Web page accessible to the blind and visually impaired. Has a directory of resources.

Adaptive Technologies for Learning & Work Environments, 2nd ed. Joseph Lazzaro. Chicago, IL: American Library Association, 2001. ISBN: 0-8389-0804-7, ISBN 13 978-0-8389-0804-4.

Comprehensive coverage of personal computer hardware basics, keyboard commands and latest technology for persons with vision impairments, persons who are deaf or hard of hearing, persons with motor disabilities, persons with speech disabilities, and persons with learning disabilities. Includes information about accessing the Internet and Intranets and funding adaptive technology.

ALAN Review. Athens, GA: Assembly on Literature for Adolescents, National Council of Teachers of English, 1979–. ISSN 0882-2840.

Three times per year. Reviews new hardback and paperback titles for adolescents. Subscription: ALAN Membership, payable to ALAN/NCTE, P.O. Box 10427, Largo, FL 33773. (http://scholar.lib.vt.edu/ejournals/ALAN)

American Book Publishing Record. New Providence, NJ: R. R. Bowker, 1960–. ISSN 0002-7707.

Monthly. Related Work: *American Book Publishing Record Cumulative*, 1984– (published annually). Compiles titles cataloged by the Library of Congress. Dewey classification arrangement. Provides full cataloging data, LC and DDC numbers, subject headings, and price. Author index.

American Foundation for the Blind.

Leading publisher in the field of blindness and visual impairment. Produces books, journals, videos, and electronic materials. Information for students, professionals, researchers, and blind and visually impaired people. (http://www.afb.org/Section.asp?SectionID=46)

The American Hero in Children's Literature: A Standards-Based Approach. Carol M. Butzow and John W. Butzow. Westport, CT: Greenwood Publishing, 2005. ISBN 1-59469-004-9, ISBN 13 978-1-59469-004-4, ISBN 0-58525-245-9 (electronic bk.).

Features more than thirty books exploring the way heroes have influenced American history, the American way of life, the lives of the people, and principles upon which the culture has developed.

American Journal of Health Education. Reston, VA: American Alliance for Health, Physical Education, Recreation and Dance, 1991–. ISSN 1932-5037.

Bimonthly. Subscription: American Alliance for Health, Physical Education, Recreation and Dance, 1900 Association Drive, Reston, VA 20191. (http://www.aahperd.org/aahe/template.cfm?template=ajhe_main.html)

American Music Teacher. Cincinnati, OH: Music Teachers National Association, 1951–. ISSN 003-0112.

Bimonthly. Covers earliest music history to the latest developments in music technology. Features articles on teaching methods and techniques. Reviews teaching materials, music publications, videocassettes, music software, and other new technology as well as issues and trends. (http://www.mtna.org/amtsi.htm)

American Printing House for the Blind.
"The world's largest source for adapted educational and daily living products—since 1858." (from Web site: http://www.aph.org/)

American Reference Books Annual. Westport, CT: Libraries Unlimited, 1970–. ISSN 0065-9959. Also ISBN 1-59158-056-0, ISBN-13 978-1-59158-056-0. Also *ARBA.* Available at http://www.greenwood.com/catalog/LU0560.aspx
Reviews reference books published in the United States and Canada. Author, title, and subject index.

Around the World with Historical Fiction and Folklore: Highly Recommended and Award-Winning Books, Grades K-8. Beth Bartleson Zarian. Lanham, MD: Scarecrow, 2004. ISBN: 0-8108-4816-3, ISBN 13 978-0-8108-4816-0.
Guide to approximately 800 highly recommended and award-winning historical fiction books for K-8.

ASHA Leader. Rockville, MD: American Speech-Language-Hearing Association, 1996–. ISSN 1085-9586. Also The *ASHA Leader.* Available at http://www.asha.org/about/publications/leader-online/
Bimonthly. Reports on emerging issues and news of the profession. Subscription: *The ASHA Leader*, 10801 Rockville Pike, Rockville, MD 20852.

Assistive Technology Journal. Jeff Jutai, ed. Arlington, VA: Publishing body: RESNA (AT Network). ISSN 1040-0435. Available at http://atnet.org/news/2005/atjv109-0401.htm
Semiannually. Rehabilitation Engineering and Assistive Technology Society of North America. Seeks to foster communication among researchers, developers, clinicians, educators, consumers, and others working in all aspects of the assistive technology arena. Subscription: RESNA 1700 N. Moore Street, Suite 1540 Arlington, VA 22209-1903. (http://www.resna.org/ProfResources/Publications/ATJournal/Subscribe.php)

AV Market Place: *The Complete Business Directory of Audio / Video.* Medford, NJ: Information Today, 1989–. ISSN 1044-0445.
Annual. Lists addresses and services of producers, distributors, production services, manufacturers, and equipment dealers.

AV Market Place, 2006: The Complete Business Directory of Products and Services for the Audio / Video Industry. Medford, NJ: Information Today, ISBN 1-57387-245-8, ISBN 13 978-1-57387-245-4.
Lists addresses and services of producers, distributors, production services, manufacturers, and equipment dealers.

Best Books for Children: Preschool Through Grade 6. 8th ed. Catherine Barr and John T. Gillespie. Westport, CT: Libraries Unlimited, 2005. Series title: Children's and Young Adult Literature Reference Series. ISBN 1-59158-085-4, ISBN 13 978-1-59158-085-0.
Includes brief annotations for 25,000 titles that had two or three recommendations in leading journals. Helps build collections by topic. Provides bibliographic and order information and citations to reviews. Indexes by author and illustrator, title, grade level, and subject.

Best Books for High School Readers: Grades 9–12. John Thomas Gillespie and Catherine Barr. Westport, CT: Libraries Unlimited, 2004. Series title: Children's and Young Adult Literature Reference Series. ISBN 1-59158-084-6, ISBN 13 978-1-59158-084-3.

Easy-to-navigate resource covering more than 12,000 titles. Includes annotations and plot summaries. Enables the evaluation of teen literature collections and assists in the creation of thematic and genre-oriented reading lists.

Best Books for High School Readers, Supplement to the First Edition: Grades 9–12. John Thomas Gillespie and Catherine Barr. Westport, CT: Libraries Unlimited, 2006. Series title: Children's and Young Adult Literature Reference Series. ISBN 1-59158-410-8.

Includes annotations and plot summaries. Enables the evaluation of teen literature collections and assists in the creation of thematic and genre-oriented reading lists.

Best Books for Middle School and Junior High Readers: Grades 6–9. John Thomas Gillespie and Catherine Barr. Westport, CT: Libraries Unlimited, 2004. ISBN 1-59158-083-8, ISBN 13 978-1-59158-083-8.

Evaluates teen literature and enables creation of thematic and genre-oriented reading lists.

Best Books for Middle School and Junior High Readers, Supplement to the First Edition: Grades 6–9. John Thomas Gillespie and Catherine Barr. Westport, CT: Libraries Unlimited, 2006. Series title: Children's and Young Adult Literature Reference Series. ISBN 1-59158-411-6, ISBN 13 978-1-59158-411-7. (U.S. Market)

Evaluates teen literature and enables creation of thematic and genre-oriented reading lists.

Best Books for Young Adults. 2nd ed. Betty B. Carter, Sally Estes, and Linda Waddle. Chicago, IL: Young Adult Library Services Association, 2000. ISBN 0-83893-501-X, ISBN 13 978-0-8389-3501-9.

Provides annotations for books published between 1966 and 1999. Organized by more than twenty-five themes. Lists formatted so they can be reproduced for handouts.

The Best of Latino Heritage, 1996–2002: A Guide to the Best Juvenile Books about Latino People. Isabel Schon. Lanham, MD: Scarecrow, 2003. ISBN: 0-8108-4669-1, ISBN 13 978-0-8108-4669-2.

Lists English in-print books for students in K-12 published in U.S. Chapters explore specific Latino countries and cultures, people, history, art, political, social, and economic problems of Latin America and Spain.

BIBZ Selection Tool. Brodart Co. at http://www.books.brodart.com/schools.htm

Web-based service for collection development and ordering. Allows user to search and access relevant titles, build customized bibliographies, select best items, and order online. Includes free full-text reviews from *Kirkus Reviews*. (http://www.books.brodart.com/onlinetools.htm)

Black Books Galore! Guide to More Great African American Children's Books. Donna Rand and Toni Trent Parker. New York: John Wiley, 2001. ISBN 0-471-37525-X, ISBN 13 978-0-471-37525-8, ISBN 0585238944 (electronic bk.).

Features 400 titles and reading plans for historical events, major holidays and seasons. Descriptions of an additional 200 recommendations. Easy-to-find listings organized by age level.

Black Books Galore! Guide to Great African American Children's Books about Boys. Donna Rand and Toni Trent Parker. New York: John Wiley & Sons, 2001. ISBN 0-471-43718-2, ISBN 13 978-0-471-43718-5.

Descriptions of over 600 books. Hundreds of young black heroes, heroines, and positive role models of every age in every category, including board books, story and picture books, fiction, nonfiction, poetry, history, biography, and fables.

Black Books Galore! Guide to Great African American Children's Books about Girls. Donna Rand and Toni Trent Parker. New York: John Wiley, 2001. ISBN 0-471-43719-0, ISBN 13 978-0-471-43719-2.

Listings organized by age level and indexed by title, topic, author, and illustrator. Reflections from famous public figures about their favorite childhood books.

Book Bridges for ESL Students: Using Young Adult and Children's Literature to Teach ESL. Suzanne Elizabeth Reid. Lanham, MD: Scarecrow, 2002. ISBN 0-8108-4213-0, ISBN 13 978-0-8108-4213-7.

Includes basic principles of teaching ESL students; a rationale for using literature in the ESL classroom; using a single work of literature for various activities; the use of picture books for basic-level learners; using fiction and nonfiction works to teach history, math, and science; using multicultural literature; and teaching special populations. Bibliography of recommended literature, activities, suggested materials for classroom use, and lesson plans.

Book Links: Connecting Books, Libraries, and Classrooms. Chicago, IL: American Library Association, 1991–. ISSN 1055-4742.

Six times per year. Discusses old and new titles. Includes "Book Strategies," "Classroom Connections," "Visual Links," "The Inside Story," and "Poetry" columns. Subscription: American Library Association, 50 E. Huron Street, Chicago, IL 60611. (http://www.ala.org/ala/productsandpublications/periodicals/booklinks/booklinks.htm)

Book Review Digest. Bronx, New York: H. W. Wilson, 1905–. ISSN 0006-7326.

Monthly (except February and July). Quarterly and annual accumulations. Available on CD-ROM and online. *Book Review Digest Plus.* Available at http://www.hwwilson.com/Databases/brdig.htm

The Book Review Index. Beverly Baer, ed. Farmington Hills, MI: Gale, 1965–. ISSN 0524-0581.(Formerly *The Book Report*).

Three times a year. Provides reviews of books, books on tape, and electronic media from a wide range of popular, academic, and professional sources. Subscription: (http://www.galegroup.com)

Bookbird: A Journal of International Children's Literature. Toronto, ON, Canada: International Board on Books for Young People, 1962–. ISSN 0006-7377.

Quarterly. Covers books of international interest and reviews of selection tools. Subscription: University of Toronto Press — Journals Division, 5201 Dufferin Street, Toronto, ON, Canada, M3H 5T8. (http://www.utpjournals.com/bookbird/bookbird.html)

Booklist. Chicago, IL: American Library Association, 1905–. ISSN 0006-7385. Also *Booklist Online* (http://www.booklistonline.com/).

Twice a month (22/year). Reviews current books, videos, and software on regular basis. Reviews foreign language materials and materials on special topics in irregular columns. Provides monthly author/title index and semiannual cumulative indexes. Includes *Reference Books Bulletin* with reviews of encyclopedias, dictionaries, atlases, and other books using a continuous revision policy. Subscription: Kable Fulfillment Services, 308 Hitt St., Mt. Morris, IL 61054-7564. (http://www.ala.org/ala/booklist/subscribe/subscribe.htm)

Books for the Teen Age. New York Public Library, Committee on Books for Young Adults, 1929–. ISSN 0068-0192.

Annual. Describes about 1,000 titles that appeal to teenagers. Subscription: Office of Branch Libraries, New York Public Library, 455 Fifth Avenue, New York, NY 10016. (http://teenlink.nypl.org/bta1.cfm)

BooksInPrint.com

An index to over 6.1 million U.S. book, audiobook, and video titles. (http://www.bowker.com/catalog/000005.htm)

Books in Print. New Providence, NJ: R. R. Bowker, 1947–. ISSN 0068-0214.

Annual. Serves as the definitive bibliographic resource with more than 1,879,000 titles of the full range of books currently published or distributed in the U.S. Related works include *Subject Guide to Books in Print, Books in Print Supplement, Forthcoming Books, Publishers, Distributors and Wholesalers of the United States*. Also *Books In Print ON DISC*. Various titles available in print, CD-ROM, and online. (http://www.booksinprint.com) *Books in Print Supplement*. ISSN 0000-0310. See *Books in Print*.

Books Out Loud: Bowker's Guide to Audiobooks. New Providence, NJ: R. R. Bowker, 1985-. ISSN 0000-1805.

Annual in two volumes. Covers more than 85,500 audiocassettes. Indexes include title, authors, reader/performer, producer, and distributor.

Books Out Loud 2006: Bowker's Guide to Audiobooks. Bowker Staff, eds. New Providence, NJ: R. R. Bowker, 2006. ISBN 13 978-0-8352-4789-4.

In two volumes. Formerly *Words on Cassette*. Over 115,000 titles by more than 80,000 authors. Listings include reader's name, price, running time, number of cassettes or CDs, content summary, release date, and abridged or unabridged version.

The Bowker Annual Library and Book Trade Almanac. Medford, NJ: Information Today, 1956–. ISSN 0068-0540.

Includes research and statistics such as average prices of books; news about legislation, associations, and grant-making agencies; lists of distinguished books; and directory information.

Bowker's Complete Video Directory. New York: R. R. Bowker, 1988–. ISSN 1051-290X.

Annual. Identifies more than 169,000 videos, in every format available, for entertainment and/or education.

Bowker's Complete Video Directory, 2006, Vols. 1–4. Bowker Staff, ed. New Providence, NJ: R. R. Bowker, 2005. ISBN 0-8352-4799-6, ISBN 13 978-0-8352-4799-3.

250,000 selections in four volumes. Indexes include title, genre, cast/director, and others. Coverage includes foreign, Spanish-language, children's, silent, and feature films.

Braille Book Review. Edmund O'Reilly, ed. Washington, DC: U.S. Library of Congress, The National Service for the Blind and Physically Handicapped (NLS), 1932–. ISSN 0006-873X.

Bimonthly. Free to blind and physically handicapped individuals. Describes books for children and adults. Provides title, order code, author, number of volumes, and date of original print edition. Indexed monthly and annually. Includes news of developments and activities in library services. Identifies new Braille books and magazines. Address: U.S. Library of Congress, National Library Service for the Blind and Physically Handicapped, 1291 Taylor Street, NW, Washington, DC 20011. (http://www.loc.gov/nls/bbr.html)

Building an ESL Collection for Young Adults: A Bibliography of Recommended Fiction and Nonfiction for School and Public Libraries. Laura Hibbets McCaffery. Westport, CT: Greenwood, 1998. ISBN 0-31329-937-4, ISBN 13 978-0-313-29937-7.

Describes titles in a wide range of subjects, grades 5 through adult. Identifies reading level, interest level, and other characteristics important for the audience. Useful indexes including author, title, and ethnic group. Appendix of nonprint materials, as well as Internet sites.

Building Electronic Library Collections: The Essential Guide to Selection Criteria and Core Subject Collections. Diane Kovacs. New York: Neal-Schuman, 2000. ISBN 1-555-70362-3, ISBN 13 978-1-55570-362-2.

Covers collecting, evaluating, and organizing Web-based information. Recommends specific sites with major subject areas. Contains annotated general and major subject webliographies and examples of information mining. Includes a section on resources to support K-12 education.

Bulletin of the Center for Children's Books. Baltimore, MD: The Johns Hopkins University Press, 1945–. (Corporate author: University of Illinois at Urbana-Champaign, Graduate School of Library and Information Science). ISSN 0008-9036.

Monthly. Summaries and critical evaluations of newly published and forthcoming books for children. Uses codes to indicate level of recommendation. Author/title index in each volume. Subscription: The Johns Hopkins University Press, 2715 North Charles St., Baltimore, MD, 21218. (http://bccb.lis.uiuc.edu/subscrip.html)

Canadian Books in Print: Author and Title Index. Toronto: University of Toronto Press, 1975–. ISSN 0068-8398.

Annual. Supplemented quarterly by *Canadian Books in Print: Update on Fiche*, 1979–. Includes English and French language titles published by predominantly English language Canadian publishers.

Captioned Media Program. National Association of the Deaf, 1447 E. Main St., Spartanburg, SC 29307. 800-237-6213 (voice) 800 237-6819 (TTY). Also *CMP Media Program* (online), *CMP En Español* (online), and *Captioned Media Program 2001–2002 Catalog.* (Formerly *Captioned Films/Videos Program*).

Offers loans of films, videos, and other teaching materials through this service of the U.S. Department of Education. (http://www.cfv.org)

CD-ROM Reference Materials for Children and Young Adults: A Critical Guide for School and Public Libraries. Stephen Del Vecchio. Englewood, CO: Libraries Unlimited, 2000. ISBN 1-56308-711-1, ISBN 13 978-1-56308-711-0.

Evaluates new children's references available on CD-ROM. Considers usability, design, and extra features.

CD-ROM Technology: A Manual for Librarians and Educators. Catherine Mambretti. Jefferson, NC: McFarland, 1998. ISBN 0-78640-501-5, ISBN 13 978-0-7864-0501-5.

Discusses criteria, installation, copyright issues, licensing, maintenance, and troubleshooting.

A Child Goes Forth (A Curriculum Guide for Preschool Children). 10th ed. Barbara J. Taylor. Upper Saddle River, NJ: Prentice Hall, 2004. ISBN 0-1304-8116-5, ISBN 13 978-0-130-48116-0.

Describes criteria for selecting materials for young children organized around areas of experience critical to a child's development. A relaxed, unstructured, but carefully planned atmosphere is emphasized, along with respect for individuality.

Children and Books. 8th ed. Zena Sutherland. Reading, MA: Addison-Wesley, 1997. ISBN 0-673-46357-5, ISBN 13 978-0-673-46357-9.

Discusses children's literature including sources of information for teachers and media specialists.

Children's and Young Adult Literature by Latino Writers: A Guide for Librarians, Teachers, Parents, and Students. Sherry York. Worthington, OH: Linworth, 2002. ISBN 1-58683-062-7, ISBN 13 978-1-58683-062-5.

Identifies literature written by Latino authors that is targeted to youth. Bibliographic information and list of additional resources provided. Genres include novels, chapter books, short stories, folklore, drama, poetry, and nonfiction.

Children's and Young Adult Literature by Native Americans: A Concept Guide for Librarians, Teachers, Parents, and Students. Sherry York. Worthington, OH: Linworth, 2003. ISBN: 1-58683-119-4, ISBN 13 978-1-58683-119-6.

Covers titles in print for fiction, folklore, drama, poetry, and non-fiction. Useful Web sites and organizations identified. Thorough index includes tribes and translators.

Children's Book Review Index. Detroit, MI: Gale Research, 1976–. ISSN 0147-5681.

Annual. Provides review citations for books recommended for children through age 10. Illustrator and title indexes.

Children's Books from Other Countries. Carl M. Tomlinson, ed. Lanham, MD: Scarecrow Press, 1998. ISBN 0-81083-4X7-2, ISBN 13 978-0-8108-3447-7.

Provides annotations for 724 titles from 29 countries. Offers suggestions for use in curriculum. Includes listings for the Hans Christian Andersen and Mildred Batchelder awards.

Children's Books in Print. New York: R. R. Bowker, 1969–. ISSN 0069-3480.

Annual. Two volumes. Related work: *Subject Guide to Children's Books in Print.* ISSN 0000-0167. Provides bibliographic and ordering information and uses Sears subject headings, supplemented by LC headings. Excludes textbooks.

Children's Books in Print 2007. New Providence, NJ: R. R. Bowker, 2006–. ISBN: 0-8352-4850-X, ISBN 13 978-0-8352-4850-1.

Two-volume set. Authoritative and unbiased. Volume 1 contains a title index of more than 385,637 books from over 21,622 U.S. publishers. Volume 2 is the author and illustrator index, which features more than 207,237 contributors and also complete contact information for all publishers, distributors, and wholesalers listed in *Children's Books In Print.*

Children's Catalog. 19th ed. New York: H. W. Wilson, 2006. ISBN 0-8242-1073-5.

Three annual supplements. Covers materials for pre-school through grade 6. Uses abridged Dewey Decimal Classification. Provides bibliographic and order information, recommended grade level, subject headings, and descriptive/critical annotations. Index lists authors, subjects, titles, and analytical references to composite works. Also available at http://www.hwwilson.com/print/childcat.cfm

Children's Magazine Guide: Subject Index to Children's Magazines and Web Sites. Westport, CT: Greenwood, 1948–. ISSN 0743-9873. Also *CMG Online* at http://www.childrensmag.com

Nine issues per year with an annual accumulation. Indexes more than sixty children's magazines. Identifies wide range of recent articles and Web sites. Provides name of article, author, magazine, issue date, and number of pages.

Choice Magazine: Current Reviews for Academic Libraries. Middletown, CT: Association of College and Research Libraries, 1963–. ISSN 0009-4978. Also *Choice Reviews Online* at (http://www.ala.org/ala/acrl/acrlpubs/choice/home.htm).

Monthly (except bimonthly July/August). Related works: *Choice Reviews on Cards.* Reviews periodicals, books, nonprint media (films, audiotapes, videos, slides, microforms, software, CD-ROMs, Web sites, and filmstrips). Annual cumulated index published separately. Subscription:

P.O. Box 141, Annapolis Junction, MD 20701, Tel: 240-646-7027 or choic-esubscriptions@pmds.com.

CM Magazine: Canadian Review of Materials. Winnipeg, MB Canada: The Manitoba Library Association, 1971–. ISSN 1201-9364.

Biweekly online. Electronic reviewing journal. Reviews books, videotapes, audiotapes, and CD-ROMs. Includes news, feature articles, interviews, and Web reviews. No charge for reading Web site or receiving their e-mail version, but they ask regular readers for annual contribution to help defray costs. Postal address: CM, 167 Houde Dr., Winnipeg MB R3V 1C6 Canada. (http://www.umanitoba.ca/cm)

Collection Assessment and Management for School Libraries: Preparing for Cooperative Collection Development. Debra E. Kachel. Westport, CT: Greenwood, 1997. ISBN 0-31329-853-8, ISBN 13 978-0-313-29853-0.

Contains the Ephrata Area School District (Pennsylvania) "Written Collection Policy Documents" including copyright, selection, acceptable use, and curriculum mapping. This guide provides new tools and techniques for analyzing, assessing, and managing collections, including "ready-to-use" collection data-gathering forms and collection assessment and analysis worksheets.

The Complete Directory of Large Print Books and Serials, 2006. New Providence, NJ: R. R. Bowker, 2006. ISBN 0-8352-4792-9, ISBN 13 978-0-8352-4792-4.

Bibliographic information on over 22,500 titles. Lists all active adult, juvenile, and textbook titles. Indicates the type size, physical size of each book, and contact information of publishers, wholesalers, and distributors. Nine indexes including title, author, general reading subject, textbook subject, children's subject, serial subject, and serial title.

Computers in Libraries: Complete Coverage of Library Information Technology. Medford, NJ: Information Today, 1981–. ISSN 1041-7915.

Ten times per year. Carries news items and general technical articles designed to provide practical information. Recent topics include e-books, licensing, virtual libraries, fundraising, and Web designing. Subscription: Information Today, Inc., 143 Old Marlton Pike, Medford, NJ 08055-8750 or custserv@infotoday.com

Connecting Boys with Books: What Libraries Can Do. Michael Sullivan. Chicago, IL: American Library Association, 2003. ISBN 0-8389-0849-7, ISBN 13 978-0-8389-0849-5.

Practical ideas, building on the unique developmental needs and interests, to connect boys with books.

Connecting Libraries with Classrooms: The Curricular Roles of the Media Specialist. Kay Bishop. Worthington, OH: Linworth, 2003. ISBN 1-58683-061-9.

Provides media specialists with guidelines to help them assume active roles in school library media centers. Includes collaboration, subject areas, special groups of students, and educational trends.

Connecting with Reluctant Teen Readers: Tips, Titles, and Tools. Patrick Jones, Maureen L. Hartman, and Patricia Taylor. New York: Neal-Schuman, 2006. ISBN: 1-55570-571-5, ISBN 13 978-1-55570-571-8.

List of over 600 books, series, and magazines with tips on types of books that will entice teens to read.

The Consumer Information Catalog. Washington, DC: Consumer Information Center, General Services Administration, 1977–. Available at http://www.pueblo.gsa.gov/catalog.pdf

Quarterly. Free. Subscription: Consumer Information Center-R, P.O. Box 100, Pueblo, CO 81002. (http://www.pueblo.gsa.gov)

Consumer Reports. Yonkers, NY: Consumers Union of the United States, 1942–. ISSN 0010-7174.

Monthly (December issue is annual buying guide issue). Provides evaluative comparisons of equipment including emerging technologies. Available online. Subscription address: Consumer Reports, P.O. Box 53029, Boulder, CO 80322. (http://www.consumerreports.org)

The Coretta Scott King Awards Book 1970–2004. 3rd ed. Henrietta M. Smith, ed. Chicago, IL: American Library Association, 2004. ISBN: 0-8389-3540-0, ISBN 13 978-0-8389-3540-8.

Provides annotation and biographical information about works by African American authors and illustrators for the designated award or honor books. Includes example of each winning illustration.

Creating a Virtual Library: A How-to-Do-It Manual. No. 91. Frederick Stielow, ed. New York: Neal-Schuman, 1999. ISBN 1-55570-346-1, ISBN 13 978-1-55570-346-2.

Provides practical guidance for designing, managing, developing policies, and selecting virtual resources.

Critical Handbook of Children's Literature. 8th ed. Rebecca J. Lukens. Boston, MA: Allyn & Bacon, 2007. ISBN 0-205-49218-5, ISBN 13 978-0-205-49218-3.

Discusses the literary elements of children's literature and facilitates use of all genres. Provides sound criteria for assessing children's books. Includes a focus on multiculturalism, a glossary of literary terms, and useful appendixes.

Crossing Boundaries with Children's Books. Doris Gebel, ed. Lanham, MD: Scarecrow, 2006. ISBN: 0-8108-5203-9, ISBN 13 978-0-8108-5203-7.

Sponsored by the United States Board on Books for Young People. Includes bibliographical references and indexes.

Culturally Diverse Videos, Audios, and CD-ROMs for Children and Young Adults. Irene Wood, ed. New York: Neal-Schuman, 1999. ISBN 1-55570-377-1, ISBN 13 978-1-55570-377-6.

Recommends over 1,000 multicultural titles, including African American, Asian, Latino, Native American, Arab, Jewish, Cajun, and various European American videos, audiocassettes, and compact discs. Grouped by age and by subject matter. Lists multicultural and foreign language CD-ROMS. Provides bibliographic information, list price, and suggested audience.

Developing Library and Information Center Collections. 5th ed. G. Edward Evans and Margaret Zarnosky Saponaro. Westport, CT: Libraries Unlimited, 2005. ISBN 1-59158-219-9, ISBN 13 978-1-59158-219-9.

Provides a comprehensive overview (including needs assessment, development policies, the selection process, an overview of publishing, print, and electronic serials, other electronic materials, government information, audiovisual materials, acquisitions, distributors and vendors, fiscal management, de-selection, collection evaluation, resource sharing, collection protection, legal issues, censorship, and intellectual freedom, with focus on the issues and processes of collection development.

Directory of Video, Computer and Audio Visual Products. (Former title: Directory of Video, Multimedia, and Audio-Visual Products). Fairfax, VA: International Communications Industries Association, 1953-. ISSN 0884-2124.

Provides photographs and specifications for video, projection systems, accessories, audiovisual products. Includes glossary, membership directory, indexes by product, company, and ICIA directory.

Education: A Guide to Reference and Information Sources. 2nd ed. Nancy P. O'Brien, ed. Reference Sources in Social Sciences Series. Englewood, CO: Libraries Unlimited, 2000. ISBN 1-56308-626-3, ISBN 13 978-1-56308-626-7, ISBN 0585333629 (electronic bk.).

Annotations describe sources in educational technology, multilingual/multicultural education, curriculum, instruction, content areas, educational research, and others. Author, title, and subject index.

Educational Leadership. Alexandria, VA: Association for Supervision and Curriculum Development, 1943–. ISSN 0013-1784. Also available at http://www.ascd.org/portal/site/ascd/menuitem. a4dbd0f2c4f9b94cdeb3ffdb62108a0c/

Eight times a year. Online version has selected full-length articles and several abstracts of articles. Reviews professional books. Subscription address: ASCD, 1703 N. Beauregard Street, Alexandria, VA 22311. (http://www.ascd.org/pubs/el/elintro.html)

Educational Media and Technology Yearbook. Vol. 32. 2007. Michael Orey, V. J. McClendon, and Robert Maribe Branch. Westport, CT: Libraries Unlimited, 2007. ISBN 1-59158-442-6, ISBN 13 978-1-59158-442-1.

Published annually in cooperation with, and cosponsored by the Association for Educational Communications and Technology and the American Society for Training and Development, Media Division. Educators Guides (annuals) available from Educators Progress Service, 214 Center Street, Randolph, WI 53956. Describes current developments and trends in the field of instructional technology. Highlights the major trends of the previous year and advances in online learning. It identifies instructional technology-related organizations and graduate programs across North America. Includes mediagraphy of journals, books, ERIC documents, journal articles, and nonprint resources. It identifies instructional technology-related organizations and graduate programs across North America. See also *FreeTeachingAids.com* at http://www.freeteachingaids.com/index.html

Titles include:

Elementary Teachers Guide to FREE Curriculum Materials

Middle School Teachers Guide to FREE Curriculum Materials

Secondary Teachers Guide to FREE Curriculum Materials

Educators Guide to FREE Videotapes Elementary / Middle School Edition

Educators Guide to FREE Videotapes Secondary Edition

Educators Guide to FREE Films, Filmstrips, and Slides

Educators Guide to FREE Internet Resources-Elementary / Middle School Edition

Educators Guide to FREE Internet Resources-Secondary Edition

Educators Guide to FREE Science Materials

Educators Guide to FREE Social Studies Materials

Educators Guide to FREE Guidance Materials

Educators Guide to FREE Family and Consumer Education Materials

Educators Guide to FREE Health, Physical Education and Recreation Materials

Educators Guide to Free Multicultural Materials

El-Hi Textbooks and Serials in Print, 2006, New Providence, NJ: R. R. Bowker, 2006. ISBN 0-8352-4793-7, ISBN 13 978-0-8352-4793-1.

   Indexes over 189,000 textbooks, reference books, periodicals, maps, tests, teaching aids, and audiovisuals by subject, author, title, series, and publisher.

Encyclopedia of Software Engineering. 2nd ed. John J. Marciniak, ed. New York: John Wiley & Sons, 2002. ISBN: 0-47-137737-6, ISBN 13 978-0-471-37737-5. Available at http://www3.interscience.wiley.com/cgi-bin/mrwhome/104554786/HOME

   Over 500 entries covering 35 taxonomic areas. Includes entries that define terms according to Institute of Electrical and Electronic Engineers standards. Topics include the Internet and Web engineering. Biographical section includes over 100 personalities who have made an impact in the field.

English Journal. Urbana, IL: National Council of Teachers of English, 1912–. ISSN 0013-8274. Available at http://www.jstor.org/journals/00138274.html

   Bimonthly. Reviews young adult literature, films, videos, software, and professional publications. Subscription: NCTE Subscription Service, 1111 W. Kenyon Road, Urbana, IL 61801-1086. (http://www.ncte.org/)

Essentials of Children's Literature. 5th ed. Carol Lynch-Brown and Carl M. Tomlinson. Boston, MA: Allyn & Bacon, 2005. ISBN 0-205-45908-0, ISBN 13 978-0-205-45908-7.

   Surveys children's literature, featuring genres, authors within the genre, and recommended titles. Includes a chapter on multicultural and international literature. Includes curriculum and teaching strategies for grades K-6.

Ethnic Book Awards: A Directory of Multicultural Literature for Young Readers Sherry York. Worthington, OH: Linworth, 2005. ISBN 1586831879, ISBN 13 978-1-58683-187-5.

Comprehensive listing of the award-winning titles of seven major multicultural awards: the Americas Award, the Asian Pacific American Award for Literature, the Carter G. Woodson Award, the Coretta Scott King Award, the Pura Belpré Award, the Sydney Taylor Book Award, and the Tomás Rivera Mexican American Children's Literature Award. Bibliographic information includes illustrator, translators, reading and interest levels, brief annotation for each title. Subject, author, editor, illustration, and translator indexes.

Evaluating the School Library Media Center: Analysis Techniques and Research Practices. Nancy Everhart. Westport, CT: Libraries Unlimited, 1998. ISBN 1-56308-085-0, ISBN 13 978-1-56308-085-2, ISBN 0-58517-544-6 (electronic bk.).

Discusses qualitative and quantitative research techniques. Guides conducting research, collecting statistics, and evaluating the media center program.

Exceptional Children. Arlington, VA: Council for Exceptional Children, 1934–. ISSN 0014-4029.

Four times a year. Research-based articles. Reviews professional books. Publishes current articles on critical and controversial issues in special education, as well as credible articles on research and developments in the field. (http://www.ideapractices.org/)

Exceptional Parent: The Magazine for Families and Professionals Caring for People with Special Needs. River Edge, NJ: Exceptional Parent, 1971–. ISSN 0046-9157.Also *EP Magazine Online* at http://eparent.com/

Twelve issues per year. Provides information and support for families with children with disabilities and the professionals who work with them. Subscription: (http://www.eparent.com/subscribe/).

Exploring Science in the Library: Resources and Activities for Young People. Maria Sosa and Tracy Gath. Chicago, IL: American Library Association, 2000. ISBN 0-8389-0768-7, ISBN 13 978-0-585-31116-6, ISBN 0-585-31116-1 (electronic bk.).

Co-published with American Association for the Advancement of Science (AAAS). Includes supplemental activities for science instruction in the library, Web references, a guide to selecting books, information about fundraising, and an annotated bibliography of science trade books.

Exploring the Environment Through Children's Literature: An Integrated Approach. Carol M. Butzow and John W. Butzow. Englewood, CO: Libraries Unlimited, 2002 ISBN 1-56308-814-2, ISBN 13 978-1-56308-814-8.

Features lessons and ideas for teaching children about nature and the environment with literature and hands-on activities.

Extreme Teens: Library Services for Nontraditional Young Adults. Sheila B. Anderson. Westport, CT: Libraries Unlimited, 2005. ISBN 1-59158-170-2, ISBN 13 978-1-59158-170-3.

Provides tips on building a collection and providing library services to connect with non-traditional young people, including juvenile delinquents, pregnant teens, the homeless, home-schooled, dropouts, GLBTQ, and many others.

Fantasy Literature for Children and Young Adults: A Comprehensive Guide. 5th ed. Ruth Nadelman Lynn. Westport, CT: Libraries Unlimited, 2005. ISBN 1591580501, ISBN 13 978-1-59158-050-8.

Comprehensive guide describing and categorizing fantasy novels and story collections published between 1900 and 2004 for readers grades 3–12. More than 7,500 titles. Organized in chapters based on fantasy subgenres and themes, including animal, alternate worlds, time travel, witchcraft, and sorcery. Complete bibliographic information, grade level, a brief annotation, and a list of review citations.

Fiction Catalog. 15th ed. John Greenfieldt. Bronx, NY: H. W. Wilson, 2006. ISBN 0-82421-055-7.

Four annual supplements. Provides access by subject and genre.

Fiction Catalog. Bronx, NY: H. W. Wilson, 1941–. ISSN 0160-4880.

Five annual supplements. Annotated list of best new and established English language fiction, with title and subject index.

Fluent in Fantasy: A Guide to Reading Interests. Diana Tixier Herald. Englewood, CO: Libraries Unlimited, 1999. ISBN 1-56308-655-7, ISBN 13 978-1-56308-655-7.

Provides an overview of the genre. Recommends titles and online resources. Includes descriptions and annotated lists of titles in various subgenres including "Sword and Sorcery," "Saga, Myth, and Legend," "Alternate and Parallel Worlds," and "Graphic Novels." Resources such as bibliographies, biographies, atlases, online resources, organizations and conventions, and awards are identified.

For Younger Readers: Braille and Talking Books. Washington, DC: National Library Service for the Blind and Physically Handicapped, U.S. Library of Congress, 1967–. ISSN 0093-2825.

Irregular. Annotates Braille, disc, and cassette books announced in *Braille Book Review* and *Talking Books Topics.* Available in Braille, sound recording, and large type. Free to blind and physically handicapped.

Free and Inexpensive Career Materials: A Resource Directory. 3rd ed. Elizabeth H. Oakes, ed. Chicago, IL: Ferguson, 2000. ISBN 0-89434-377-7, ISBN 978-0-89434-377-3.

Lists more than 800 sources of career information materials. Provides fax numbers, Web sites, and e-mail addresses for many of the organizations. (Market: Canada)

From Biography to History: Best Books for Children's Entertainment and Education. Catherine Barr, ed. Westport, CT: Greenwood Publishing Group, 1998. ISBN 0-8352-4012-6, ISBN 13 978-0-8352-4012-3.

Biographies of 600 notable men and women, as well as 600 related books. Lists are organized by age-group.

Genreflecting: A Guide to Popular Reading Interests. 6th ed. Diana Tixier Herald and Wayne A. Wiegand. Englewood, CO: Libraries Unlimited, 2005. ISBN 1-59158-286-5, ISBN 13 978-1-59158-286-1.

More than 5,000 titles classified by genre (including historical fiction, westerns, crime, adventure, romance, science fiction, fantasy, horror, Christian fiction, and women's fiction/chick lit), subgenre, and theme.

Chapters on Christian fiction and emerging genres. Indexes are by subject or author and title.

Genreflecting: A Guide to Reading Interest in Genre Fiction. Diana Tixier Herald. Englewood, CO: Libraries Unlimited, 2000. ISBN 1-56308-638-7, ISBN 13 978-1-56308-638-0.

Describes eight fiction genres and subgenres, including romance, westerns, fantasy, crime, science fiction. Identifies more than 6,000 titles. Includes information on such genre topics as trade magazines, critical works, book clubs, specialized publishers, and conventions.

Gifted Books, Gifted Readers: Literature Activities to Excite Young Minds. Nancy J. Polette. Westport, CT: Libraries Unlimited, 2000. ISBN 1-56308-822-3, ISBN 13 978-1-56308-822-3 (teacher's edition).

Suggestions to help children connect reading content to their own experiences.

Gifted Child Quarterly. Paula L. Olszewski-Kubilius, ed. Washington, DC: National Association for Gifted Children, 1957–. ISSN 0016-9862.

Quarterly. For educational researchers, administrators, teachers, and parents of gifted children. Publishes research and theoretical papers on the nature and needs of high-ability children. (http://www.nagc.org)

Gifted Child Today Magazine: The Nation's Leading Resource for Nurturing Talented Children. Waco, TX: Prufrock Press, 1978-. ISSN 1076-2175.

Quarterly. Includes bibliographies, illustrations, book reviews designed to meet the needs of parents and teachers of gifted, creative, and talented youngsters. (http://www.prufrock.com/client/client_pages/prufrock_jm_giftchild.cfm)

Global Voices: Using Historical Fiction to Teach Social Studies. Susan B. Ouzts. Tucson, AZ: Good Year Books, 1998. ISBN 0-673-36395-3.

Provides lessons incorporating contemporary literature from many cultures for use in language arts and social studies classes in middle schools.

GPO Access. U.S. Government Printing Office.

Free electronic access to information products produced by the Federal Government. (http://www.gpoaccess.gov/about/index.html)

Grantsmanship for Small Libraries and School Library Media Centers. Frank W. Hoffmann, Sylvia D. Hall-Ellis, Doris Meyer, and Ann Jerabek. Englewood, CO: Libraries Unlimited, 1999. ISBN 1-56308-484-8, ISBN 13 978-1-56308-484-3.

Describes the planning, project design, project narrative, project personnel, budget development, and project evaluation for grants. Includes appendixes with an annotated bibliography, frequently asked questions, and a glossary.

Great Books for African-American Children. Pamela Toussaint. New York: Plume, 1999. ISBN 0-452-28044-3, ISBN 13 978-0-452-28044-3.

Lists and annotates 250 books (from pre-school to young adult) that celebrate the African American culture. Includes quotations from notable African Americans and biographical information about Black authors and illustrators.

Great Books for African Americans. Pamela Toussaint. Caledonia, MN: Turtleback Books, 1999. ISBN 0-606-17070-7, ISBN 13 978-0-606-17070-3.

Reviews 250 titles and provides ordering information.

Great Web Sites for Kids Selection Criteria. Children and Technology Committee of the Association of Library Service to Children. Chicago, IL: American Library Association.

Helps parents evaluate authorship/sponsorship, purpose, design, stability, and content. Recommends sites for children. (http://www.ala.org/ala/alsc/greatwebsites/greatwebsitesforkids/greatwebsites.htm)

Guide to Microforms in Print: Author/Title. Munich, Germany: K. G. Saur, 1975–. ISSN 0164-0747.

Annual. Lists microforms by author and title. (http://www.saur.de)

Guide to Popular U.S. Government Publications, 1997–1999. Frank W. Hoffmann and Richard J. Wood. Boulder, CO: NetLibrary. ISBN 0-585-45472-8, ISBN 13 978-0-585-45472-6.

Covers 2,500 publications. Provides bibliographic information, illustrative material, stock number, price, SuDocs classification number, and annotation.

Guide to Reference Materials for School Library Media Centers. 5th ed. Barbara Ripp Safford. Englewood, CO: Libraries Unlimited, 1998. ISBN 1-56308-545-3, ISBN 13 978-1-56308-545-1. Boulder, CO: NetLibrary. ISBN 0585257027 (electronic bk.).

Covers more than 2,000 titles including electronic resources with age and reading levels, presentation styles, strengths and weaknesses, comparison with other works, and citations to reviews.

Halliwell's Film Video and DVD Guide 2006. 21st. ed. John Walker, ed. New York: HarperCollins, 2006. ISBN 0-00-720550-3, ISBN 13 978-0-00-720550-9.

Includes more than 23,000 reviews. Provides country of origin, rating, format, year releases, alternate title, brief description, quotes from reviews, and awards. Arranged alphabetically by title. Lists Academy Award winners, four-star reviews by title and by year, three-star reviews by title and year.

High/Low Handbook: Best Books and Web Sites for Reluctant Teen Readers. 4th ed. Ellen V LiBretto and Catherine Barr. Westport, CT: Libraries Unlimited, 2002. ISBN 0-31332-276-7.

A ready reference for those who work with students who have poor reading skills and need materials that will entice them to read. Contains book titles and URLs in subject categories such as fiction, subdivided by genre; biography and memoirs; health and fitness; history; science; and sports. A section of magazine titles provides descriptions and ordering information. Appendixes include a publishers' list and Web resources.

The History Teacher. Long Beach, CA: Society for History Education, 1967–. ISSN 0018-2745.

Quarterly. Reviews books, textbooks, supplementary readers, and professional books. Subscription: Society for History Education, P.O.

Box 1578, Borrego Springs, CA 92004. (http://www.thehistoryteacher.org/html)

Hoagies' Gifted Education Page.
"Consists of about 900 pages of information on gifted children and adults, including 400+ pages of my collection, plus 500+ pages of ERIC Clearinghouse for Disabilities and Gifted Education (ERICEC)." (from Web site: http://www.hoagiesgifted.org/reading_lists.htm)

Hooked on Horror: A Guide to Reading Interests in Horror Fiction. Anthony J. Fonseca and June Michele Pulliam. Genreflecting Advisory Series. Englewood, CO: Libraries Unlimited, 2003. ISBN 1-56308-904-1, ISBN 13 978-1-56308-904-6.
Describes approximately 1,000 contemporary and classic titles for English literature classes and horror fans. Focuses on widely available titles. Annotated bibliography of adult horror novels and films arranged by thirteen subgenres. History of the horror genre. Identifies additional reading and sources for research on the subject of horror, lists of award winners.

The Horn Book Magazine. Boston, MA: Horn Book, 1924–. ISSN 0018-5078.
Six issues per year. Related work: *The Horn Book Guide to Children's and Young Adult Books*, 1989–. ISSN 1044-405X. Two issues per year. Reviews and ratings hardback and paperback books. Includes books in Spanish. Subscription: The Horn Book, Inc., 56 Roland Street, Suite 200, Boston, MA 02129. (http://www.hbook.com/publications/magazine/default.asp)

Huck's Children's Literature in the Elementary School. 9th ed. Charlotte S. Huck and Barbara Zulandt Kiefer. Boston, MA: McGraw-Hill, 2006. ISBN 0-07-312298-X, ISBN 13 978-0-07-312298-4.
Guides teachers and media specialists in the selection and use of all genres of literature with children. It helps the user to plan and evaluate children's understandings of literature.

Including Families of Children with Special Needs: A How-to-Do-It Manual for Librarians. Sandra Feinberg, Kathleen Deerr, Barbara Jordan, and Michele Langa. New York: Neal-Schuman, 1999. ISBN 1-55570-339-9.
Offers suggestions for selecting materials, including services, toys, and resources for parents. Four appendixes, including a bibliography for parents and librarians and a list of children's books that feature special needs characters.

Index to Poetry for Children and Young People, 1993–1997: A Title, Subject, Author, and First Line Index to Poetry in Collections for Children and Young People. Bronx, NY: H. W. Wilson, 1998. ISBN 0-82420-939-7.
Covers approximately 8,700 poems from more than 186 sources. Indexes by title, author, first line, and subject.

Information Power: Building Partnerships for Learning. American Association of School Librarians and Association for Educational Communications and Technology. Chicago, IL: American Library Association, 1998. ISBN 0-83893-470-6, ISBN 13 978-0-8389-3470-8.

Guidelines for school library media centers. Includes the national information literacy standards.

Informational Picture Books for Children. Patricia J. Cianciolo. Chicago, IL: American Library Association, 2000. ISBN 0-83890-774-1, ISBN 13 978-0-8389-0774-0.

Annotates 250 titles published between 1994 and 1999, of interest to pre-schoolers through middle school students. Wide bibliographic scope. Useful guidelines for evaluating other titles.

Instructional Technology and Media for Learning. Sharon E. Smaldino, James D. Russell, Robert Heinich, and Michael Molenda, Upper Saddle River, NJ: Prentice Hall, 2004. ISBN 0-13-113682-8, ISBN 13 978-0-13-113682-3.

Discusses selection and use of media. Includes software package for teachers to use in creating, maintaining, printing, and evaluating lesson plans and the materials used in them. Includes educational resources and technology, teaching skills and techniques.

Intellectual Freedom Manual. 6th ed. ALA Office of Intellectual Freedom. Chicago, IL: American Library Association, 2005. ISBN 0-83893-561-3, ISBN 13 978-0-8389-3561-3.

Includes policies and their interpretations. Offers guidelines for developing policies and practices.

Internet Books for Educators, Parents, and Students. Jean Reese. Englewood, CO: Libraries Unlimited, 1999. ISBN 1-56308-697-2, ISBN 0585116423 (electronic bk.).

Recommends approximately 100 titles. Index for author and title.

Internet Resource Directory for K–12 Teachers and Librarians. Elizabeth B. Miller. Englewood, CO: Libraries Unlimited, 2004. ISBN 0-31300-958-9, ISBN 13 978-0-313-00958-7.

Describes selected resources on a wide range of subjects including resources to help teachers and media specialists, lesson plans, AUP, copyright, intellectual freedom, and selections. Posts changes and updates monthly at (http://lu.com/bookext.cfm).

Internet Technology for Schools. Catherine Mambretti. Jefferson, NC: McFarland, 1999. ISBN 0-78640-727-1, ISBN 13 978-0-7864-0727-9.

Moves from a general overview of the issues faced in planning for and developing technology in the schools to good Internet practices, and to providing technical guidelines. Glossary.

Journal for the Education of the Gifted. Tracy Cross, ed. Waco, TX: Prufrock Press, 1978–. ISSN 0162-3532.

Quarterly. "Offers information and research on the educational and psychological needs of gifted and talented children." (from Web site: http://www.prufrock.com/client/client_pages/prufrock_jm_jeg.cfm)

Journal of Adolescent and Adult Literacy. (JAAL) Newark, DE: International Reading Association, Inc., 1957–. ISSN 1081-3004.

Eight times a year (September–May; December & January combined) "Published exclusively for teachers and older learners. Practical, classroom-tested ideas grounded in research and theory."(from Web site: http://www.reading.org/publications/journals/jaal/index.html)

Journal of Family and Consumer Sciences. Washington, DC: American Home Economics Association, 1909–. ISSN 1082-1651. (Formerly *Journal of Home Economics* ISSN 0022-1570.)

Five times a year. Reviews trade and professional books covering family relations, children, food and nutrition, household affairs, and teaching methods. Subscription: American Association of Family and Consumer Sciences, 1555 King St., Alexandria, VA 22314. (http://www.aafcs.org/resources/jfcs.html)

Journal of Geography. Macomb, IL: National Council for Geographic Education, 1902–. ISSN 0022-1341.

Bimonthly. Reviews textbooks and professional materials; has a column on free and inexpensive materials. Subscription: National Council for Geographic Education, Jacksonville State University, 206A Martin Hall, Jacksonville, AL 36265. (http://www.ncge.org)

Journal of Physical Education, Recreation and Dance. Reston, VA: American Alliance for Health, Physical Education, Recreation, and Dance, 1896-. ISSN 0730-3084.

Monthly (9/year). Index. Features by-lined articles and short features on all aspects of physical education, recreation, dance, athletics, and safety education as taught in schools and colleges. Covers administration, curriculum methods, and equipment. (http://www.aahperd.org/aahperd/template.cfm?template=johperd_main.html)

Journal of Secondary Gifted Education. Bonnie Cramond, ed. Waco, TX: Prufrock Press, 1993-. ISSN 1077-4610.

Quarterly. "Offers education professionals comprehensive and critical information needed for building an effective educational environment for gifted adolescents." (from Web site: http://www.prufrock.com/client/client_pages/prufrock_jm_jsge.cfm)

Journal of Visual Impairment and Blindness. Alan J Koenig, ed. New York: American Foundation for the Blind, 1977-. ISSN 0145-482X.

Monthly. Available in regular print or in Braille. Available in microform, on audiocassette, and online at http://www.afb.org Subscription: (http://www.afb.org/Section.asp?SectionID=54)

Junior Genreflecting: A Guide to Good Reads and Series Fiction for Children. Bridget Dealy Volz, Lynda Blackburn Welborn, and Cheryl Perkins Scheer. Genreflecting Advisory Series. Englewood, CO: Libraries Unlimited, 2000. ISBN 1-56308-556-9, ISBN 13 978-1-56308-556-7, ISBN 0-58533-352-1 (electronic bk.).

Describes titles for children in grades 3–8. Arranges titles by specific themes and subtopics.

Kirkus Reviews. New York: Kirkus Service, V N U Business Publications, 1933–. ISSN 0042-6598.

Monthly. Available online. Reviews trade books. Entries provide bibliographic/order information, paging, month and day of release, type of book, and grade level. Subscription: Information Marketing, 770 Broadway, 6th Floor, New York, NY 10003. (http://www.kirkusreviews.com/)

Kliatt: Reviews of Selected Current Paperback Books, Hardcover Fiction, Audiobooks, and Educational Software. Wellesley, MA: Kliatt, 1978–. ISSN 1065-8602.

Six issues per year. Reviews software, paperbacks, and audiobooks for ages 12–19. Subscription: Kliatt, 33 Bay State Road, Wellesley, MA 02481. (http://hometown.aol.com/kliatt/index.html)

Language Arts. Urbana, IL: National Council of Teachers of English, 1924–. ISSN 0360-9170.

Bimonthly (September through May). Reviews children's books and professional materials. Subscription: National Council of Teachers of English, 1111 Kenyon Road, Urbana, IL 61801. (http://www.ncte.org/store/journals/105389.htm)

Learning and Libraries in an Information Age: Principles and Practice. Barbara K. Stripling, ed. Englewood, CO: Libraries Unlimited, 1999. ISBN 1-56308-666-2, ISBN 13 978-1-56308-666-3, ISBN: 0585113955 (electronic bk.).

Blends latest research and theory with effective practices. Discusses the role of the media center in meeting informational and instructional needs and in establishing collaborative efforts with teachers.

Lesbian and Gay Voices: An Annotated Bibliography and Guide to Literature for Children and Young Adults. Frances Ann Day. Westport, CT: Greenwood, 2000. ISBN: 0-313-31162-5, ISBN 13 978-0-313-31162-8.

Thoughtful and thorough annotations of more than 275 titles featuring lesbian and gay characters appropriate for young readers, including picture books, fiction, short stories, nonfiction, biography, and autobiography. Suggested guidelines for evaluating books. Profiles sixteen gay and lesbian authors.

Less Is More: A Practical Guide to Weeding School Library Collections. Donna J. Baumbach and Linda L. Miller. Chicago, IL: American Library Association, 2006. ISBN 0-8389-0919-5, ISBN 13 978-0-8389-0919-5.

Practical guide outlining the steps for making weeding part of a library's ongoing procedures. Explains how to use automation tools.

Libraries, the First Amendment, and Cyberspace: What You Need to Know. Robert S. Peck. Chicago, IL: American Library Association, 2000. ISBN 0-8389-0773-3, ISBN 13 978-0-8389-0773-3.

Answers questions relating to censorship and access. Appendixes include important First Amendment documents.

Library Journal. New York: Reed Business Information, 1876–. ISSN 0363-0277. *Library Journal Digital* at http://www.libraryjournal.com/

Twenty-two times a year, plus Buyer's Guide, ten supplements and weekly review. Available in microform. Reviews books, magazines, videos, CD-ROM, software, and audiobooks. Monthly author index to reviews. Includes annual buyer's guide to hardware and equipment. Subscription: Reed Business Information, PO Box 16027, North Hollywood, CA, 91615. Phone (800)-588-1030.

Library Media Connection: Magazine for Secondary School Library Media and Technology Specialists. Worthington, OH: Linworth, 2003- ISSN 1542-4715 (*Library Talk* merged and incorporated into this publication).

Seven times a year. Blending practical information, professional development, and book and technology reviews by educators. (http://www. linworth.com/lmc.html)

Literary Market Place: The Directory of Book Publishing (LPM). Medford, NJ: Information Today, 1973–. ISSN 0000-1155. Also available at http://www.infotoday.com

Annual. Lists publishing and publishing-related businesses, including distributors, literary agents, small presses, events, editorial and art devices, printers and binders. Also lists recent mergers and acquisitions and company reportage of publishers, i.e. divisions, subsidiaries, and imprints.

Literary Market Place 2007. Medford, NJ: Information Today, 2006. ISBN 1-57387-255-5, ISBN 13 978-1-57387-255-3.

Two volumes. Over 14,000 listings covering all aspects of the business. Fifty-four sections organize everyone and everything in the business including publishers, agents, ad agencies, associations, distributors, and events. (http://www.infotoday.com)

Literature Connections to American History, K–6: Resources to Enhance and Entice. Lynda G. Adamson. Englewood, CO: Libraries Unlimited, 1998. ISBN 1-56308-502-X, ISBN 13 978-0-585-10883-4, ISBN 0-58510-883-8 (electronic bk.).

Identifies thousands of historical fiction novels, biographies, history trade books, CD-ROMs, and videotapes on American history from before 1600 to current times.

Literature Connections to American History, 7-12: Resources to Enhance and Entice. Lynda G. Adamson. Englewood, CO: Libraries Unlimited, 1997. ISBN: 1-56308-503-8, ISBN 13 978-1-56308-503-1, ISBN 0-58513-346-8 (electronic bk).

Identifies thousands of historical fiction novels, biographies, history trade books, CD-ROMs, and videotapes on American history from before 1600 to current times.

Literature Connections to World History, Grades K–6: Resources to Enhance and Entice. Lynda G. Adamson. Englewood, CO: Libraries Unlimited, 1998. ISBN 1-56308-504-6, ISBN 13 978-1-56308-504-8, ISBN 0-58513-389-1 (electronic bk.).

Identifies thousands of historical fiction novels, biographies, history trade books, CD-ROMs, and videotapes covering prehistory to the modern era. Includes annotated bibliography.

Literature Connections to World History, 7–12: Resources to Enhance and Entice. Lynda G. Adamson. Englewood, CO: Libraries Unlimited, 1998. ISBN 1-5630-8505-4, ISBN I3 978-1-56308-505-5, ISBN 0-58513-342-5 (electronic bk.).

Identifies thousands of historical fiction novels, biographies, history trade books, CD-ROMs, and videotapes covering prehistory to the modern era. Includes annotated bibliography.

Literature Lures: Using Picture Books and Novels to Motivate Middle School Readers. Nancy J. Polette and Joan Ebbesmeyer. Westport, CT: Libraries

Unlimited, 2004. ISBN 0-313-01010-2, ISBN 13 978-0-313-01010-1 (electronic bk).

Tool for exploring important themes and motivating students to become involved in the literature experience. Titles carefully chosen, using as criteria the quality of the writing, the importance of its message, and how easily it could serve as a springboard to junior novels that explore the same theme. Grades 6–10.

Mathematics Teacher. Reston, VA: National Council of Teachers of Mathematics, 1908–. ISSN 0004-136X. Also online *ON-Math* (ISSN 0025-5769) at http://my.nctm.org/eresources/journal_home.asp?journal_id=4

Nine times a year. Features on the improvement of mathematics instruction in junior and senior high schools, two-year colleges and teacher education colleges. The column "Reviewing and Viewing" covers teaching materials, including games, videotapes, workbooks, software, and books for teachers. About 100,000 mediagraphic items covered. Subscription: NCTM, Drawer A, 1906 Association Drive, Reston, VA 20191. Phone (800) 235-7566. (http://www.nctm.org/membership/application/)

Mathematics Teaching in the Middle School. (MTMS) Reston, VA: National Council of Teachers of Mathematics, 1994–. ISSN 1072-0839.

Nine times a year (September–May). "Offers activities, lesson ideas, teaching strategies, and problems through in-depth articles, departments and features." (from Web site: http://my.nctm.org/eresources/journal_home.asp?journal_id=3)

Media Review Digest: Reviews of Educational Non-Book Media. Ann Arbor, MI: Pierian Press, 1970–. ISSN 0363-7778.

Available in print and online. Lists reviews and evaluations of all forms of non-book print media appearing in a variety of periodicals and reviewing services. Subscription: Customer Service Dept., The Pierian Press, P.O. Box 1808, Ann Arbor, MI, 48106. (http://www.pierianpress.com/index.php?section=databases&content=mrd)

Middle and Junior High School Library Catalog. Juliette Yaakov, ed. Bronx, NY: H. W. Wilson, 1965–. (ISSN not provided). Available at http://www.hwwilson.com/print/mjhscat.cfm and in book format, 9th ed. Bronx, NY: H. W. Wilson, 2005. ISBN 0-8242-1053-0.

Quinquennial plus four annual supplements. Recommends more than 4,200 fiction and nonfiction books in the main volume. Arranged by Abridged Dewey Decimal Classification. Indexes: author, title, subject, and analytics.

Monthly Catalog of United States Government Publications. Washington, DC: U.S. Government Printing Office, 1895–. GP 3.8. ISSN 0362-6830.

In print and online. Identifies publications by major branches, departments, and bureaus of the U.S. government. Provides depository and order information. (http://www.access.gpo.gov/su_docs/dpos/adpos400.html)

More Hot Links: Linking Literature with the Middle School Curriculum. Cora M. Wright. Greenwood Village, CO: Libraries Unlimited, 2002. ISBN 1-56308-942-4, ISBN 13 978-1-56308-942-8.

Includes more than 300 additional fiction and nonfiction annotated titles chosen for recreational reading and curriculum connections for students from fifth to ninth grade. Sections on humor, series, and picture books for all ages. Recommends titles arranged by curriculum areas. Indicates high interest/low reading level titles.

More Rip-Roaring Reads for Reluctant Teen Readers. Betty DeBruyne Ammon and Gale W. Sherman. Englewood, CO: Libraries Unlimited, 1999. ISBN 1-56308-571-2, ISBN 13 978-0-585-12352-3, ISBN 0-58512-352-7 (electronic bk.).

Describes forty titles (fiction and nonfiction) in terms of ways to motivate reluctant readers in middle and high school. Listings include genre, themes, and reading and interest levels.

More Virtual Field Trips. Gail Cooper Markunas and Carry Cooper. Englewood, CO: Libraries Unlimited, 1999. ISBN 1-56308-770-0, ISBN 13 978-1-56308-770-7.

Allows travel throughout the world (back and forth in time) to study natural phenomena and participate in cultural and scientific activities.

Moving Library Collections: A Management Handbook. Elizabeth Chamberlain Habich. Westport, CT: Greenwood, 1998. ISBN 13 978-0-313-00780-4, ISBN 0-313-00780-2 (electronic bk.).

Offers suggestions for planning effective moves handled by staff or professional movers. Includes pest-management advice.

Multicultural Children's Literature: Through the Eyes of Many Children. Donna E. Norton. Upper Saddle River, NJ: Prentice Hall, 2005. ISBN 0-1311-7806-7, ISBN 13 978-0-1311-7806-9.

Compact guide of selected high-quality examples of multicultural literature. Focuses on incorporating the best multicultural books into the classroom, honoring and respecting both the literature and the cultures in the classroom, and using literature to motivate and nurture a culturally responsive classroom.

Multicultural Picturebooks: Art for Illuminating Our World. 2nd ed. Sylvia S. Marantz and Kenneth A. Marantz, eds. Lanham, MD: Scarecrow Press, 2004. ISBN: 0-8108-4933-X, ISBN 13 978-0-8108-4933-4.

Evaluates the quality and classroom appropriateness of picture books with a multicultural theme for grades K-4. Reviews storylines and special features, look and style of illustrations, design and layout. Includes bibliographical references and index.

Multicultural Projects Index: Things to Make and Do to Celebrate Festivals, Cultures, and Holidays Around the World. 4th ed. Mary Anne Pilger. Medford, NJ: Libraries Unlimited, 2005. ISBN 1-59158-236-9, ISBN 13 978-1-59158-236-6.

Index of multicultural projects that promote diversity and cross-cultural understanding in more than 1,700 books; indexed by subject and author. Also has indexes to educational games, crafts, activities.

Multicultural Resources on the Internet: The United States and Canada. Vicki L. Gregory, Marilyn H. Karrenbrock Stauffer, and Thomas W. Keene. Englewood, CO: Libraries Unlimited, 1999. ISBN 1-56308-676-X, ISBN 13 978-1-56308-676-2.

Annotates valuable information about URL sites for Native American, African American, Hispanic American, Asian American, Chinese American, Japanese American, Asian Indian American, Jewish American, Americans of Middle Eastern descent, French Canadian, Cajun, Creole, and Hawaiian American cultures.

MultiCultural Review: Dedicated to a Better Understanding of Ethnic, Racial and Religious Diversity. Tampa, FL: Goldman Group, 1992–. ISSN 1058-9236.

Quarterly. Includes articles on current issues related to multiculturalism, bibliographic essays, articles on non-profit resources, practical applications, and reviews of materials for juvenile and adult audiences. Subscription: (http://www.mcreview.com/subscribe.html).

Neal-Schuman Authoritative Guide to Evaluating Information on the Internet. Alison Cooke. New York: Neal-Schuman, 1999. ISBN 1-55570-356-9, IBSN 13 978-1-55570-356-1.

Discusses criteria for a range of types of sources including Web sites, electronic journals, newsgroups, databases, current awareness services, and FAQs. Available at http://www.neal-schuman.com/db/7/177.html

Neal-Shuman Internet Policy Handbook for Libraries. Mark Smith. New York: Neal-Schuman, 1999. ISBN 1-55570-345-3, ISBN 13 978-1-55570-345-5.

Includes examples from school library media center policies, describes the process of developing policies, and discusses the issues involved. Material for measuring Internet use and handling challenges to Internet-related policies and procedures.

Negotiating the Special Education Maze: A Guide for Parents and Teachers. 3rd ed. Winifred Anderson, Stephan Chitwood, and Deidre Hayden. Bethesda, MD: Woodbine House, 1997. ISBN 0-93314-972-7, IBSN 13 978-0-933149-72-4. Also available in Spanish Guiándose Por la Intrincada Senda de la Educación Especial: Una Guía Para Padres y Maestros. 1999 ISBN 1-89062-707-0.

Covers changes in disability laws, including the Americans with Disabilities Act (ADA) and Individuals with Disabilities Education Act (IDEA); reviews early intervention services for children from birth to age 3; and covers transitioning young adults out of school. Presents an effective approach for obtaining appropriate instruction and therapy designed to meet the unique needs of every child with special needs. Process is explained, including eligibility, testing, evaluation, and the Individualized Education Program (IEP). Includes bibliographical references and index.

The New Grove Dictionary of Music and Musicians. 2nd ed. Stanley Sadie and John Tyrrell, eds. New York: Oxford University Press, 2001. ISBN 0-19-517067-9, ISBN 13 978-0-19-517067-2. Also available at http://www.grovemusic.com

First edition's 22,500 articles have been reviewed and revised, with many expanded. Thousands of new articles, topics, cross-references, and areas of scholarship. Previously neglected or under-represented areas are examined, explored, and explained. Articles cover more than 5,000 years of music history, instruments, composers, institutions, performers, and genres. Extensive, authoritative contributions on non-Western music. Valuable appendixes.

Newbery and Caldecott Awards: A Guide to the Medal and Honor Books. Chicago, IL: American Library Association, 2006. ISBN 0-83893-565-1, ISBN 13 978-0-8389-3565-1.

Annual. Provides background information about the titles and their creators.

Newsletter on Intellectual Freedom. Judith F. Krug, ed. Chicago, IL: Intellectual Freedom Committee of the American Library Association, 1952–. ISSN 0028-9485. Available at http://www.ala.org/nif

Bimonthly. Reports events relating to intellectual freedom and censorship. Subscription American Library Association, 50 E. Huron St., Chicago, IL 60611. (http://cs.ala.org/nif/subscribe.html)

Online: The Magazine of Online Information Systems. Medford, NJ: Information Today, 1970–. ISSN 0146-5422. Available at http://www.infotoday. com/online/default.shtml

Six times per year. Provides articles about online applications and in-depth evaluative reviews. Subscription: Information Today, 143 Old Marlton Pike, Medford, NJ, 08055. (http://infotoday.stores.yahoo.net/ onlinemagazine.html)

Output Measures for School Library Media Programs. Frances B. Bradburn. New York: Neal-Schuman, 1998. ISBN 1-55570-326-7, ISBN 13 978-1-55570-326-4.

Describes how to use traditionally-collected data to talk about existing programs or document the need for change. Describes and provides fully developed case studies using various measures.

Picture Books by Latino Writers: A Guide for Librarians, Teachers, Parents, and Students. Sherry York. Worthington, OH: Linworth, 2002. ISBN 1-58683-052-X, ISBN 13 978-1-58683-052-6.

Features sixty-five picture books by Latino authors. Biographical information about authors, illustrators, and translators. Identifies literary awards won by the books; includes publisher and distributor information. Also has a bibliography of additional Latino-related picture books.

Popular Series Fiction for K-6 Readers: A Reading and Selection Guide. Catherine Barr and Rebecca L. Thomas. Westport, CT: Libraries Unlimited, 2004. ISBN 1-59158-203-2, ISBN 13 978-1-59158-203-8.

Introduces best and most popular fiction series of today, covering more than 1,000 series with over 10,000 titles, appropriate for elementary readers. Annotations also indicate series and titles accepted by some of the popular electronic reading programs (e.g., *Accelerated Reading, Reading First*). Appendixes include "Books for Boys," "Books for Girls," "for Reluctant Readers/ESL Students," and "Developing Series."

Popular Series Fiction for Middle School and Teen Readers: A Reading and Selection Guide. Catherine Barr and Rebecca L Thomas. Westport, CT: Libraries Unlimited, 2005. ISBN 1-59158-202-4, ISBN 13 978-1-59158-202-1.

Introduces best and most popular fiction series of today, covering approximately 800 series. Annotations describe the series' appeal, lists characters and location. Annotations also indicate series and titles that are accepted by some of the popular electronic reading programs (e.g., *Accelerated Read* and *Reading* ed. *Counts.*).

Preservation: Caring for Your Collections. Library of Congress. Available at http://www.loc.gov/preserv/careothr.html

Covers books, motion picture films, photographs, manuscripts, prints, posters, maps, audiorecordings, and the drying of water-damaged materials.

*Programming with Latino Children's Material*s: *A How-to-Do-It Manual for Librarians.* Tim Wadham. New York: Neal-Schuman, 1999. ISBN: 1-55570-352-6, ISBN 13 978-1-55570-352-3.

Provides background information on the Latino culture, book reviews, folktales, annotated bibliographies, suggestions for selection policies, and identifies acquisition sources. Includes the full text (in Spanish and English) for almost 100 fingerplays and nursery rhymes, programs. Special features include the Dewey Decimal Classification in Spanish, Latino holiday programs, a section on speaking Spanish, and ready-to-copy bilingual publicity materials.

Publishers, Distributors, and Wholesalers of the United States: A Directory of Publishers, Distributors, Associations, Wholesalers, Software Producers and Manufacturers Listing Editorial and Ordering Addresses, and an ISBN Publisher Prefix Index. New Providence, NJ: R. R. Bowker, 1979–. ISSN 0000-0671.

Annual, in two volumes. Lists more than 50,000 publishers, wholesalers, distributors, software firms, and museum and association imprints. Access by name, imprint, subsidiaries, divisions, state, firms with toll-free numbers, ISBN prefix, and publisher's field of activity. Also includes discount schedule and return policies.

Publishers Weekly. New York: Reed Business Information, 1872–. ISSN 0000-0019.

Weekly. Reviews books and audiovisual materials. Discusses news and trends in the book industry, including author interviews, advance book reviews, marketing and book design, and manufacturing articles. (http://www.publishersweekly.com/)

The Pura Belpré Awards: Celebrating Latino Authors and Illustrators. Rose Zertuche Trevino, ed. Chicago, IL: American Library Association, 2006. ISBN 0-8389-3562-1, ISBN13 978-0-8389-3562-0.

Covers the first ten years of the Pura Belpré Awards. Annotates the award-winning titles and provides biographies of the authors and illustrators.

Quill and Quire: Canada's Magazine of Book News and Reviews. Toronto: Key Publishers, 1935–. ISSN 0033-6491.

Monthly. Available online. Reviews books and has advertisements for tapes and records. Subscription: (https://www.quillandquire.com/profile/order_magazine.cfm).

Reaching Reluctant Young Adult Readers: A Handbook for Librarians and Teachers. Edward T. Sullivan. Lanham, MD: Scarecrow, 2002. ISBN: 0-8108-4343-9, ISBN 13 978-0-8108-4343-1.

Offers strategies, tools, and resources to entice reluctant readers with characters and themes that are appropriate on an intellectual and maturity level. Cultural relevance to Asian, Black, and Latino students addressed. Includes fiction, comics, graphic novels, nonfiction, picture books, magazines, and audiobooks.

Readers' Guide to Periodical Literature. Bronx, NY: H. W. Wilson, 1901–. ISSN 0034-0464.

Monthly. Available in print and online. Author and subject indexes to selected general interest periodicals of reference value in libraries, including book reviews. Related source: *Abridged Readers' Guide to Periodical Literature, Readers' Guide Full Text, Mega Edition* (online), *Readers' Guide Full Text, Select Edition* (online). (http://www.hwwilson.com/Databases/Readersg.htm)

Reading in Series: A Selection Guide to Books for Children. Catherine Barr, ed. New Providence, NJ: R. R. Bowker, 1999. ISBN 0-835243-011-8.

Covers more than 1,000 series. Provides author, current publisher, genre, grade level, brief description, list of all titles in the series, and reference to similar series. Includes a series for ESL readers. (UK)

The Reading Teacher. Newark, DE: International Reading Association, 1948–. ISSN 0034-0561.

Eight issues per year (print and online). Includes teaching tips, insights into theory, research findings, and reviews of children's literature. Subscription: International Reading Association, Inc., 800 Barksdale Rd, Newark, DE 19714. (http://www.reading.org/publications/journals/rt/index.html)

Recommended Books in Spanish for Children and Young Adults: 2000–2004. Isabel Schon. Lanham, MD: Scarecrow, 2004. ISBN 0-8108-5196-2, ISBN 13 978-0-8108-5196-2.

Critical annotations for more than 1,300 books in Spanish, including reference, nonfiction, and fiction. Section on publishers' series. Appendix of dealers. Indexes of authors, titles, and subjects.

Recommended Reference Books for Small and Medium-Sized Libraries. Bohdan S. Wynar, ed. Westport, CT: Libraries Unlimited, 1981–. ISSN 0277-5948.

Annual. Reviews coded to identify titles of interest to school library media centers. (http://www.lu.com)

Recommended Reference Books for Small and Medium-Sized Libraries and Media Centers. 2006. Graff Hysell Shannon, ed. Westport, CT: Libraries Unlimited, 2006. ISBN: 1-59158-288-1, ISBN 13 978-1-5915-8380-6.

Based on *American Reference Books Annual*; written by over 200 subject specialists; identifies best, most affordable and most appropriate new reference materials in any field.

Recommended Reference Books in Paperback. 3d ed. Jovian P. Lang and Jack O'Gorman. Englewood, CO: Libraries Unlimited, 2000. ISBN 1-56308-583-6, IBSN 13 978-1-56308-583-3, ISBN 0-58532-511-1 (electronic bk.).

Annotates approximately 1,000 titles covering a wide range of subjects.

Reference and Research Guide to Mystery and Detective Fiction. 2nd ed. Richard Bleiler. Reference Sources in the Humanities Series. Englewood, CO: Libraries Unlimited, 2004. ISBN 1-56308-924-6, ISBN 13 978-1-5630-8924-4.

Provides a comprehensive guide to mystery and detective titles for use as reference and research tool and aid to collection development.

Reference Sources for Small and Medium-Sized Libraries. 6th ed. Scott E. Kennedy, ed. Chicago, IL: American Library Association, 1999. ISBN 0-83893-568-5, ISBN 13 978-0-8389-3468-5, ISBN 0-58534-178-8 (electronic bk.).

Comprehensive buying guide. Describes reference sources recommended by the Reference Sources for Small and Medium-sized Libraries Editorial Committee, Collection Development and Evaluation Section, Reference and User Services Association of the American Library Association.

Resources in Education (RIE). Kerri Nine, ed. U.S. Department of Education, Office of Educational Research and Improvement, National Library of Education, Educational Resources Information Center, Lanham, MD. ERIC Processing and Reference Facility, 1966–. ISSN 0098-0897.

Monthly. Also available from ERIC as part of a computer file, online sources, and CD-ROMs. Provides summaries of the documents and abstracts available from the ERIC Document Reproduction Service (EDRS). Distributor: U.S. Government Printing Office, Washington, DC 20402. (http://www.eric.ed.gov/)

Romance Fiction: A Guide to the Genre. Kristin Ramsdell. Genreflecting Advisory Series. Englewood, CO: Libraries Unlimited, 1999. ISBN 1-56308-335-3, ISBN 13 978-1-56308-335-8, ISBN 0-58514-753-1 (electronic bk.).

Provides background information. Identifies selected titles for young adults.

S B & F (Science Books and Films). Washington, DC: American Association for the Advancement of Science, 1965–. ISSN 1533-5046. Also *S B & F Online* at http://www.sbfonline.com/

Bimonthly. Reviews books, films, videos, and software. Lists Public Broadcasting System materials. Covers pre-school through professional materials. Subscription: American Association for the Advancement of Science, 1200 New York Ave., Washington, DC 20005.

(http://www.sbfonline.com/subscribenow.htm)

Scholastic Reading Counts! Software Manual. New York: Scholastic Inc., 2006. ISBN 0-439-78484-0, ISBN 13 978-0-439-78484-9.

Manages and motivates independent reading, grades K-12. Also available at http://teacher.scholastic.com/products/readingcounts/overview.htm

School Libraries in Canada Online. Canadian Association for School Libraries, 1980–. ISSN 1710-8535. Free online at www.schoollibraries.ca

Quarterly. Reviews books, films, videos, and CDs for grades K–12.

School Library Journal: The Magazine of Children, Young Adults, and School Librarians. New York: Reed Business Information, 1954–. ISSN 0362-8930.

Twelve issues per year. Reviews books (pre-school through adult titles for young people, Spanish language, references), videos, recordings, CD-ROMs, and software. Includes checklists of pamphlets, posters, and free materials. Includes monthly index, annual author/title book review index, and audiovisual index. (http://www.slj.com/)

School Talk. Urbana, IL: National Council of Teachers of English, 1995–. ISSN 1083-2939.

Quarterly. Each issue focuses on a theoretical or pedagogical topic of interest to elementary school teachers of English language arts.

Schwann Online. Woodland, CA: Schwann Publications and Paratext

"Schwann online is an electronic edition of the classical recording catalog information of Schwann Opus and the non-classical recording information of Schwann Spectrum. It is not designed specifically as a resource for ordering musical recordings, but rather as a reference tool for music bibliographers, catalogers and enthusiasts." (from Web site: http://schwann.odyssi.com/)

Science. Washington, DC: American Association for the Advancement of Science, 1880–. ISSN 0036-8075.

Weekly. "Journal of original scientific research, global news and commentary." (from Web site: http://www.sciencemag.org/magazine.dtl)

Science & Children: The Journal for Elementary School Science Teachers. Washington, DC: National Science Teachers Association, 1963–. ISSN 0036-8148.

Eight times per year (September through May) and available at http://www.nsta.org/pubs/sc/ Presents ideas and activities for science educators from preschool through middle school. Reviews software, curriculum materials, and children's books. Subscription: NSTA, 1840 Wilson Boulevard, Arlington VA 22201-3000. (http://www.nsta.org/memcategories)

Science Scope: A Journal for Middle-Junior High Science Teachers. Kenneth L Roberts (Managing Editor). Arlington, VA: National Science Teachers Association, 1978–. ISSN 0887-2376.

Eight times a year. "Fresh ideas on what to teach and how to teach it." (from Web site: http://www.nsta.org/pubs/scope).

The Science Teacher. National Science Teachers Association, 1934–. ISSN 0036-8555. Available at http://www.nsta.org/highschool#journal

Nine times a year. (September–May). Reviews software, books for students, and professional books. Subscription: National Science Teachers Association NSTA, 1840 Wilson Boulevard, Arlington VA 22201-3000. (www.nsta.org)

Science Through Children's Literature: An Integrated Approach. 2nd ed. Carol M. Butzow and John W. Butzow. Englewood, CO: Libraries Unlimited, 2000. ISBN 1-56308-651-4, ISBN 13 978-1-56308-651-9, ISBN 0-58525245-9 (electronic bk.).

Features more than thirty instructional units and offers lesson ideas and activities. Identifies useful books with science in the storyline.

Selecting Books for the Elementary School Library Media Center: A Complete Guide. Phyllis Van Orden. New York: Neal-Schuman, 2000. ISBN 1-55570-368-2. ISBN 13 978-1-55570-368-4.

Describes the selection process and identifies criteria for picture books, fiction, folk literature, poetry, information books, reference works, and professional books. Glossary.

Senior High School Library Catalog. 16th ed. Juliette Yaakov, ed. New York: H. W. Wilson, 2002. ISBN 0-8242-1008-5. Also available at http://www.hwwilson.com/print/srhscat.htm

Four annual supplements. Abridged Dewey Decimal Classification. Provides bibliographic and order information, availability of paperback editions, Sears subject headings, and descriptive/critical annotations. Index by author, title, subject, and analytics.

Social Education. Arlington, VA: National Council for the Social Studies, 1937–. ISSN 0037-7724.

Seven issues per year. Reviews books for children and young adults. Subscription: National Council for the Social Studies, 8555 16th Street, Silver Spring, MD 20910. (http://www.socialstudies.org/publications/se/)

Social Studies and the Young Learner. Kristen Page, ed. Silver Spring, MD: National Council for the Social Studies, 1988–. ISSN 1056-0300.

Quarterly. Offers K-6 social studies educators practical tips in all aspects of social studies instruction. (http://www.socialstudies.org/publications/ssyl)

Software Encyclopedia: A Guide for Personal, Professional, and Business Users Including Application Software on CD-ROM. New Providence, NJ: R. R. Bowker, 2006. ISBN 0-8352-4813-5, ISBN 13 978-0-8352-4813-6.

Annual. Provides annotated listings for over 44,600 software programs. Entries classified under 668 subject headings containing title, subtitle, version number, publication date, compatible system, memory, and application requirements.

Software and CD-ROM Reviews on File. New York: Facts on File, 1985–. ISSN 1087-6367.

Monthly. Reviews over 600 software programs per year. Indexes by subject and company. Provides publisher, address, price, and publisher's description. Condenses and cites reviews.

Some of My Best Friends Are Books: Guiding Gifted Readers for Preschool to High School. 2nd ed. Judith Wynn Halsted. Scottsdale, AZ: Great Potential Press, 2002. ISBN 0-910707-51-0, ISBN 13 978-0-910707-51-0.

Contains summaries of about 300 books and research on the reading needs of gifted students. Index of books organized by grade, subject, and author. (http://giftedbooks.com/index.htm)

Speaking Out! Voices in Celebration of Intellectual Freedom. Ann K. Symons and Sally Gardner Reed. Chicago, IL: American Library Association, 1999. ISBN 0-83890-763-6, ISBN 13 978-0-8389-0763-4.

Brief essays provide insight, breadth of perspective, and challenges to your personal and professional position. Offers examples of how to defend and preserve intellectual freedom in the library. (http://www.alastore.ala.org/SiteSolution.taf?_sn=catalog2&_pn=product_ detail&_op=557)

Special Education and the Law: A Guide for Practitioners. 2nd ed. Allan G. Osborne Jr. and Charles J. Russo. Thousand Oaks, CA: Corwin Press, 2006. ISBN 1-4129-2622-X, ISBN 13 978-1-4129-2622-5.

Information on every facet of special education law: federal mandates, statutes, regulations, and special education case law. Discusses rights to a free appropriate public education, related services, assistive technology, and transition services; due process procedures for evaluation, development of IEPs, and placement; student discipline, dispute resolution, remedies for failure to provide a free appropriate public education, conflict management, and IDEA compliance.

The Special Educator's Survival Guide. 2nd ed. Roge Pierangelo. Somerset, NJ: John Wiley & Sons, 2004. ISBN 0-7879-7096-4, ISBN 13 978-0-7879-7096-3.

Practical guide covering current American laws and standards. Identifies various stages of the referral process, parent intakes and conferences, evaluation, interpretation, diagnosis, remediation, placement, individual education plans, classroom management, medication, educational law, and more. Offers essential tools including reproducible forms, checklists, and sample letters.

Subject Guide to Books in Print. See *Books in Print.*

Subject Guide to Children's Books in Print. See *Children's Books in Print.*

SUNLINK Weed of the Month Club. 1999–2005. Florida Department of Education. Archive available at http://www.sunlink.ucf.edu/weed/

Offers practical suggestions and criteria for weeding collections, one subject at a time. Recommends over 100 weeding subjects with suggested Dewey numbers and weeding criteria for each.

Talking Books Topics. Edmund O'Reilly, ed. Washington, DC: U.S. Library of Congress, National Library Service for the Blind and Physically Handicapped National Service for the Blind and Physically Handicapped (NLS), 1935–. ISSN 0039-9183.

Bimonthly. Annotates magazines and books available through the cooperating libraries. Contains news of developments and activities in library services and announcements of new recorded books and magazines. Titles are available free to the blind and physically handicapped individuals. (http://www.loc.gov/nls/tbt/)

Teaching Children Mathematics. Andy Reeves (Editorial Director). Reston, VA: National Council of Teachers of Mathematics, 1954–; New Series 1994–. ISSN 1073-5836.

Monthly (September–May) "Offers activities, lesson ideas, teaching strategies, and problems through in-depth articles, departments, and features." (from Web site: http://www.nctm.org)

The Teaching Librarian. Toronto: Ontario School Library Association, 1974–. ISSN 1188-679X. (Formerly *The Reviewing Librarian.* ISSN 0318-0948).

Three times a year. Reviews books, audiovisual materials, government publications, and magazines. Ontario Library Association, 100 Lombard St, Ste 303, Toronto, ON M5C 1M3 Canada.

Teacher Librarian. David Loertscher, ed. Blue Ridge Summit, PA: Scarecrow Press, 1973–. ISSN 1481-1782. (Formerly *Emergency Librarian.* ISSN 0315-8888).

Five times a year. Available online. Reviews professional reading, magazines, paperbacks, software, videos, and Web sites. Subscription: Teacher Librarian, 15200 NBN Way, Blue Ridge Summit, PA 17214. (http://www.teacherlibrarian.com)

Teaching Exceptional Children. Reston, VA: The Council for Exceptional Children, 1968–. ISSN 0040-0599.

Six times a year. Articles deal with current issues and practical methods and materials for classroom use. Subscription: Council for Exceptional Children, 1110 North Glebe Rd., Suite 300, Arlington, VA 22201. (http://www.cec.sped.org/bk/abtec.htm)

Tech Trends: For Leaders in Education and Training. Association for Educational Communications and Technology, 1985–. New York: Springer. ISSN 8756-3894, ISSN 1559-7075 (online).

Six times a year. Included in membership dues "Copyright and You," a regular column. "A leading publication for professionals in the educational communication and technology field. Its major purposes are: to provide a vehicle for the exchange of information among professional practitioners concerning the management of media and programs, the application of educational technology principles and techniques to instructional programs, corporate and military training, and any other kinds of information that can contribute to the advancement of knowledge of practice in the field." (from Web site: http://www.aect.org/Intranet/Publications/index.asp). Subscription: AECT, 1800 North Stonelake Drive, Suite 2, Bloomington, IN 47404-1517. (http://www.springer.com/sgw/cda/frontpage/0,11855,4-40109-70-75666525-0,00.html)

Technology and Copyright Law: A Guidebook for the Library, Research, and Teaching Professions. 2nd ed. Arlene Bielefield and Lawrence Cheeseman. New York: Neal-Schuman, 2006. ISBN 1-55570-570-7, ISBN 13 978-1-55570-570-1.

An exhaustive, scholarly examination of copyright history and law. Covers international developments in copyright law, judicial decisions, and congressional guidelines, and offers examples of applying the law to real-life situations.

Technology and Learning. New York: NewBay Media, 1980–. ISSN 1053-6728.

Ten issues per year. Reviews computer software and multimedia for elementary and secondary students. Provides hardware requirements, emphasis, grade level, publisher, description of software manuals and guides, rating, strengths, and weaknesses.

Teen Genreflecting. 2nd ed. Diana Tixier Herald. Englewood, CO: Libraries Unlimited, 2003. ISBN 1-56308-996-3, ISBN 13 978-1-56308-996-3.

Guide covers nearly 1,400 titles and authors for popular teen genres of historical novels, science fiction, fantasy, mystery, suspense, horror adventure, sports, romance, and contemporary novels.

Teen Legal Rights. Kathleen A. Hempelman. Westport, CT: Greenwood, 2000. ISBN 0-31330-968-X, ISBN 13 978-0-313-30968-7.

Covers discrimination issues, freedom of expression, school libraries, and school newspapers.

Teen Rights: A Legal Guide for Teens and the Adults in Their Lives. Traci Truly. Westport, CT: Sourcebooks, 2002. ISBN 1-57248-525-6, ISBN 13 978-1-57248-221-0.

Legal responsibilities and rights of teens, what to do if rights are abused or revoked. (http://www.sourcebooks.com/cart/shopdisplayproducts.asp?Search=Yes&sppp=10)

Television Production: A Classroom Approach. 2nd ed. Keith Kyker and Christopher Curchy. Westport, CT: Libraries Unlimited, 2004. ISBN 1-56308-774-X (instructor edition.), ISBN 13 978-1-56308-774-5.

Reflects advances in television production in the last ten years, including digital imaging and equipment, equipment use, project planning instruction, newsgathering methodology, studio production, and movie production. The teacher's guide has instructional notes, answer sheets, instructional ideas, and evaluation notes.

Thematic Guide to Popular Nonfiction. Lynda G. Adamson. Westport, CT: Greenwood Press, 2006. ISBN 0-313-32855-2, ISBN 13 978-0-313-32855-8.

Identifies popular works of nonfiction related to particular themes. Included are alphabetically arranged entries on fifty prevalent themes, such as animals, exploration, genocide, immigrants, poverty, and race relations. Lists of additional nonfiction for further reading, additional themes and related works, bibliography of works on popular nonfiction.

Through Indian Eyes: The Native Experience in Books for Children. 4th ed. Contemporary American Indian Issues, No. 7. Beverly Slapin and Doris Seale. Los Angeles, CA: American Indian Studies Center, 1998. ISBN 0-93562-646-8, ISBN 13 978-0-935626-46-9.

Expands on earlier editions of *Books Without Bias: Through Indian Eyes.* Critically evaluates and offers guidelines for selection of books on Native Americans.

Through the Eyes of a Child: An Introduction to Children's Literature. 7th ed. Donna E. Norton and Saundra E. Norton. Upper Saddle River, NJ: Prentice Hall, 2007. ISBN 0-132-20296-4, ISBN 13 978-0-132-20296-1.

Prepares reader to evaluate, choose, and share quality literature with children. Focus on classroom-tested teaching strategies and new teaching ideas. Treats multicultural literature as a separate chapter as well as integrated throughout.

TV Guide.

Provides a daily listing of television programs. (http://www.tvguide.com)

University Press Books Selected for Public and Secondary School Libraries. Association of American University Presses, 1991–. ISSN 1055-4173. Available at http://aaupnet.org/librarybooks/

Annual. Selections rated by a committee from the American Association of School Libraries (AASL) and the Public Library Association (PLA). Rates books in terms of general audience, regional interest, and in-depth collections for students in grades 6–12. For publishers listed, see Web site for the AAUP On-Line Catalog (http://aaupnet.org/librarybooks/). Members of AASL and PLA automatically receive copies. Librarians can obtain a free copy of the bibliography by writing on their school's stationery to the Association of American University Presses, Inc., Marketing Department, 71 West 23rd Street, Suite 901, New York, NY 10010.

U.S. Government Books. U.S. Government Printing Office, (formerly *U.S. Government Book: Publications for Sale by the Government Printing Office.* ISSN 0734-2764). Now available at http://www.gpoaccess.gov/index.html

Lists available books.

U.S. Government on the Web: Getting the Information You Need. 3rd ed. Peter Hernon, Robert E. Dugan, and John A. Shuler. Portsmouth, NH: Libraries Unlimited, 2003. ISBN 1-59158-086-2, ISBN 13 978-1-59158-086-7.

Serves as a directory, as a map to the government's structure, and as a play-book outlining strategies for locating information. Describes issues, types of publications, search engines, and Web sites. Includes a chapter about Web sites for children. Indexes by government body, title, and author. (http://lu.com/search.cfm)

Venture into Cultures: A Resource Book of Multicultural Materials and Programs. 2nd. ed. Olga R. Kuharets. Chicago, IL: American Library Association, 2001. ISBN 0-8389-3513-3, ISBN 13 978-0-8389-3513-2.

Rich stories, illustrations, traditions, and music from around the world, including African, Caribbean, Indian, Jewish-American, Korean, Latin American, Middle Eastern, Native American, and Russian items. Recommends books, Web sites, videos, audiotapes, and directions for programming materials. Includes bibliographical references and index.

Vertical File Index: Guide to Pamphlets and References to Current Topics. New York: H. W. Wilson, 1955–. ISSN 0042-4439.

Bimonthly. Provides order information for over 3,000 sources of free and inexpensive materials including reading lists, charts, posters, maps, and government publications. Arranged by subject with title index. Subscription: H. W. Wilson, 950 University Avenue, Bronx, NY 10452. (http://www.hwwilson.com/print/vfi.html)

The Video Librarian: Video Review Guide for Libraries. Randy Pitman, ed. Seabeck, WA: Video Librarian, 1986–. ISSN 0887-6851.

Bimonthly. Reviews nearly 200 videos for public, school, and university libraries. The magazine's supplement is available online at http://www.videolibrarian.com/ Subscription: *Video Librarian*, 8705 Honeycomb Court NW, Seabeck, WA 98380. (http://www.videolibrarian.com/about/subscription.html#Anchor-form.)

Video Source Book. Jim Craddock, ed. Farmington Hills, MI: Gale Group, 1979–. ISSN 0748-0881.

Annual. Covers pre-recorded video programs currently available on videocassette, videodisc, and videotape. Provides date of release, running time, major plot, theme, closed captions, or signing for people with a hearing impairment, and availability. Order from: Gale Group, 27500 Drake Rd., Farmington, MI 48331. (http://www.gale.com)

The Video Source Book. 26th ed. Detroit: Thompson Gale, 2001. ISBN: 0-78767-3698-3, ISBN 13 978-0-7876-3698-2.

Comprehensive coverage of video offerings with listings for more than 130,000 complete programs, encompassing more than 160,000 videos.

VOYA: Voice of Youth Advocates. Metuchen, NJ: Scarecrow Press, 1978–. ISSN 0160-4201. Available online.

Monthly. Reviews books (trade, paperbacks, reprints, professional), reference titles, and media of materials for or about adolescents. (http://www.voya.com)

Weaving the Literacy Web: Creating Curriculum Based on Books Children Love. Hope Vestergaard. St. Paul, MN: Redleaf Press, 2005. ISBN 1-929610-70-X, ISBN 13 978-1-929610-70-9.

Introduction to book-based webbing and ideas for activity planning, as well as helpful tips for observing children's interests and evaluating books for the classroom library.

Web Braille. Library of Congress, National Library Service for the Blind and Physically Handicapped.

Provides information on how to access electronic Braille books. (http://www.loc.gov/loc/lcib/9911/braille.html)

Weeding Library Collections: Library Weeding Methods. 4th ed. Stanley J. Slote. Englewood, CO: Libraries Unlimited, 1997. ISBN 1-56308-511-9, ISBN 13 978-1-56308-511-6.

Discusses the policies and practices used in weeding collections.

The World of Work Through Children's Literature: An Integrated Approach. Carol M. Butzow and John W. Butzow. Englewood, CO: Libraries Unlimited, 1999. ISBN 1-56308-650-6, ISBN 13 978-1-56308-650-2.

Features lessons, activities, and ideas based on a variety of themes about work, including local economy, work skills, work communities.

The World Through Children's Books. Susan Stan. Lanham, MD: Scarecrow, 2002. ISBN 0-8108-4198-3, ISBN 13 978-0-8108-4198-7.

Annotated bibliography organized geographically by world region and country, and containing nearly 700 books representing over 70 countries.

WWW Evaluation Guide. Tana Hudak. Takoma Park, MD: Takoma Park Maryland Library. (http://www.takomapark.info/library/reference/eval.html)

Evaluation guide listed under "School Resources." Helps the evaluator assess the identifying factors for the site, analyze content and sources, and evaluate visuals.

Youth with Special Needs. Broomall, PA: Mason Crest Publishers. Fifteen-volume set.

Unique collection that "combines factual information with fictional stories to bring to life the struggles, challenges, and triumphs of youth with special needs and educates about realities of living with different physical, mental, and emotional conditions." (from Web site: http://www.masoncrest.com/series_view.php?seriesID=21)

Index